Managing Service Operations

Managing Service Operations

Design and Implementation

Bill Hollins and Sadie Shinkins

Los Angeles | London | New Delhi
Singapore | Washington DC

First published 2006

Reprinted 2009

SAGE Publications Ltd
1 Oliver's Yard
55 City Road
London EC1Y 1SP

SAGE Publications Inc.
2455 Teller Road
Thousand Oaks, California 91320

SAGE Publications India Pvt Ltd
B 1/I 1 Mohan Cooperative Industrial Area
Mathura Road
New Delhi 110 044

SAGE Publications Asia-Pacific Pte Ltd
33 Pekin Street #02-01
Far East Square
Singapore 048763

British Library Cataloguing in Publication data

A catalogue record for this book is available from the British Library

ISBN-13 978-1-4129-2952-3
ISBN-13 978-1-4129-2953-0 (pbk)

Library of Congress Control Number: 2006927097

Typeset by C&M Digitals (P) Ltd, Chennai, India
Printed and bound in Great Britain by CPI Antony Rowe, Chippenham, Wiltshire
Printed on paper from sustainable resources

FSC
Mixed Sources
Product group from well-managed
forests and other controlled sources
Cert no. SGS-COC-2953
www.fsc.org
© 1996 Forest Stewardship Council

CONTENTS

ACKNOWLEDGEMENTS

We thank the following for their help in compiling this book:

Design Council London, as part of the material in this book was produced with their support, although it represents the personal view of the authors.

Mark Fuller, known as 'Feltham Bee', for the offer of a photo for the case study in Chapter 15.

Lavrans Lovlie of Live/Work, Gill Wildman of Plot and Jane Minardi for figures.

Taner Ozsumer and Oscar Santacruz for figures.

Bill's wife, Gillian, for her tolerance and proof reading, Ranjan Madenayke for the original idea, and Alan Topalian for parts of Chapter 14.

Special thanks are due to John, Patrick and Matthew for their patience during this project.

And finally, this book is dedicated to Raja, because it is his turn.

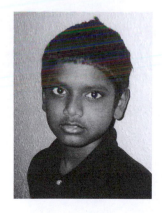

PREFACE

The only thing that gives an organization a competitive edge ... is what it knows, how it uses what it knows, and how fast it can know something new.

Laurence Prusak, Managing Principal IBM
Global Services Boston (1996)

[That's three things!]

The main focus of this book is 'the product' (service), that which actually brings in the money, and as such, it takes a broader view than many operations management books. There is **operations management, design management** and some **marketing** in this because, although the three subjects often tend to be taught separately, it is not possible, in practice, to treat these as such. The actions in managing one have an effect on the others. By a greater linkage of these topics under one umbrella there will be a greater understanding of the realities of management.

Another feature of this book is that it is for those involved in management in the service sector. This will include those managing in the not-for-profit sector, health provision, transport, banking, hotel and catering etc. Employment in the service sector in industrialized countries now exceeds that in manufacturing. In Europe and the United States 80% of people are now employed in services and even in Japan employment in services started to exceed manufacturing this century (Sakao and Shimomura 2004). Services are becoming a key focus in management education as, increasingly, employment and wealth generation in industrialized countries moves from making things towards the provision of services often associated with products manufactured in low wage economies. This does not mean that manufacturing will be ignored, as many of the techniques used in service operations have their roots in manufacturing but have then been adapted to make them more 'people-centric' and thus more applicable to the service sector.

The scope will cover services from the original 'trigger' or idea right through the market research, service development, implementation and performance improvement to the eventual termination and disposal of the service. This follows the realization and increasing acceptance that a product or service cannot be fully successful if its various components are managed independently, in a series of 'over the wall' operations. Decisions taken early in the process must relate to decisions and activities at the later stages.

This should encourage readers (you) to explore the relationships between customers' needs and an organization's products and services. It should aid readers to understand the interrelationship between service design (in its total sense) and operations to deliver these services that satisfy customers within the framework of the organization's objectives and capabilities. Additionally, it provides an understanding of the requirement for quality in operations and outputs and the need and methods for monitoring performance and implementing change as necessary.

The structure of this book

The text has been divided into four parts that follow a continuum of managing products and services. It will start with an introduction to services management, explaining why services are different from manufactured products. Also, this section will explain what is meant by operations management. This section also contains a chapter on the 'people side', acknowledging the fact that service operations management is undertaken *by people* and *for people* and the performance of the former must be optimized for the benefit of the latter.

The second part will be about the development of new services and will include our research findings showing that, generally, service design management is poor.

Part 3 will focus on the management of service operations and will include service quality management, supply chain management and managing service capacity.

Throughout this book there are illustrative case studies, but in Part 4 there will be an extended case study relating to a struggling football club. In this case study various operations techniques introduced throughout the book will be used within the story.

The authors have a website that can be used in conjunction with this book – www.sagepub.co.uk/hollins. This site includes some PowerPoint slides on each chapter for lecturers who adopt this text in their teaching. There are also Student Activities at the end of each chapter.

Detailed contents of the book

Services operations management will be explored from the business proposal, through market research, development, implementation and on to termination and disposal of the service, bearing in mind the highly iterative nature of any development. Each section of the book will describe the underpinning theory.

PART 1

Services, Strategy and People

1 Introduction to Services Management: The Customer-Led Organization
This explains why this book is needed, showing various types of services and how services have grown. The operations manager's role and the role of operations management itself is then described. Considering the customer-led organization, customer care versus customer service is considered and this includes relationship marketing, customer satisfaction and improvement. There is also coverage of buyer behaviour as well as of the impact on selling and delivering products and services.

2 Service Operations Strategy
This chapter will include the strategic role and objectives of operations, customer satisfaction versus resource utilization, and adding value. It will include an analysis and evaluation of operations strategies and frameworks for effective management of the operations process. In this there will be the recognition of different operating systems and the circumstances that determine their appropriateness, optimizing of scheduling and allocating resources. Job design and work organization will be included, as well as how to develop the implementation plan.

3 People, Leadership and Management
This book and the tools and techniques described herein cover the whole area from trigger to disposal. Managing this total process is far from easy, as it is necessary to coordinate a large number of people. In this chapter we look at who should be involved and how to coordinate these experts. This includes how to organize teams and how to lead them as well as leadership and communications. Working methods and design teams will be included, and also how to manage creative people. Job design and aspects of motivation are also inculded.

1 INTRODUCTION TO SERVICES MANAGEMENT: THE CUSTOMER-LED ORGANIZATION

> When the rate of change outside exceeds the rate of change inside, the end is in sight.
>
> Chairman and CEO, General Electric, 1980–2000
>
> Jack Welch

Services are products (of a special type); services need to be designed, and these services and their operation needs to be managed. This is the operations management of services in the fullest sense. It has been said that 'The British service industry is not known for high service standards' (Munoz 2004). Hopefully, this book will go some way to showing how to improve things.

There is growing realization that many techniques generated in the manufacturing sector (there are still 365,000 manufacturers in the UK) also work in the much larger service sector (TQM, JIT, MRP etc.). The same good practices that apply in getting the right manufactured products apply, by and large, to services.

> Know your customers, your products, your services and your capabilities, and get it right first time.

There are a lot of management fads and panaceas that are supposed to turn the organization into an instant success: follow eight rules and suddenly all your problems will disappear. Unfortunately, it isn't that easy; if it were, then we would all be rich. This book advises the use of various rules and tools and techniques but not every one applies in every situation and most only work if you also apply a good deal of hard work. Some can take several years to implement effectively.

In this book we will introduce some ideas that can be used to identify the right products and services that are worth pursuing into production or implementation as well as indicate those products that should be avoided or abandoned. Remember that there is no one suit that fits all organizations. Some of the procedures described may not be applicable in a particular situation.

A company must offer products or services that customers want, that can be made or supplied, at a price people are prepared to pay and return a profit for the company. Without fulfilling all these criteria the product can be deemed to be a failure, and in time, so will the organization.

The focus is on the very early stages of the service. The processes as described throughout tend to take a 'top to bottom' approach but will, in practice, be iterative. This means that as new and better information becomes available those involved in the process may need to backtrack to check on, or change, some of the earlier work. This is quite normal in good management as long as this iteration is kept under control and it is realized that there comes a point where further changes are unnecessarily disruptive, time-consuming and expensive.

Various people will be responsible for the implementation of each of these stages and these people should have this responsibility included as part of their job description. This should also indicate areas where additional training must be given to enable those involved to do these tasks.

Before we go any further, however, you ought to know where we are starting from and how we got here.

An instant guide to the history of management gurus

Management gurus, write fashionable things that tell the top bosses and 'young men of potential' how to win world markets with a couple of easily implemented ideas. Unfortunately, life isn't that easy, so every couple of years, after the failure of one management fad, the latest gimmick appears with a new fancy title and content not dissimilar to the last. Two years is about the lifespan of these, unless you hit on a real 'biggie', like adding a few extra 'Ps' to the Marketing Mix, and then you can drag the mileage out for a few more years.

In this section you can learn about the management gurus of the past to provide you with a springboard for the future. If nothing else, it may help you to make a winning impression at cocktail parties.

The history

Interchangeability of parts was achieved by the American Eli Whitney (1765–1825). In 1798 the American government gave him a contract for 10,000 muskets and these were produced so that the individual parts could be used in any musket. This was first shown in the UK in the Great Exhibition of 1851. It was fundamental to the subsequent development of mass production. Prior to this, parts had to be individually made for any device by skilled craftsmen. Mass production meant a large number of workers and that meant communication and management problems that remain to this day. Eli Whitney was not a guru but an engineer, which is far superior.

Around 1860 Weber invented bureaucracy as an efficient way of organizing large numbers of people. Essentially it was a pyramid organizational structure with the boss at the top (it was Fayol who first drew the organizational chart). In spite of many themes and variations, such as matrix management, if you ask someone to draw the structure of their organization they will still draw it in the shape of a pyramid with the boss at the top.

Around the same time Marx was telling us that those at the point of production would take over companies in a workers' revolution. His drinking mate Engels (Engels bought all the drinks) noticed that rather than take up cudgels against the bosses in fact workers were trying to copy their lifestyle (clocks for the mantelpiece etc.). This was later called (by Bottomore) 'embourgeoisement of the working classes'. Marx once said 'the group seemed so ill assorted as to risk being torn apart by their own internal contradictions' – that seems to sum up most attempts so far seen at implementing Total Quality Management.

Frederick Winslow Taylor's work was couched in early twentieth century terminology but with 1980s thinking that dragged through the 'caring nineties' and into the 'bomb you' new century. He started a rudimentary form of work-study: 'get an ox to do an ox's work'. Through the Gilbreths and their measurement of hand movements of people assembling work (therbligs – not quite their name back-to-front), Henry Ford and his Highland Park car factory, Bedeaux and his implementation of work study, they all tried to get more work out of the workforce.

Then came Elton Mayo and his chums with their Human Relations School. With their milk-cow called psychology (contented cows produce more milk) they also did their bit to push up production but did so in the belief that it could be done with smiles. Keeping up production through a happy workforce was the continuing theme for the next fifty years of management theories.

We grinned through Herzberg with his motivation and hygiene factors. We were confused by Douglas McGregor with 'Y' carrots and 'X' sticks with which to motivate the workforce.

Chinoy never reached 'guru' status as he considered that not all workers were the same. Some sought promotion in work and others placed a greater emphasis on outside activities. Furthermore, he indicated that their priorities moved from in-firm ambition to outside interest – and back as their careers progressed. All far too complicated for your average manager to cope with.

Around the late 1970s there was a bit of a lull as gurus moved from looking at people to looking at the process. Gurus took the whole operation by the scruff of the neck and shook it with downsizing – later called 'right sizing' (redundancy), empowerment (those that are left work harder) and flattening (everybody who knows how to do the job gets axed). Hammer is one of the men to blame. Hammer's house of horror, known as Business Process Re-engineering (BPR), might have been

Taylorism revisited, producing corporate myopia and more redundancy. So far we have only found one attempt at BPR that did not end in redundancy, and that was at Leicester Royal Infirmary.

Total Quality Management (TQM) is an area thick with gurus. Deming said that quality problems were 85% management problems – that is why he had to leave the United States to get listened to. Juran told us that improvement is always possible. Ishikawa did his bit for quality with his seven rules followed by seven more. Crosby's book *Quality is Free* (1979, still available) became a hit with managers who rarely get beyond the title of books that they purchase. As a result, many companies tried to introduce TQM without a budget. Crosby actually meant 'quality is free – eventually'. It costs a lot in time and commitment as well as money at the start but you get all this back eventually, through lower total quality costs. Unfortunately managers thinking that you get all this for free is the main reason behind the 80% of TQM initiatives that fail.

Between them these gurus have managed to destroy most of industry and those companies that remain have their sights set firmly on the short term. They then turned on the services aimed at the health service, transport and education. And what is happening to these?

We get gurus to investigate, philosophize and plan, disrupt, reorganize, flatten, focus, make lean to the point of anorexia and generally foul up, but what of the people who blindly accept all these fashions and fads – the managers?

Today computers and automation and other technology more determine the speed of things, along with the essential of good design, so 'management gurus' have turned their attention to middle managers. We now have job enrichment – getting the workers to do several jobs – and now the workers are responsible for the job, we can kick out the middle managers.

Those of you who go to lectures will have noticed how lecturers try to emulate the fashionable guru of the time. In the Herzberg era lectures were presented behind a haze of cigarette smoke and were interspaced with long pregnant pauses. Fortunately, now that the Peters era is drawing to a close, lecturers no longer feel that they have to get bathed in perspiration and shout at the audience. They now rather take on the 'comfy' presentation style of a talk show host.

Up to the present nobody has questioned the top management and their dubious right to manage. We always make the assumption that they make decisions that are best for their organization. The assumption is also made that the other employees only have their own selfish interests at heart. The truth seems to be a bit of both. Both groups want the company to survive and thrive and both want a fair cut from it. So perhaps there aren't two groups at all.

Gurus and consultants never question the rights of the top management or rarely draw into consideration their own interests that may conflict with those of the organization. Any proposals must ensure that the manager's self-interest is not dented and that they can continue to wallow in wealth as well as self-glory from their flame-proof seats in their ivory towers – and, of course, they only have the interests of their shareholders at heart. This is because management gurus and other consultants know who pays their fees. They don't question it, they just count the money. Perhaps you should begin to question their actions more.

Where there is growth in manufacturing

The manufacturing sector worldwide will continue to be dominated by rich indus-trialized countries that have large home markets for their output and can afford the economies of scale brought about by a high investment in capital equipment (e.g. the United States). The other and main area for growth for manufactured prod-ucts will be those large countries that have very low cost labour, a large potential home market and can attract inward investment. The most notable of these are India and China.

So where does this leave the rest of us? Although in some countries low cost labour delays the introduction of automation, increased introduction of farm mechanization will cause the number of people directly employed in growing things to decline. In these countries there may be a small (in world terms) manufacturing sector.

In most industrialized countries (sometimes called 'post-industrialized countries) the number of people employed in the service sector has grown way beyond those employed in manufacturing. In the UK 80% of employment is in services (and 72% of the UK economy) with 13% in manufacturing and the rest in mining and agri-culture. The service sector now makes up 70% of European GDP growth (Brown and West 2006).

Increasingly, business will appreciate the advantages that can be gained from adding value through services. The importance of 'services' to the economy of the country will continue to grow in the foreseeable future. This means that there will be an increasing demand for new services. So how should these new services be developed?

The service sector is growing both in size, employment and importance to the economies of all industrialized countries as the manufacturing sector declines. In industrialized countries worldwide there is an increase in the contribution of the GNP and in the level of employment derived from non-manufacturers, or more especially, the service sector. The percentage of those employed in the service sector is rising throughout the EU and the United States, as might be expected, but it is also rising in developing countries. Also, the Incomes Data Services show that the fastest growing areas of employment in the UK are all in customer service roles.

The importance of 'services' to the economy of countries worldwide will continue to grow in the foreseeable future and economic prosperity has contributed to this growth of services. Higher disposable incomes have led to an increase in financial ser-vices, entertainment, eating out, travel, personal health care and fitness. There are stand-alone services, but most manufactured products will also contain a large ser-vice element on which the product will be judged. Even in manufacturing organi-zations it is estimated that 20% of employees are working in a service role.

As Raymond Turner (who managed the design of the very successful Heathrow Express) has stated, 'Design acts as an interface between company and customer, ensuring that the company delivers what the customer wants in a way that adds value to both' (Turner 2002).

Only recently have some managers in organizations involved in the service sector realized that a conscious effort in applying 'design' techniques to services can result in greater customer satisfaction, greater control over their offerings and greater profits. Unfortunately, there are few resources available that can assist these managers in the application of design to their service products, although the British Design Council has gone some way to rectifying this with part of their Knowledge Cell Asset website being devoted to service design management (Design Council 2002).

As services are the growth area, well-designed services can be very profitable. The opportunities for innovation through technology, marketing and throughout the life of a service are currently changing the whole way that customers are contacted, served and retained. Service design can be applied at all these stages where customers interface with the organization to improve their satisfaction and company profits.

All of these areas will benefit from an injection of good design and good operations management.

What is a service?

A **service** has been defined by Kotler et al. (1986) as 'any activity or benefit that one party can give to another that is essentially intangible and does not result in the ownership of anything. Its production may or may not be tied to a physical product'.

It has been more fully defined as:

(a) A set of functions offered to a user by an organization.
(b) Results generated by activities at the interface between the supplier and the customer and by supplier internal activities to meet the customer needs.

Note 1: *The supplier or the customer may be represented at the interface by personnel or equipment.*
Note 2: *Customer activities at the interface with the supplier may be essential to the service delivery.*
Note 3: *Service is intangible and as such cannot be stored.*
Note 4: *Delivery or use of tangible products may form part of the service delivery.*
Note 5: *A service may be linked with the manufacture and supply of tangible products.*
   (BS 7000-3, BS 7000-10, BS EN ISO 9000)

So how does this affect service management?

Generally, services differ from manufacturing in up to five ways. Service design can be both tangible and intangible. It can involve artefacts and other things including communication, environment and behaviours. Whichever form it takes it must be consistent and easy to use.

1 **Tangibility:** One can physically touch a manufactured product but most services are intangible. One cannot touch legal advice or a journey, though one can often see the results. There are stand-alone services but most manufactured products will also contain a large service element on which the product will be judged. Even in manufacturing organizations it is estimated that 20% of employees are working in a service role. Also, many services 'ride on the back' of manufactured products.

2 **Transportability:** Most services cannot be transported and, therefore, exported (though the means of producing these services often can). It is estimated that only about 14% of services are exportable, although this is fast changing. The increase in the power and availability of information technology and ease of communication and other technological advances mean that it is now possible to operate services across borders and continents and this growing trend will continue. For example, insurance and telephone banking and call centres can easily operate across the world. This opens up new threats and some service companies will become vulnerable to overseas competition. But also this opens up business opportunities to home-based service organizations to 'attack' overseas markets. As a result, a 'world-wide' dimension needs to be considered in the specification of new services. This will include potential threats and opportunities.

3 **Storability:** Because services tend to be intangible, it is usually impossible to store them. For example, a car in a showroom if not sold today can be sold tomorrow but an empty seat on an aeroplane or room in a hotel is lost once the plane has left or the night has passed.

4 **Customer contact:** Generally, in manufacturing the customer may be unaware of how the product came about. In services, production and consumption tend to occur at the same time (Simultaneity). As production and consumption occur at the same time in a service (Kelley et al. 1990), customers cannot fail to notice if the service has been poorly designed (Edvardsson and Olsson 1996). Of course, this can relate to the physical surroundings but, increasingly, users are looking to the 'totality' of the service. That which is offered must, at least, meet their perceived expectations. These customer expectations are continuing to rise. Service that was acceptable in a shop, hospital outpatients department or railway station just a few years ago is now considered unacceptable.

5 **Quality:** In manufacturing, quality tends to be measured against drawings etc. The measures tend to be quantitative. The measures of quality in a service tend to be qualitative and there are few quantitative measures. As a result, there is a wider variability in services and it is more difficult to control the quality of a service – which is often down to the person giving it. Quality Assurance (QA) (BS EN ISO 9001:2000) is still growing in the service sector. So is the application of TQM. Many of the aims of QA and TQM can be achieved through service design.

The above five features may present themselves as **heterogeneity**. Every time a service is offered, it may be different due to a different type of person receiving it and giving it. For example, some customers may need more personal attention when buying a computer to have the many features explained. Others may be more knowledgeable and not require (or want) such personal attention. This often leads to the need for further training so that the different types of customer can be recognized and the service that they receive tailored to that best suited to their needs.

The above is sometimes known as the **'SHIP' model – Simultantaneity** (customer contact), **Heterogeneity, Intangibility** (tangibility), **Perishability** (storability).

The **service value exchange** is well demonstrated in Figure 1.1, developed by Lavrans Lovlie of Live/Work, a service design consultancy. This shows the often intangible relationships between customer, intermediaries and service provider.

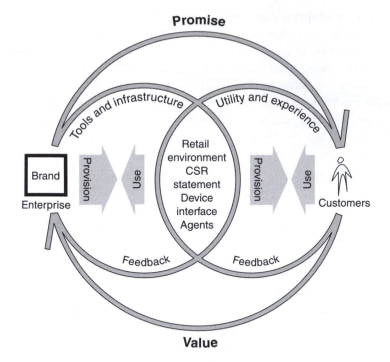

FIGURE 1.1   TYPICAL SERVICE VALUE EXCHANGE. (REPRODUCED COURTESY OF LAVRANS LOVLIE, LIVE/WORK: www.livework.co.uk)

Importance to public services

Often, public services are serving large numbers of people and must operate within tight financial constraints and budgets. Although it may not be possible to increase the finance available, through effective operations management, it is often possible to make the available finance stretch further. This will result in a more efficient use of the resources available within these tight constraints.

Importance to charities

Most charities are both raisers and spenders of finance but from and to quite distinctive groups. The needs of both of these are likely to be very different. When designing charities it is necessary to balance the funds raised from one group with the commitment (spending) to the other (Hollins and Hollins 1991).

In practice this requires a service design process for raising the finance and a design process for spending the finance. These two processes run in parallel (concurrency) and are highly iterative and dependent on each other (you can't spend what you haven't raised).

Features of a service

Quality starts with design and quality needs to be built into the design of the service provision rather than being added later. The application of tools such as SERVQUAL (Parasuraman et al. 1988, 1994; Mills 1990; Mattsson 1994) is an attempt to match (or exceed) service provision with customer expectations.

Services cannot be patented and therefore intellectual property in services is more difficult to protect and copying of competing services is easier – another reason to keep applying serial innovation (BS 7000-1: 1999) to retain that competitive edge.

From looking at just the product, companies should be moving towards designing the product, process and service interface and moving towards a 'whole life' consideration as a method for adding value and maximizing profit throughout the value chain (Porter 1985), right through to disposal (Bush and Sheldon 1993). This places a greater emphasis on the post-production stage of products, distribution, marketing, customer and market support – the service end of the process – as well as corporate development.

By putting customer convenience and satisfaction at the forefront, managers are forced to think (and then develop) the customer experience. Often this starts by blueprinting (Shostack 1984) the likely customer experience then improving the proposed service through the elimination of 'blockages' to efficiency and satisfaction.

More new technology will be used in services. This will make transactions faster and more efficient and more repeatable. The repeatability will make it easier to control and increase the quality of the service. The standardization brought about by the application of technology may reduce the personal interaction and thus the 'individual' nature of services. The 'service' dimension could be lost from the service transaction and that may not be to the satisfaction of all customers. The difference in the 'bespoke' nature of some services compared with some others (the difference between a restaurant and a 'fast food' outlet) will result in both types of service being available. The segmentation choices will be part of the service design.

On the other hand, further 'discrete' applications of advanced technology (especially in communication) and IT in services can allow the benefits of apparent 'individual' service combined with the benefits that can be achieved with repeatability and 'selective' standardization. This can also allow the service providers to spend more time with customers.

Who are the customers?

In most manufactured products the customer is the person who buys it and uses it. There are exceptions, a parent may buy a toy, which a child will use. In services the number of customers or stakeholders is much wider. For example, in primary school education the customers/stakeholders will include the children, the parents, the local authority, central government and taxpayers, all of whom have a stake and this stake is not equal and may alter at different times and in different circumstances. Likewise, the X-ray department in the local hospital: here the stakeholders will include the patient, the doctor, the local health trust, the hospital management, government and, again, taxpayers. This makes the design of successful services more difficult as it is necessary to understand and provide the needs of these stakeholders and appreciate the relative importance of each to succeed.

SUMMARY OF KEY POINTS

In the growing international market for services:

- There will be an increasing reliance on technology and automation.
- There will be a greater customer emphasis on quality.
- The importance of the service sector in terms of profit and employment will continue to grow throughout the world.

Much of the above will be expanded upon in subsequent chapters.

2 SERVICE OPERATIONS STRATEGY

Of course strategy is hard – it's about making tough choices.

Professor Michael E. Porter, 2001, Harvard Business School

Organizations need to understand their operational world. In the classic definition, the two concerns of strategy are the 'external environment' and the 'future'. Mintzberg (1994) states that 'an organization needs a sense of where it is going and what forces in its environment are going to help or hinder it in achieving its goal'. Porter (1985) suggests that it helps the organization to explore a limited number of possible directions and create a model of how their actions are going to affect that environment.

LEARNING OUTCOMES

When you have completed this chapter you should be able to:

- Discuss the nature of competitive advantage.
- Identify the components of a business strategy.

The history of strategy

It has been written that strategy comes from the military writings of Sun Tzu, who wrote, in 360 BC in *The Art of War*, that 'strategy is the great work of the organization' (Grant 1995; Mintzberg 1998). Other authors have described the origin of the word strategy as being derived from the Greek *strategos*, itself derived from the words for 'army' and 'lead' (Grant 1995; Kare-Silver 1997; Trott 1998; Whittington 1993). Lynch (1997) states that 'strategy is likely to concern itself with the survival of the business as the minimum objective and the creation of value-added as a maximum objective. Porter's definition, quoted in Kare-Silver (1997), is 'a combination of the ends for which the firm is striving and the means by which it is seeking to get there'. Bennett (1996) has a similar definition, 'the totality of management decisions that determine the purpose and direction of the enterprise and hence its fundamental goals, activities and the policies it selects in order to attain its objectives'. All of these certainly point to the future and how to get there, but do not define the type of products and services that are needed in this future. Much strategic management is still locked into the Porteresque eighties. A SWOT and PEST analysis (see below) is still a good start, but it works much better if linked to a *specific* product/market.

So, if strategy is a statement of how an organization expects to achieve its missions and goals, it can be seen very much as a road map outlining how the organization is going to reach these goals, the steps that need to be taken.

Any organization is concerned not only with survival in the short term but also with how to stay in business in the long term. Planning for this often involves a statement of the organization's mission, which should set out the purpose or rationale for the organization's existence. Mission statements are often so overblown as to be viewed with ridicule or so banal as to be meaningless. However, it is easier to develop a good strategy if the mission or the intent of the strategy has been well expressed. They do give an organization an opportunity to set out its vision of the desirable future for the organization. An example from Tesco states: 'Our core purpose is **to create value for customers to earn their lifetime loyalty**'. Its plan for long-term growth is based around: growth in the core UK market, growth internationally, developing the non-food market as the food one and following customers into new retailing services.

Objectives or statements of what we want to do are drawn up after an analysis of the environment and an appraisal of where competitive advantage could be derived. Environmental scanning using tools such as identifying Strengths, Weaknesses, Opportunities and Threats (SWOT analysis) or identifying Political, Economic, Social and Technological factors (PEST analysis) is a fundamental feature of strategy development (see Tables 2.1 and 2.2).

The PEST model assesses a market while the SWOT analysis is commonly used to appraise a business unit, a proposition or idea. These are the two basic building blocks in any assessment of the internal and external environment. Some writers have extended the PEST model to seven factors, named PESTELI, by adding Environmental, Legislative and Industry factors to the original. Of course you might expect these issues to be covered in the PEST analysis since Industry should surely be considered under the Economic heading, Legislative factors should arise under the Political heading and Environmental factors could well be discussed under all four PEST headings.

Such analyses help identify customers' needs, current and future, which should then help the organization plan how to meet those. Of course, such plans have to take account of the existing competition and the likelihood of new entrants affecting the competitive position of the organization. An assessment of the role of suppliers and their bargaining power impacts on the cost analysis undertaken by an organization to underpin its planned strategy.

Competitive advantage

So what do we mean by competitive advantage? Where an organization has a unique advantage over its competitors it can be deemed to have a competitive advantage.

TABLE 2.1 BUSINESS ANALYSIS TOOL (SWOT)

Strengths	Weaknesses
e.g. innovative product design	e.g. inflexible supply chain
Opportunities	**Threats**
e.g. changes in delivery technology	e.g. new entrants to market

TABLE 2.2 ENVIRONMENTAL SCANNING (PESTELI)

Political factors
Economic factors
Social factors
Technological factors
Environmental factors
Legislative factors
Industry factors

Such advantage usually manifests itself by the achievement of profits higher than the average for their sector. Michael Porter (1980) identified two basic ways of achieving competitive advantage. The first occurs when an organization is able to deliver the same benefits as its competitors but at a lower cost, thereby gaining a **cost advantage** for itself. The second is when the organization **differentiates** itself by offering superior benefits to its competitors. Such improved benefits and services usually command a higher price. Such a position is only sustainable of course if consumers believe they are getting added value for those higher prices.

A third type of strategy has been described as a **focus strategy**, whereby a company applies a cost leadership or differentiation strategy within a particular target market in some specialized way that delivers an advantage over those firms applying their generic strategy in a wider market.

Differentiation will come from anything and everything that influences the value that customers derive from the product or service. So the operations manager has a role to play in defining everything about a product that will influence its potential value to customers. This can be tweaking the design of the product features, influencing its convenience for customers through decisions on the location of distribution centres or retail outlets, or affecting how delivery, installation or repair and maintenance services are implemented.

The differentiation may come from achieving a quality advantage or through timely, reliable delivery or from offering a flexible performance that is extremely responsive to customer needs. In the airline industry Singapore Airlines aims to create competitive advantage for themselves by focusing on maximizing the value created for the customer, which then commands a price premium. Policies such as offering branded goods, extending the product range, making use of economies of scale, offering highly personalized procedures are commonly found in a differentiation strategy.

Competing on cost is the strategy adopted by budget airlines Ryanair and easyJet. Ryanair proudly declares itself to be Europe's original low fare airline (founded in 1985) and is still Europe's largest low fare carrier in 2005. Ryanair commits, itself to offer the lowest available prices to passengers, on all routes on which they operate. In doing so they are following the same strategy pioneered by Southwest Airlines in the United States since their launch in 1971. This is founded on the use of secondary airports and terminals, first-come first-served seating, no-meal flights, smaller crews flying more hours and the use of Internet booking.

The low cost airlines make effective use of their capacity. Both Southwest Airlines and Ryanair use Boeing 737s. Ryanair has just replaced its current fleet of Boeing 737-200s with 737-800s which are designed to have less of an adverse impact on the environment with less emissions, lower fuel burn, greater seat density and quieter engines. Standardizing the fleet in this way has the advantage of making spares and maintenance easier to organize and less costly.

Costs are taken out of the value chain by minimizing the amount of time their planes actually spend on the ground. Faster turnarounds can be achieved by speeding up the cleaning process, hence no peanuts or meals. Drinks and snacks are of course available for purchase, not distributed for free as the full cost airlines do. Ryanair is quite obvious about its aim, which is to continue to offer low fares that will encourage growth in passenger traffic. Its ability to offer these low fares is founded on its policy of focusing on containing its costs through delivering operating efficiencies.

A low cost strategy should not be confused with low value or low quality. Retailers like Wal-Mart that pursue a low cost strategy focus on reducing distribution costs, shrinkage in the stores, reduced warehousing costs and through keen management of their supply chain achieve a high inventory turnover. Discount retailers like Aldi and Lidl have also successfully pursued a cost leadership strategy through limiting the product range offered in their stores, simplifying business processes, standardizing, making use of automation and offering non-branded goods.

Levels of strategy

If one accepts a top-down hierarchical approach to strategy there are three main levels of strategy: corporate, business and functional. Under this model the corporate goals are handed down to the business and then to functional areas (see Figure 2.1). Strategy at the corporate level sets out the direction of the whole organization, acknowledging the key stakeholders the organization is seeking to satisfy. These stakeholders will be both internal and external. Such a strategy is a statement of how the organization wants to position itself in its economic, political, social environment. It details the types of business the corporation wants to be in and what parts of the world it wants to operate in. In large diversified companies the second level of strategy, business level strategy, is at the Strategic Business Unit (SBU) level. This strategy sets out the plan for how the business unit will deal with its customers, markets and competitors and also how this will contribute to the overall corporate strategy. Growth and profitability targets and return on investment are considered at

Corporate goals

Business Unit level

Functional areas

FIGURE 2.1   STRATEGY DEVELOPMENT

Four-stage model

Stage 1   Internal neutrality
Stage 2   External neutrality
Stage 3   Internally supportive
Stage 4   Externally supportive

FIGURE 2.2   HAYES AND WHEELWRIGHT'S (1984) FOUR-STAGE MODEL

this level. The third level of strategy is where the business functions, operations or finance or marketing, formulate their long-term plans which support the aims being pursued by the business strategy. Different business objectives would probably require different operations strategies in that they would demand a different set of priorities. Under the top-down model the role of the operations function is to implement business strategy formulated elsewhere.

Hayes and Wheelwright (1984) claimed that overall operations capability drives the success of organizations and developed a model to help identify the strategic role of the operations function. The four-stage model (see Figure 2.2) progresses from a passive, largely reactive approach to a proactive approach in Stage 4. The stages can be described as follows.

Stage 1: Internal neutrality   At this stage the operations function is attempting to reach a certain minimum standard. It is seen as a hindrance in the delivery of competitive advantage by the other business functions. Its focus is on avoiding mistakes so it tends to be inward-looking and is reactive. The bad publicity that comes from organizations being let down by their operations can be damaging.

Stage 2: External neutrality   Here the operations function compares its perfor-mance with competitor organizations. Benchmarking its performance against its competitors enables it to identify the best ideas to copy. In trying to match the benchmarks it has identified, the operations function is attempting to be externally neutral.

Stage 3: Internally supportive   At Stage 3 operations are broadly up there with the best but have aspirations to continue to improve and be the very best in the mar-ket. The operations function has developed appropriate operations processes and resources to excel in those areas in which the company needs to compete effectively. The internally supportive element comes from the development of a credible oper-ations strategy which supports the corporate strategy.

Stage 4: Externally supportive   At this level the operations function is playing a lead role in strategy-making and is forming the foundation for future competitive success. It might be doing so by organizing resources in innovative ways or in design-ing in flexibility so it is capable of adapting as markets change. At Stage 4 a long-term perspective is taken and capabilities developed that will enable the organization to compete in future market conditions. It is about redefining the market and its expectations.

Operations performance objectives

Slack, Chambers and Johnston (2004) identified five performance objectives that apply to all types of operation. Focusing on one or more of these can provide a source of competitive advantage to the organization.

Quality, whether you are running a hospital or a retail superstore, is about doing things right so that error-free goods and services are delivered that are fit for their purpose. We talk further in the quality chapter (Chapter 9) about the various definitions of quality which can be adopted. Quality encompasses both the quality of the design of the product in terms of aesthetics, reliability and per-formance and the quality of the process that delivers the product or service. Quality of delivery process impacts on costs and dependability. Quality is a major source of customer satisfaction or dissatisfaction. Poor quality products or poor quality of service are likely to put the customer off returning, leading to future lost sales.

Flexibility is about the operation being able to change what it does quickly. How quickly can the organization change the mix of products and services it is offering to the customer? Changing consumer tastes affects demand levels and the product range desired, and for an organization to stay competitive it needs to be able to respond to these changes with flexibility. Can the organization react to demand changes and increase or decrease the volume of output in response? Is a wide range of products or services on offer? Can the organization bring new product/service designs to market quickly so it is in a position to meet changing customer needs?

Providing flexibility in delivery options, both the manner and the timing give an opportunity for differentiation.

Speed is all about how long customers wait before receiving their service. Addressing the speed objective requires the organization to pay attention to the cycle time involved in their new product development. How long does it take to bring new products to market? As we shall discuss later, adopting a multidisciplinary team approach to design, seeing it as an iterative process with activities being undertaken in parallel, reduces the design cycle time. An organization also has to pay attention to its scheduling and capacity planning as well as inventory management to be able to deliver on the speed objective. Reducing inventory will also impact on obtaining a cost advantage.

Dependability is, of course, about consistency. An organization's processes have to be geared up to consistently meeting a promised delivery time for a product or service. Customers are unlikely to be satisfied by an increase in delivery speed if it is not matched by consistent performance. This will require that an organization has systems in place to identify problems early and be flexible enough in its planning to be able to move to a plan B as necessary.

Cost is the last objective to be discussed but clearly not the least. For organizations that have adopted a low cost strategy it is the most important objective. The lower the cost of producing the goods the lower price that can be offered to customers, which in turn will boost sales and profits. Even organizations that seek to gain their competitive advantage through differentiation are keen to lower their cost basis because that will lead to improvements in profit levels. To be able to deliver a cost advantage an organization has to analyse where operation costs are incurred. The major cost categories are staffing, facilities that include technology and equipment costs, and materials. The proportions vary between these categories but broadly an organization spends around 55% of its costs on materials, 30% on facilities and 15% on staffing (Greasely 2006). So focusing on reducing the cost of materials will have the biggest impact on reducing costs. It is not surprising then to see the current emphasis on supply chain management and procurement. These sorts of cost breakdown hold good for the manufacturing sector such as automobile plants or for supermarket retailers. In contrast, when considering a hospital the biggest cost element will be staff costs, then facility and technology costs followed by bought-in materials and services. Many costs in a hospital operation are fixed and will not vary according to the number of patients treated. That is to say that facilities like beds, operating theatres or laboratories are as expensive as are the highly specialized staff. These are *all* needed to be available if not all of the time, then most of it. That obviously has cost implications.

Generally the level of costs depends on the volume and variety of output and how variable is demand. Variety of outputs leads to greater levels of complexity and therefore increased costs.

Cost is dependent on the other performance objectives. Improvements in each of the other four will lead to cost reductions. The relative priority of the performance objectives is determined by the demands of customers and the actions of competitors. Making these decisions on priorities links back to the statement in the strategy of what business the organization is in and who are its customers. Selling to customers who insist on error-free products requires the organization to concentrate on its quality performance. Consumer segments that are looking for low-priced products or services will lead the organization to emphasize its cost performance.

Effective market research will help the organization to identify different competitive factors such as innovative products and services, a wide range of products and services, low price, reliable delivery, fast delivery, high quality and the ability to be flexible and change the timing or quantity of output. In terms of being able to make appropriate business decisions an operations manager needs to be able to judge the relative importance of such competitive factors.

Order winning and qualifying factors

Such factors can be distinguished between those that are 'order winning' and those that are 'qualifying factors'. As the name suggests, order winning factors contribute directly and in a significant manner to the winning of business. They will be the factors identified by customers as the reason they made a purchase. So improving performance around the order winning factors is likely to result in improving the organization's opportunity of winning more business. Qualifying factors perform an important function, like the hygiene factors in Herzberg's motivation model. They may not be the crucial determinants of success but they have to be there just for the organization to be considered by the customer. Performance below such a qualifying level could disqualify the company from being considered. This has to be weighed up with the realization that further improvements in performance around those factors are unlikely to result in improved business. To put it another way, the organization is unlikely to gain a return on its investment in the further development of qualifying factors.

These factors have to be considered by each of the customer segments an organization is selling into. For example, the judgements of personal banking customers will be quite different from those of corporate banking services. The weighting given to various factors differs in importance according to the product life cycle stage reached (see Figure 2.3).

The Platts–Gregory procedure

Platts and Gregory (1990) developed a procedure to help formulate an operations strategy which starts at Stage 1 with an analysis of the market position of the organization. Given its external focus at this stage, it looks at opportunities and threats in the competitive marketplace. In particular it identifies the factors that are required by the market and then compares those with the achieved performance so it enables an organization to chart how the operation performs with what the market is looking for. Profiling in this way shows where the gaps are, which should then be addressed by the operations strategy.

The capabilities of the operation are then assessed in Stage 2 of the procedure. What are the current operations practices and how far do these achieve the performance levels identified in Stage 1 as being important?

	Introduction	Growth	Maturity	Decline
Order winners	Performance or novelty	Availability of quality products and services	Low price, dependable supply	Low price
Order qualifiers	Quality, the product range	Price, the product range	Product range, quality	Dependable supply

FIGURE 2.3 THE ROLE OF ORDER WINNERS AND QUALIFIERS AT DIFFERENT STAGES OF THE PRODUCT LIFE CYCLE

Reviewing the options open to the organization takes place at Stage 3 and results in the selection of options that best satisfy the criteria identified in the earlier stages. While this procedure explicitly identifies the gaps between operations performance and the market requirements, this model is regarded as being over-simplistic by those authorities in the strategy area. It does provide a framework for asking some important questions though. Whatever model is chosen it is important to identify what will be the critical success factors for an organization to sustain its long-term well-being.

A crucial part of the formulation of operations strategy is to prioritize competitive factors such as quality, cost, flexibility, dependability and speed. A simple 2×2 matrix of importance/performance is rather crude. Slack (1994) derived a 9-point importance scale (Table 2.3) which takes account of some of these issues just discussed. An assessment of importance and performance leads to decision-making that identifies where urgent action is needed, where the areas for improvement are, at what level performance is appropriate and where it is excessive in terms of what is appropriate as far as customers are concerned.

Although a lot has been written on company strategy, little of this has focused on the actual products (and services) that organizations will need to provide to ensure their survival in that future. How far ahead is this future? Johnson and Scholes (1984) do imply a longer view in their definitions, 'strategy is the direction and scope of an organization over the long term'. Other writers who have said that strategy requires a long-term perspective are Grant (1995) and Schwartz (1998). Although all of these certainly point to the future and how to get there, they do not define the type of products and services that are needed in this future.

Strategy is still considered the important topic to be studied and acted upon by those right at the top of the organization, but recently doubts have crept in (Kare-Silver 1997; Mintzberg 1994). It could be suggested that the belief by some that strategic management is falling from grace is because it does not actively consider the product element. The strategy depends very much on what products and services an organization can and wants to produce.

TABLE 2.3   A 9-POINT IMPORTANCE/PERFORMANCE SCALE

For this product or service does each performance objective meet the following?

Order winning objectives:

1 Provide a crucial advantage with customers;

2 Provide an important advantage with most customers;

3 Provide a useful advantage with most customers.

Qualifying objectives:

4 Need to be at least up to good industry standard;

5 Need to be around the median industry standard;

6 Need to be within close range of the rest of the industry.

Less important objectives:

7 Do not usually come into customers' consideration;

8 Very rarely come into customers' considerations;

9 Never come into consideration by customers and are never likely to do so.

In this market sector, or for this product group, is our achieved performance in each of the performance objectives:

Better than competitors:

1 Consistently considerably better than our nearest competitor;

2 Consistently clearly better than our nearest competitor;

3 Marginally better than our nearest competitor.

The same as competitors:

4 Often marginally better than most competitors;

5 About the same as most competitors;

6 Often within striking distance of the main competitors.

Worse than competitors:

7 Usually marginally worse than most competitors;

8 Usually worse than most competitors;

9 Consistently worse than most competitors?

Slack, 1994

Product strategy

The organization must have a strategic plan and this must be described to all managers in the organization. This is *not* a mission statement as most mission statements are too bland to be of any practical use and too vague to be implemented. Steer clear of mission statements at this stage (and probably every stage). Sociologist and broadcaster Laurie Taylor recounted the following experience quoted in *People Management* (19 April 2001, vol. 7, no. 8): 'I would speak to managers and they would say "It is going marvellously – we've got this great new mission statement." Then I would go down the hall and the staff would be rolling around laughing at the new mission statement. Management theory is often a subject of derision down the corridor.'

A strategic plan should be a detailed description of where the company intends to go *over the next few years*. It is surprising how many strategic plans (and strategy books) only consider their actions over just the next year. Such a plan simply demonstrates that senior managers are not in control of their business, nor do they give due consideration to the abilities and capabilities of their employees. As many product and service developments can take several years to fully implement, sometimes, development programmes in organizations stretch beyond the written strategic plan. Often these are government or local authority funded organizations. The reverse should be the reality: company strategy should lead the product development otherwise who is running the company? Not the top managers.

As G. Peters (1996) has written: 'We are invariably caught unaware of the trends affecting our business because we don't spend enough time looking to the future. Our day-to-day lives are spent managing one crisis or another.'

People managing new products and services can do their bit to revitalize strategy. In fact, with the latest work on design and innovation management and the resulting standard BS 7000-1 *Guide to Managing Innovation* (1999), these managers are taking their work a lot further than many strategic thinkers and planners.

With experience and a new service programme linked in to a well-written strategic plan, a more effective delivery of profitable new products and services will be the result. This will not happen overnight but the logic is clearly there to be seen, so persuading people for its implementation will not be a serious design management problem.

But ... the environment?

Perhaps oddly, despite what people say when asked, very few will go out of their way to buy something that is more environmentally friendly, especially if they have to pay more for it. It was reckoned, at an environmental workshop in Croatia (McAloon and Andreasen 2004), that in Europe there are about 5% of people who will buy environmentally friendly products. A market does exist and may be enough to support niche players but it does not win over big markets. On the other hand, being environmentally friendly coupled with other advantages can be a successful product strategy.

With the enormous success of the ISO 9000 series the standards bodies thought they might achieve similar success with the Environment Management Audit Schemes, such as BS 7750, EMAS and EN 14000. These have not been anywhere near as successful and the reason seems to be fairly obvious. With schemes to improve quality it could be shown that there was a definite marketing edge that would result, as said, in customers demanding it and only purchasing from companies that had acquired it. Although companies often give lip service to their support for environmental policies, they are often not prepared to put their money forward to support companies that are kinder to the environment when their products may cost more. In short, being better to the environment does not always give the marketing edge that providing better quality does.

SUMMARY OF KEY POINTS

- Even in a dynamic, competitive global economy productivity gains are possible and they are likely to be driven by the operations manager.
- Organizations identify their strengths and weaknesses and then develop strategies that take account of those strengths and weaknesses and place the organization in a position to meet the opportunities and threats identified through environmental scanning.
- Organizations can achieve competitive advantage through low cost or product differentiation or a focus strategy.

STUDENT ACTIVITY 2.1

1 Identify three retail companies that follow one of the three generic strategies (cost leadership, differentiation and focus). How have they implemented these strategic plans?
2 How does an operations management strategy change during a product's life cycle?
3 Thinking of the automobile industry, select a car company of your choice and discuss how you think their operations strategy has changed over the Past ten years.

3 PEOPLE, LEADERSHIP AND MANAGEMENT

In this century high performance is only achieved through people, and we can only achieve what the business needs by meeting their needs.

Greg Dyke, former Director General of the BBC, in a talk entitled 'Why did they cry?' reported by Duncan Brown, *People Management*, 27 October 2005

Throughout this book we tend to talk about processes – what activities are needed to get things to work right. None of this happens without people, so in this chapter we look at the people side.

LEARNING OUTCOMES

When you have completed this chapter you should be able to:

- Understand the contribution good job design can make to effective operations.
- Appraise motivational strategies.
- Understand empowerment and leadership.
- Organize groups of people to perform effectively.
- Be able to attribute roles and responsibilities.
- Be aware of the problems that can occur in joint ventures.
- Know how the 'people' side can be improved.

Remember, it is not *companies* that are easy to work for or work with, it is *the people* in those companies that make them easy to work for or with, and as was said to one of the authors at Rover some years back, 'people and politics are more than 50% of any process'.

People are even more important in the service sector as, by definition, people are often part of the process and, therefore, interfacing directly with the organization's customers. A badly trained employee can do a great deal of damage to an organization through poor liaison with the customer.

The processes involved in the management of service operations are now so big that they can certainly no longer be mastered by one person. Management is now undertaken by teams of people expert in particular areas. Also, in certain sectors, design will be done by people who do not have design as part of their job title (Dumas 1990). So just as in operations management, as the activities encompassed under the heading of 'new product development' grow, so the difficulty of its management increases.

Looking at the 'people side' can also be profitable. In the United States the retailer Sears found that a 10% increase in employee satisfaction was associated with a 2.5% increase in customer satisfaction and a 1% rise in sales (Brown and West 2006).

Managing people requires trust

It is quite likely that the growth in activities within an organization probably results in an exponential growth in the difficulty of its (people) management. All the more reason for sound, well-thought-out and documented processes, which includes satisfactory channels of formal and informal communication. Formal communication is that which takes place in organized meetings or by work processes. Informal communication is, as the name implies, that which takes place outside of the organized systems – often people just 'chatting' to each other.

Both are important and necessary in an organization and it has been shown that it is the informal communication that is often more effective. Unfortunately, informal communication cannot be controlled and this can result in unfounded rumours that can damage the smooth operation of an organization. Generally though, if an attitude of openness and trust exists in a company, informal communication can and should be encouraged. Often the negative side of informal communication flourishes when there is too much secrecy within a company and this is rooted in a lack of trust between managers and operators. One of the authors has worked in a company that kept everything a secret. This included an embargo on stating how many company cars there were. Why? How could this affect the running of the company? Generally, the more a management team tries to keep secrets the more rumours will spread. Be open and inform people of what is happening and this will help to generate trust and reduce those damaging management and worker 'them and us' attitudes.

Later in this chapter we will be describing how involving all 'internal customers' can make the daily work lives of all more enjoyable.

FAILURES IN COMMUNICATION

The Space Shuttle 'Challenger' of 1985 exploded shortly after take-off with the loss of all ten of the crew. The accident was due to an oil seal on the fuel tank which only became pliable at temperatures above freezing point. The Challenger took off early in the morning, when the air temperature was cold and the seal was not pliable.

(Continued)

Fuel leaked past the seal and exploded. The resultant enquiry highlighted the poor communication between the various parties involved, as the specification of the oil seal used was known but the information had not reached those in the command centre before NASA had committed themselves to a demanding schedule of take-offs, which did not allow time for reworking of the design.

Experts – internal and external

Always remember that any company is full of 'experts'. Some of these are employed as such and it is part of their job. With others, they may have useful knowledge that has not been harnessed and may not even be known about. Over the past ten years, many organizations have launched 'knowledgement' programmes to explore how they can best tap into this tacit knowledge in their organization. One of the present authors, as part of consultancy work, has developed lists of abilities that employees have in a 'Skills Audit' of some organizations. It is often these hobbies and outside interests that can be quite useful to an organization when it is entering an unfamiliar area.

To take the other extreme, the University of Westminster never used their 'internal experts' in the belief that any employee could have a 'vested interest' in twisting things to their advantage. A good (or rather, very bad) example of this was shown when they ignored their various experts in questionnaire design to develop a questionnaire to identify their new corporate identity. Not only was the outside consultant much more expensive than using people from inside, the final questionnaire was so laughably bad that it is still used by lecturers in several universities as an example of how not to write a questionnaire. This shows a lack of trust from top management. Always trust the workforce. As Herzberg put it rather simply, 'a worker wants to do a good job because he wants to do a good job'. He went on to say that they must also be given the right tools to be able to do a good job, the training to use those tools, the freedom to 'enrich' their job and the motivation. When it is considered that Herzberg et al. (1957) wrote all this about half a century ago it shows that there is quite a bit of catching up to do in many organizations.

Some years ago the former head of Matsushita Electric, Konosuki Matsushita, predicted the failure of Western companies. He said:

We are going to win and the Industrial West is going to lose out. There is nothing much you can do about it because the reason for your failure is within yourselves.

Your firms are built on the Taylor model; even worse, so are your heads. With your bosses doing the thinking, while the workers wield the screwdrivers, you are convinced deep down that this is the right way to run a business.

For you the essence of management is getting the ideas out of the heads of the bosses and into the hands of labour.

For us, the core of management is precisely the art of mobilizing and pulling together the intellectual resources of all employees in the service of the firm.

Damning words, but there has been an attitude change in the minds of top management in this country. The way in which Business Process Re-engineering was dismissed as a second-rate fad by most of British industry suggests that, increasingly, management are trying to pull together and work with all employees. Good management is often about having the trust and confidence to delegate.

Motivation

Motivation can be increased by the following means.

Job rotation

One way of attempting to keep motivational levels high is job rotation, where, to avoid employees getting stale through doing the same specialized job all the time, the job each person does is rotated on a daily, weekly or monthly basis, whichever makes sense for operational reasons. This can help employees develop a broader portfolio of skills and let them have experience of more varied work. Improved motivation and thereby productivity may not last though if the employees come to see the rotation as merely exposing them to a series of boring jobs, each as boring as the last.

Job enlargement

A number of similar jobs on the same level are combined into a larger one with a view to generating jobs with more variety and interest. Again this may result in only a temporary uplift before cynicism about a bigger boring job sets in. Horizontal expansion is one way to characterize this.

Job enrichment

Adding more responsibility to a job, such as responsibility for quality, makes it more interesting. This method of job design gives responsibility for some of the planning and control necessary for achievement back to the employee. This can be seen as vertical expansion.

Ergonomics

Ergonomics or the study of work examines the interface between human and machine. It examines the physical environment within which work is conducted. Understanding ergonomics can lead to improved job performance. If we consider the optimum height for a desk, we take into account the task to be performed at the desk and the size of the individual. Standard desk height is usually 29 inches, yet it should be lower for typing or data entry. Having the desk or chair at the wrong height will affect the posture of the worker and can lead to back and neck pain. Many of the tools, handles, computer keyboards in use put the wrists in an unnatural position. This combined with the repetitive movements of typing can contribute to carpal tunnel syndrome. This syndrome affects thousands of workers annually at great cost to employers, insurers and the health service. Concerns about the incidence of repetitive strain injury among office workers have led to the redesign of keyboards away from the traditional 'qwerty' style, but the familiarity of the existing inefficient layout has prevented these generally from being adopted. There is, perhaps, a design lesson to be learned here – as we shall see later in this book.

Over the years, research has built up large data banks of body measurements, for example the distance most people can reach while remaining seated, important if, for example, the job involves leaning forward to adjust a lever.

The physical environment concerns light, noise and vibration, temperature and humidity. Most people achieve their optimum performance in temperatures of between 18 and 22°C. There are legal limits on the time people can work with loud noise and a maximum permitted decibel standard. Severe noise and vibrations can damage hearing. Pollution or fumes can be irritating to the skin or cause breathing difficulties. Filters need to be fitted to minimize the impact these will have on the workforce. Safe working conditions are expected. Health and safety at work legislation set out the responsibilities of employers to provide a safe environment with extensive use of guards and other fail-safe devices as necessary, and the duty of employees not to work in unsafe conditions.

Empowerment

This involves loading the enrichment so that employees take responsibility for decisions that might naturally belong to specialists. It flows from the idea that those most closely involved with operations are in the best position to make decisions about them. It gives employees a sense of ownership of their jobs so that they can use their own knowledge and expertise to manage the details of the jobs.

Case Study: Allow people to manage

The New Deal for Communities (NDC) is a government-financed scheme that was set up with the good intentions of improving conditions in poorer areas. Fairly small areas were identified as having poor housing, high unemployment, high crime and/or poor education facilities. The community runs these well-meaning schemes and the finance involved is not insubstantial. Typically, a scheme will last ten years, involve a community of around ten thousand people and will be funded to the tune of up to £4 million a year, which is quite a lot of money per person. Of course, such an investment will be well justified if it achieves the aims of improving the area, and many NDCs can be proud of their performance.

One of the authors was employed as a consultant by one of these schemes and unfortunately his experiences show that there were serious deficiencies in that particular scheme. The flaw in the basic idea, in this particular case, lay in the well-meaning theme of 'for the community by the community'. Any such scheme needs well-trained, well-informed and well-meaning leadership.

The author became involved when the scheme was just entering the third year of its ten-year operation. They had a 'shop' where local residents could call in for advice or information and they also had offices with very competent staff. The community decisions were made by an un-elected body of local people on various committees. In principle this sounds effective, and below the leadership level it was. It was the make-up of these committees which was deficient. Ideally, they should have been involved in strategic decision-making, which could then be implemented by the competent full-time employees. In practice, in this case, the committees tended to be made up of people with a bit of spare time, little formal training and (a personal opinion) little ability to deal with this important function.

The main problem was 'micro-management' or, in fact, it was worse than that, it was 'minutia management'. The committees insisted on making every decision, however small. As was overheard, 'If you make any decision without my say-so I will block it' – and this was meant. Furthermore, the various committees disagreed with each other, and as some of the committee members had fallen out with others they seemed more concerned in blocking others' actions than improving the lot of the community. The level of decision-making taken by those on the ground was restricted. Even small decisions had to be taken by a committee, such as what colour they should paint the wall in the office. With committee meetings held once a month and few decisions coming out of these meetings, most initiatives seemed to stagnate. For example, it took the committee two months to decide the colour of some cobblestones for a small part of the pavement. The attempt to introduce a new logo (see Box) was perhaps one of the most ridiculous occurrences.

A graphic designer was commissioned to produce some designs to a specification that had been (eventually) agreed by the relevant committee. Five designs were supplied which were generally considered excellent by those in the office. These were enlarged and laminated, and displayed in the shop on a residents' open day. Members of the local community were invited to stick a smiley face on the logo they liked best. This showed that one logo was significantly more popular than the others.

At the next marketing meeting it was therefore announced that this was to be the new logo, to which one member of the committee responded, 'Who says?' The procedure that had been followed was explained, and that local residents had voted for the chosen logo. To which the reply came, 'They are just people off the street. We represent the community.'

At the same meeting the committee not only threw out all the logos but they threw out the original (agreed) specification from which the logos were designed. After two further meetings they had still failed to reach any decision on how to proceed and it was decided to keep the existing, drab logo for a further 12 months. The whole process had taken four months in which time the new notepaper, signage in the borough and the website had been delayed waiting on the logo decision.

The net effect of this was to make the employees focus on small areas on which they had already obtained permission and do these to death. The other effect was that employees soon became disillusioned, demoralized and sought jobs elsewhere.

When some of the decision-making deficiencies were pointed out to committee members, initially the author was called 'unprofessional', and then all subsequent attempts to implement anything were blocked. The ultimate example of this was a marketing budget proposal that was written for the following two years. This was not unexpectedly 'thrown out', which was the committee's prerogative. What the committee did not consider was that when they threw out the new budget proposal they should also have made provision to maintain the status quo. If they had looked smug in announcing that £0 had been allocated to marketing, they looked less pleased when the Internet went down shortly afterwards and when the monthly newsletter was not delivered and all the planned signage for the area was cancelled as there was no budget to keep going initiatives previously agreed.

After six months of failing to achieve anything, the author declined when asked if he would like to extend his commitment for another six months.

Roles and responsibilities

In many areas we rely on acting in teams. Using multidisciplinary skills collectively can be very powerful if done correctly, and organizations consist of teams of individuals. An understanding of teams and good team orientation will assist individuals and organizations to perform better.

The project may demand a range of skills, which are unlikely to be held by one person. Furthermore, individuals like being in teams as it satisfies social and affiliation need. It is a way of sharing risk and work load with others, a way of establishing self-esteem and also a means of gaining support.

Design circles

Everybody who can make a contribution to the improvement of a service should be involved, but this can cause problems if teams get too big to function efficiently. They become difficult to organize and communication breaks down. Clearly, if everybody who ought to be involved is to be heard, a system needs to be devised so that this can happen. This is called the 'Design Circle'. This name originally came from 'Quality Circles', which were devised by Ishikawa and are used in TQM. The idea was taken into earlier stages of the process – hence the name.

The Design Circle can work from the market research stage through the whole operations process, or for any improvement in any aspect of the service where a process is involved. Of course, in practice, not everybody who would be involved at sometime or another would be included all the time. The personnel in the Design Circle will change as the various stages of the process are completed. New faces will join and others will leave, perhaps to rejoin at a later stage as their particular expertise again becomes relevant. Membership of the Design Circle is, therefore, fluid and will include those best suited to meet the objective – which is to progress to the next stage of the process. In design, as the design progresses through the various stages of the process the Design Circle will develop until it could eventually be transformed into a Quality Circle when the product is established on the market.

With more people being involved in the decision-making process, the better these decisions are likely to be, up to a point. That point, or rather the maximum size of the group, has been determined by the occupational psychologist Edgar Schein (1969) as nine or under. Above nine the group tends to break down into sub-groups and communication generally is less effective. So the maximum size of the Design Circle should be nine at any one meeting.

Occasionally in the design process the number of people who can make a relevant input exceeds nine. When this occurs two Design Circles should be formed, operating in parallel. This should only be for a short period and as soon as possible the circles must be merged into a single Design Circle again.

Roles and responsibility matrix

With different people coming in at different stages in the process, it can be quite difficult to control the roles and responsibilities of those involved. In many organizations a RACI chart is compiled. This is an acronym for **Responsibility** (the persons who complete the task), **Accountability** (the individual ultimately responsible), **Consult** (the persons to be consulted) and **Inform** (those individuals who need to be told of the decision).

We developed a matrix (Figure 3.1) as another way to do this, and this is now used in a couple of British Standards (BS 7000 Parts 1 and 3).

On the vertical axis are shown all the stages of the process and on the horizontal axis the various people who will be involved in completing that particular stage. This can be combined with the RACI chart to make it more effective.

By doing this at the start you will identify shortages within the skills available, but this need not be a problem. For example, if you discover at the start that in 15 months' time you require three people with particular skills, but you in fact only have one person with these skills, there is plenty of time either to employ or retrain people or subcontract this stage of the work to another organization. Potential problems are significantly reduced if they are predicted sufficiently far in advance so that it is possible to cure them before they become a problem.

This matrix will result in a box for each person at each stage of the process. Put a tick in each box to identify if a particular person will be required to take part at any stage. The last column is headed 'Number in the Design Circle' and in this the total number of people involved at that stage of the process should be written. If this number exceeds nine, it would be advisable to split the design circle into two. Alternatively, it may be possible to divide this stage into two parts to be undertaken in series or, preferably, in parallel.

Job function	Product champion	Financial director	Marketing director	Detail designers	Suppliers	Sales personnel	Service managers	Customers	Implementers	Number in the Design Circle
PROCESS STAGE:	INSERT THE NAMES OF THE PEOPLE WHO ARE TO BE INVOLVED AT EACH STAGE OF THE PROCESS									
Design concept										
Detail design										
Testing										
Provision for delivery										
Service launch										
Selling										
In service										
Monitoring and improvement										
Evaluation										
Decommissioning, termination and disposal										

FIGURE 3.1 ROLES AND RESPONSIBILITY MATRIX

Having identified those involved in the improvement process, and where they make their contribution, the next stage is to give each their role and responsibility, as in the RACI chart. The matrix shown is an over-simplification. Usually at each stage there are several activities that must be completed. These should all be placed on the vertical axis, with roles and responsibilities for all parts of these assigned.

These process stages can also be developed into a Gantt chart, with time scales placed on the horizontal axis to aid with the scheduling of the design process.

Most recently the Roles and Responsibility Matrix has been taken further to identify whether people with the right skills and training are being used in each role. It is even taken as far as to see whether they have the right psychological profile, this being measured through psychological and psychometric testing. For example Belbin (1981) identified various team roles that would make up 'balanced' teams and these can be used in conjunction with the Design Circle.

The most recent extension to this is to see if it is possible to identify whether those apportioned a particular role are likely to be capable of performing that particular role successfully. This could result in further training or perhaps people being reassigned to other activities that might better suit their psychological mindset. For example, an introverted character would not suit a role where one has to sell for a living. Such a role requires a more extrovert (and empathetic) character. A few companies are already 'aligning' their staff into roles that best match their personality to make more effective teams.

Key success factors

Research from Henley-Incubator (2003) identified five key success factors necessary to take a new product from the concept stage through to reality. Most of these are 'people-centred'. They specified the need for the following:

1 'A relentless focus on solving a customer problem', this being more important than inspirational ideas or technological innovation.
2 'A leader and a team with a passion to achieve.' A strong commitment of the people associated with the opportunity is a major determinant of the project's success.
3 'A common language for communicating and charting progress.' Design, being multidisciplinary, requires people from various backgrounds and with various skills to be able to understand what the problems are and what progress is being made with the project.
4 'Relevant and quantifiable assets and skills to contribute.' It is necessary to really understand the true nature of the skills needed for a design project and those that are available if success is to be achieved.
5 'Networking is critical.' This is necessary, both internal and external to the organization.

The three key questions that need to be answered when considering a new product's potential are: Is it real? Can we win? Is it worth winning? The same applies to much in operations management.

Leadership and product champions

Organization of communication is extremely difficult and it would be glib to over-look the difficulties of dealing with people and personalities. Having an effective process is vital but whether it works or not comes down to good leadership and coordination.

Leadership needs to be coordinated. It needs to be well informed and educated/skilled in areas in which decisions are to be taken. There is nothing wrong with devolving part of decision-making to those 'experts' who have greater knowledge in those areas. Leadership does not necessarily need to be strong but it must be focused and in sympathy with the aims of the organization and the whole range of products. It should also welcome change if change means improvement.

> The final test of a leader is that he leaves behind him in other men the conviction and will to carry on.
>
> Walter Lippmann

Good leaders should motivate and encourage others and be able to justify decisions (and not be afraid to defend them) once taken in the light of all available information. And the leader must actually take decisions. No decision at all is often worse than a slightly wrong decision made with the best information available at that time.

Also, the long-term effects of any decisions need to be considered and, if the company is to be visionary, so must be the leadership.

A **product champion** has been defined as 'a person dedicated to the promotion and introduction of a new product, although not necessarily responsible for any aspect of the programme' (BS 7000-10: 1995). A more common usage of the term is someone who is not a director but has the power of a director and is supported by the directors for that one project. It is someone who is actively involved at all stages of the process and knows why the decisions were taken at each stage of the process. As seniority tends to decline at the later stages of the process it would be a waste of resources to have a director involved at these later stages.

The product champion must be an optimist and an enthusiast, who pushes the new product forward. They must encourage the others involved in the project and push them to achieve what are often difficult targets within tight financial constraints. On the other hand, they must be a realist, in as much as when things go wrong and it is apparent the targets or specification cannot be achieved they should recommend that the project be abandoned.

The product champion is the person who makes the ultimate decision to abandon the project once it is apparent that it will be a failure. In reality this often means that the final decision for abandoning is taken by the directors on the product champion's advice, having scrutinized earlier stages of the process to see if the problem could be overcome by, perhaps, changing aspects of the specification. Obviously, the role of product champion is most important in the team. The objective of a leader is to control and organize the activity of the design team, using the resources available in the best possible way.

A product champion is always needed to fairly overcome the natural differences that occur within any product development. The ideal person to be a product champion is someone who can see the big picture. There are natural differences that appear, for example, between marketing and production, the former wanting a different product for every customer and the latter wanting all products the same to ease automation and economies of scale. It is the product champion who can resolve differences.

The leader should be encouraging the members of the team to perform optimally, while achieving the design team's objectives. They must help the members to understand their roles and their expected contribution. It will be necessary to encourage them to put their personal objectives in second place where these conflict with the team's objectives and to give positive feedback on their contribution and performance. Group leaders must be able to smooth over disagreements and unproductive competition between the team members, using tact, insight, detachment and firm control.

Empowerment and recent improvements in service

Several things have come together over the past ten years to improve the face-to-face service that customers receive. Staff are an expensive necessity so there tends to be fewer of them but they are better educated and better trained. With the wider adoption of TQM and QA these employees are empowered to take responsibility and make decisions. Furthermore (an important aspect of service management), the occasional mistake is tolerated by management and is an indication where further training is required rather than a reason for punishment.

All this helps when things go wrong. Where possible, the service provision should be blueprinted and all eventualities considered and planned for at the design stage. When people are interfacing with people no blueprinted process will always run exactly as written. It is therefore important that employees who face customers are sufficiently flexible to cope with the unexpected and sufficiently skilled to solve the problem.

By and large, in Europe and some parts of the United States this is now the case. When something goes wrong the person in front of the customer will sort things out. Ability and willingness to make snap decisions is a function of good service delivery nowadays.

There are exceptions, the UK's National Health Service being one. Owing to the trend in the UK (following that seen in the United States) for patients to litigate against the health provider, people working in the health service are less prepared to make fast decisions. They first demand a bank of test results, which increases the cost to the health service and delays the onset of treatment.

The inability to take responsibility often occurs in countries where labour costs are low. It is easier to employ a large number of staff but their individual abilities are often lacking. It is when things do not follow the blueprint that staff are not trained to cope with the unexpected and are 'chastised' if they opt to think for themselves. The immediate loser is the customer who has to wait and suffer on indecision. The final loser will be the service supplier itself.

The training of those who will deliver the service must be included as part of the service design. In manufacturing, staff will be trained to 'do the job'. In services, due to the coincidence of production and consumption and people being part of the service delivery, the staff must also be trained in how to effectively serve the customers. This will involve a larger human relations context within the training.

Case Study: A proverbial tale of failure, or how the road to hell is paved with good intentions

Recent literature has described the importance of alliances in developing products and services (e.g. BS 7000-1: 1999). Generally, alliances between different organizations or the involvement between an organization and a university can be beneficial, as each can have expertise that the other needs to provide a successful service in the full sense. So, by and large, they are 'a good thing'. But the case study below shows that they can go wrong and here we see the 'communication' problems that were experienced in a multinational joint venture. The case relates to a manufactured product but the lessons learned are equally applicable to companies operating in the service sector.

Introduction: 'There is many a slip between cup and lip'
Often more can be learned from a failure than a success. This case describes a project involving three quite different companies operating at a great distance from each other. It is hard enough to develop a successful product within the bounds of one company. It is even harder when three companies are involved and each may have differing interests, strategies or objectives, and this is such a case.

It seemed like the perfect combination. Company A had patented an invention that could have clear advantages over processes currently used. Company B had extensive experience in the market in which this innovation could be used and they possessed all the necessary test equipment required for the product development. Company C produced some of the raw material that would be used in the product but, also, being a large and successful company, had adequate finance to see the idea through all the design stages, into production and beyond. On paper, with the combination of these companies, it would appear that the project couldn't fail – but it did.

Company A, based in the southern states of America, had invented a new product idea that company B, based in the UK, could sell when developed. There was initially a tie-up between these two small companies and at the low cost, early stages of the design process there was sufficient finance available to fund this highly innovative product. It soon became apparent though that more finance would be needed to complete the development process and productionize the item.

Up to this point the communication between the two parties had been satisfactory, aided by many trips from the United States by the head of company A. But the development of the product was slower than it needed to be as the cost of the project essentially had to be covered by profits from existing product sales and specified in the development budget. Of course, there were differences of opinion between the two groups in the direction and emphasis in different aspects of the project – the 'scientific' side being led by company A and the market knowledge side led by company B – but these tended to be resolved easily.

'Many hands make light work'

The tie-up with company C seemed likely to solve all the problems. They had adequate finances to fund this development, including all the high costs associated with productionizing the process, which is typically almost half the total cost of any manufactured product (Hollins and Pugh 1989), as shown in Figure 3. 2.

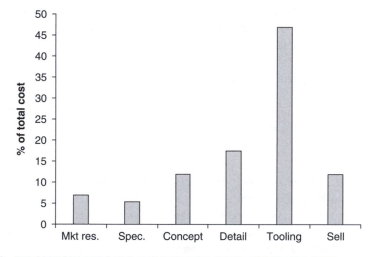

FIGURE 3.2   THE COST OF DEVELOPING NEW PRODUCTS (AFTER HOLLINS AND PUGH, 1990). THE PRODUCTIONIZING STAGE IS STILL, BY FAR, THE MOST EXPENSIVE STAGE OF THE PROCESS

Pause for Thought

The cost of the stages given here relate to manufactured goods. Why are there no equivalent figures available for services?

Initially, the set-up worked well, but as the product was essentially an invention in its first market form, the time for the various stages of the design proved difficult to predict. The time scale for this highly intensive scheme began to fall behind schedule, but the expenditure of the project was still relatively low at this stage.

'He who pays the piper calls the tune'

At this stage of the development, company C set milestones and stage gateways (Cooper 1988; BS 7000-3: 2006), which had to be achieved before the next financial investment for the development to companies A and B was triggered. Something, often assumed in the design literature, is that the milestones to be reached by each stage gateway should be on a logical progression to the successful conclusion of the design process – which is a successful profitable product operating within its market. Unfortunately, these milestones bore little resemblance to the real needs of this known market but were more related to the relatively unsophisticated test (proving) equipment owned by company C.

The dilemma then arose in companies A and B. Should they develop the product according to the needs of company C or should they go for the market requirements? The pragmatic decision was taken – develop the needs of company C and take the money. After all, this would be a stage towards the needs of the market. The alternative would be to abandon the whole programme or develop the product at a much slower pace than before using the small development budgets of companies A and B.

'Too many cooks'

One of the successes of Japanese industry has been explained as the close link between product design and process design (design of the method of manufacture). Even so, at this detail and embodiment stage (Pahl and Beitz 1996; Pugh 1982) of the design process there had been little real thought given to how the product could be manufactured in the large quantities anticipated.

Both A and B had always realized the potential of the product and, if it could be mass-produced at low cost, new markets would then become open to the device. A decision had been taken, early on by A and B, not to quickly 'commoditize' the product, that is, mass produce for low cost high volume markets.

> *With any new product (MP3 and DVD players for example) the initial product is introduced at a high cost and in small quantities and then the price and costs fall. This is due to the high cost of R&D being paid off and the initial high introductory promotion slows as customers become familiar with the product. Also, the high cost of productionizing and automation (if any) can more easily be clawed back.*
>
> *Best (2005), amongst others, has discussed how people purchase new products that are introduced on to the market. Initially, the purchasers are called 'innovators' and in the next stage of the product life cycle they are called 'early adopters'. These people do not mind paying the high introductory price because they want the special features of the product (or want to impress their neighbours). As production builds, economies of scale are introduced and competition appears, the price will fall and this results in greater market penetration. The product will eventually become a 'commodity' that can be afforded by almost any user.*

With the finance available from company C it would be possible to quickly move towards commodity markets so the design could be produced not only for the high value end but for the lower value market also.

'In the land of the blind the one-eyed man is king'

Productionizing was taken up by company C as they had a vast experience in both batch and mass production. Unfortunately, this experience did not include knowledge of the specific techniques needed for this development. Company C tested many of their own prototypes but, when samples came to company B for test on their more advanced equipment, it was clear that they were some way from being reliable – the most important aspect of any product or service (Hollins and Pugh 1989). As the product was performing, it was not competitive with company B's existing offerings.

> For a product to succeed it must demonstrate advantages over that already on the market – benefits, which may also be 'Unique Selling Propositions' (Dibb et al. 2001: Hollins et al. 2003). Competition is always wider than most companies realize (Levitt's Marketing Myopia, 1960).

Communication

At this stage of the process, lack of 'empathy' between the participants meant that it was difficult to sort out the problems in frank discussion. At last there was a degree of concurrency within the design process as the product design and process design was occurring together. But, as said by Andreasen (1994), one of the most important aspects of simultaneous engineering is the need for effective communication, but communication across countries proved to be a problem. Initially, the various parties made visits for face-to-face meetings but this was expensive. Then telephone conferencing was used and, at first, this was thought to be beneficial, as it was not expensive and saved valuable director time spent in travel.

After a couple of months of such negotiations, however, they were abandoned in favour of a return to face-to-face meetings. This was because the barriers between the three parties seemed to be growing. The 'non-verbal' communication was missing and, after some phone meetings ended in acrimony, it was realized that communication really is better when undertaken round a table. The informal discussion on the weather, family and social events tends to be missing in a formal link-up and a 'them and us' situation is enforced. This was partly overcome by the parties all meeting together in the United States for a social get-together, where talk of work was out and the aim was purely to have a good time and increase the informal communication.

Leadership

What the project really lacked was an independent product champion. Usually differences of opinion, when they occur, do so between different departments with different priorities but all within the same organization. This was magnified in this case, where the participants were from different companies. Within a single company it should be fairly easy to ensure that the product champion has the best aims of the company at heart. But in this case (and similar multi-company projects), who could be an impartial product champion?

> *Some years ago the author was involved in consultancy with a company that made wind generators. Senior managers who were extremely competent and well qualified made technical decisions but their abilities were focused on the small area of their expertise. In a particular project a product champion was selected who was aged 25. He was not as senior as the other managers involved but he was capable of seeing the 'big picture'. Each manager would give his or her expert opinion and the young product champion then decided the overall direction for the project. In this particular project it worked.*

Over the months effective communication became less efficient as the various groups battled with the difficulties that arose in the development. A satisfactory solution in this project was never found, and to our knowledge, there has been nothing researched that solves this problem. How can an independent product champion be selected in multi-company developments?

Perhaps an outside consultant would have helped to solve the problem. This would come at significant cost if someone was to have sufficient involvement in the project to know the 'ins and outs' of each company as well as being able to understand the technology.

Concurrency

Concurrent engineering (doing aspects of the development in parallel to save time) often works well when the detailed stage and implementation takes place in parallel. This is more difficult with an innovative product that, by its very nature, is not fully understood (Hollins and Hollins 1991). In this development the attempts were being made to productionize at the concept stage, where fundamental changes were still being made to the design. This caused much 'stalling' in company C where they would start to embark on production tools only for the basic elements of the concept to be changed by company A rendering the new tooling obsolete.

A lesson to be learnt is that concurrent engineering can only be effective when the basic concept has been finalized (agreed and signed off). Those implementing a service need a fair degree of stability. Concurrent engineering does *not* mean that all stages of a design process can be undertaken in parallel. At many stages (and between several of those stages) concurrency is inappropriate.

Conclusions

It is hard enough to develop a successful product within the bounds of one company. It is even harder when three companies are involved and each may have differing interests, strategies or objectives.

In retrospect, one could see that the demarcation lines were too strongly drawn. Company A (leading the scientific side) tended to ignore design improvements proposed by company B, ignoring the latter's vast experience in developing solutions (albeit less scientifically based) in their home market. This was similar to 'over the wall' design as first described by John Crawford of Cranfield University in the mid-1980s. It also ignored the observations of Osborne (1993) and others that the most senior people or specialists do not necessarily have all the best ideas at the concept (creative) stage of the design process.

The study shows the importance of specifying the *right* milestones in a stage gate process (Cooper 1993). In this project they were related in terms of technological 'breakthroughs' rather than the needs of the market.

A lot has been made of the effectiveness of video and conference calls in multinational projects. Certainly this saves money and time, but in this case the loss in the informal and non-verbal communication had serious damaging effects on the trust between participants and the likely success of the venture.

Leadership (a product champion) is necessary in a design project (BS 7000-2: 1997). It must be recognized that the richest and largest company may well harm their own position by taking a too dominant role in the leadership and operation of such developments (Badke-Shaub and Stempfle 2004). The results confirm that understanding of technology and the market can be equally as important as adequate finances in design.

'A rolling stone gathers no moss'

It should be said that the product was eventually successful and is now on the market.

Case Study: Cool Logistics – the profit is in the service

As has been said, many services 'ride on the back' of manufactured products – for example, car sales need cars. What is often overlooked is that the service side can often be designed and developed to be the greater part, and the most profitable part, of the offering. Such is the case with Cool Logistics, a company based in Leighton Buzzard that specializes in the design and manufacture of insulated shipping systems.

The company

Cool Logistics was started in December 2000 to design, validate, manufacture and test products. The actual product is essentially very simple but to meet the customer requirements often entails some very innovative solutions and these are backed by exhaustive testing. Turnover has grown dramatically in each year of operation through incorporating service principles throughout the organization. They now employ about 60 people.

The key to the company's success has been to focus on customer requirements and to be flexible enough to develop tailor-made solutions to meet these requirements. This means getting close to customers, allowing a personal relationship to be built between customer and company. Beyond merely reacting to customer requests, the service is designed to offer solutions to meet unusual customer requirements. Doing such 'specials' has been the undoing of companies in the past but in Cool Logistics it has been found that going that bit further to provide help often results in being placed on the customer list as a 'preferred supplier'.

Blueprinting

When the company was set up the directors envisaged the 'customer journey' for each service eventuality. These processes were blueprinted in some detail and these blueprints analysed to determine and fully understand the 'customer touch points', that is, the customer journey and where the customers might contact or need help from the company.

As was said in 1980 by Jan Carlzon, then President of Scandinavian Airlines, 'All instances where customers come into contact with our organization constitute "moments of truth" – unique, never-to-be-repeated opportunities for us to distinguish ourselves memorably from competitors.' And this is still true today.

Processes were designed to optimize the efficiency in each of these contacts. Of course, it was not possible to envisage each eventuality, especially in a company growing so fast. The basic blueprints have been enlarged and adapted and are now endemic within the organization and do appear to ensure a good service.

This 'service element' has been taken further in the company. Occasionally a customer will ring up with an urgent request for product testing or validation. Quite often this is because the customer has 'blundered' in anticipating their own requirements. The company communications have been designed to solve these 'crises' at short notice and 'getting customers out of a hole' usually results in longer-term benefits. This means losing other operational advantages to meet this goal: for example, the company finds that it has to hold large quantities of stock in order to provide this service – JIT from suppliers would not provide a sufficiently good service.

Customer relationship management and total quality management

One other feature of the service (from the blueprint) is that, before invoices are sent out, all customers are telephoned to obtain customer feedback and to ensure that they are pleased with the service that has been provided. As problems are immediately solved this has virtually eliminated customer complaints. This is all part of relationship management which is a growth area in service provision and is based on the principle that it is easier to retain existing customers than it is to attract new ones. There is a close link between this and Total Quality Management. The instigator of TQM (W. Edwards Deming) said that the aim was to 'delight' customers – to go beyond what they expect. This is further enhanced through an effective and easy-to-use website and literature, all of which has been designed by qualified designers.

As in many organizations, the staff undergo continuous training but in Cool Logistics the staff are also trained in areas such as teamwork and creativity. It is believed that this training enhances their flexibility to cope with the unexpected and does improve their performance. This informal and 'organic' approach to the company organization is a further example of how design principles permeate throughout the company.

Employees are also empowered to make decisions and to offer suggestions to improve the way the company works. Originally, this was just for the office staff but this has now been extended to involve everybody in the company. Prizes are awarded for the best ideas.

But what of the internal customers?

There is another dimension to this. In such a fast-growing company trying to respond to 'instant' customer demands, the stresses and strains within the company grew along with the success. The spectacular growth of Cool Logistics has had its 'down side'. Everybody was working harder and faster and, as a result, some people were feeling that 'working here is not as much fun as it used to be'. The solution was sought to this problem through an 'internal market research' investigation to see if these difficulties could be overcome through better communication or better processes.

The key again came from Total Quality Management. An aspect of TQM is 'internal customers', who are those people with whom one directly works inside the company. Cool Logistics was responding instantly to the needs of outside customers and these were being achieved at the expense of the internal customers.

The research

Using a questionnaire, all the employees were interviewed over a period of two days. Questions covered aspects of work, processes and communication but also enquired as to any problems or ideas that could improve their work or make life at Cool Logistics less 'stressful'. If they could think of ways to make their life easier (and the life of those they worked with) all would benefit. The company would be a happier and more efficient place in which to work. Some of the discussion ventured into other areas and this unearthed further opinions and perceptions.

The results

It was found that almost everybody felt, in most cases, they were helped by others to do their job and that people rallied around when there were problems. Also, quite a few stated how much they liked the informal and relaxed way the organization was managed. They also enjoyed the company outings that further endorsed the informal nature of management within Cool Logistics. It is important to maintain this informal approach even though it is accepted that this becomes increasingly more difficult in any growing company. When one stated that his only complaint was that he 'had to work through Friday afternoon' then there clearly were not too many problems. Another man stated that this was the happiest company in which he had worked.

Generally, internal communication appeared to be good but a few of the operatives stated that they had been working for Cool Logistics for some time before they realized what the company did ('I didn't know what the products were used for'). This was easily resolved. A two-page leaflet to hand out to all new starters has been produced stating a little about the company, what it does and where its products are used.

On the broader front, most felt that they were not getting enough information from the directors as to where the company was going ('information comes down the grapevine from directors'). By the amount of work people were doing everybody realized that the company was growing fast, but several were unsure if this was a general trend or just a short-term happening. On this basis, a newsletter was produced once every two months and the general opinion was that this newsletter should not show long-term plans but should concentrate on particular jobs and customers. Furthermore, the directors now hold monthly meetings with all staff to state what has been happening and to answer any questions. They also now make a point of regularly wandering around production thanking people for their efforts and praising their work and asking if they have any questions or suggestions.

Another area that needed to be resolved was the lack of 'people skills' from line managers. As one respondent said, 'it would be nice to be asked to do things rather than just being told to do it'. These people had often been employed when the company was small but now were managing groups of workers but had no skills in this area. To this end human resources training has been given and this will focus on taking a more friendly approach to managing those with whom they work.

The questionnaire unearthed one major surprise. It was discovered that there was one important and growing product that almost all the production operatives hated having to make. The solution in the short term was to organize a rota that, at least, ensured that all did equal stints on the job. For the longer term, process design has come to the rescue and production of this particular product has been automated. The unpopular job, but not the product, has been designed out of the company.

Conclusions

Managers tended to focus on dealing with customers and often overlooked the 'internal customers' – their staff. Their involvement and efficiency can often be improved through following the initial 'trigger', in this case that there were problems due to the fast growth of the company. Market research was undertaken to fully understand the needs of the (internal) customers. From the results of this market research several small specifications were written and these were then discussed in a brainstorming session. In this (concept) session various solutions were proposed and the 'best' of these agreed and then implemented. In this case they had to meet the needs of the staff but also had to be viable and not interfere with the effective operation of the company.

The mission of the company is 'striving to be a pleasure to do business with'. They achieve this through designing then implementing a good service. The company has been structured and runs on good service, its continuing success suggesting that such a principle works.

Managers – you are often the weakest link

Management have often been the weak link in the chain. *Management Today* proudly announced in the September 1999 edition that 50% of British managers have a management qualification. A step in the right direction you might say, but only 50%? How many of you would use an unqualified dentist, doctor, accountant or welder? Why do we put up with unqualified managers? Many organizations have suffered at the hands (and minds) of these unqualified managers – the sort who have shelves of the latest management books all of which have never been opened (the information is imparted by some form of osmosis).

And on what do these top managers base their decisions? The one-day conference is where these managers become educated to the point of expertise. Choosing the conference is a tricky business. First the conference must have an elaborate title, which can then be shortened to a handy acronym, such as Rationalization over Technomation

(ROT): Then it must have a decent lunch included, and it must have a formidable fee attached to keep the riff-raff out (say, £800/day). Then, armed with this little learning (which is a dangerous thing) they become influenced into accepting the importance of the latest fad. Unfortunately, although they have been convinced of its importance, they haven't been shown enough so that they can actually implement it.

They return to work charged up with ideas for change. Change doesn't necessarily mean improvement. As they only have half the ideas worked out, they then call in the management consultants (are they qualified?) – and then the fun really starts.

From probably well before the Boer War we British have a history of being 'lions led by donkeys' in more than just war. Sometimes it is amazing that in spite of all this stacked against us, we often manage to succeed. You, as users of this book, are learning to be managers, and (if you do it properly) you will be better able than many to cope with managing processes and people.

DOES THIS STRIKE A CHORD?

Once upon a time there was a boat race between a Japanese crew and a National Health Service team. Both practised hard to reach their peak performance but on the big day the Japanese won by a mile.

The NHS team became discouraged and morale sagged. Senior managers decided the reason for the crushing defeat must be found and set up a working party to investigate the problem. After six months of deliberation, they came up with a substantial report and a recommendation for action.

The working party concluded that the Japanese had eight people rowing and one steering while the NHS team had eight steering and one rowing. It immediately hired a consultancy to look at the team's structure. Millions of pounds and several months later the consultants reported that too many people were steering and not enough rowing.

To avoid losing again the team structure was changed to give three assistant steering managers, three steering managers and one executive manager, and a director of steering services. A performance and appraisal system was also set up to give the person rowing the boat more incentive to work harder.

The Japanese were challenged to another race – and won by two miles. The NHS managers responded by laying off the rower for poor performance, selling the oar and cancelling orders for a new boat. The money was used to finance higher than average pay awards for the steering group.

(Anon.)

In the end, an organization is nothing more than the collective capacity of its people to create value. Lou Gerstner, CEO of IBM

SUMMARY OF KEY POINTS

- This chapter has been about how to do things through people. Processes are essential to get things done but who does these things and how they lead and communicate need to be effective if any process is to be efficient.
- Good management needs delegation and this needs trust and empowerment.
- Good leadership is essential and a product champion can provide this.
- The Roles and Responsibility Matrix can show who should be involved and when. People can be profiled so that they are given the right job for their personality.
- The several case studies have indicated where good and bad people management has occurred. One case showed that internal customers can be almost as important as those a company sells to, if the operation is to work effectively.

STUDENT ACTIVITY 3.1

1   What is the role of ergonomics in job design?
2   How could you select a suitable product champion?
3   What is the purpose of the Roles and Responsibility Matrix?
4   What is the 'internal customer?'
5   What is the difference between informal and formal communication?
6   There are two different descriptions of the role of the product champion, what are these?

STUDENT ACTIVITY 3.2

You are a director who wants to (a) start a new service and (b) improve an existing service.

1   What sort of information should you give your project manager?
2   What sort of information do you want back?
3   When do you want this information back?
4   How will you decide that it isn't worth pursuing any particular product?

Guidance

As you consider this you will see that much of the information that is required is quite different for a product improvement than for a completely new product. In the former those involved are familiar with the product, what it does and where it sells. In the latter the whole point of the product is often not clear and much more information is required at the start of the process.

As a director you will not want the small day-to-day information but broader information regarding the time scales and cost of the development. The project manager will want to know what parameters he/she must operate within. Essentially, this is what is allowed by the company and specified by the director.

STUDENT ACTIVITY 3.3

Describe the role of the product champion.

Guidance

The role of the product champion depends a lot on how the term is defined. In some circles it is a term to describe somebody who supports but does not actually take part in the day-to-day development activities. Elsewhere the term is used to describe someone who is actively involved in day-to-day activities. Take the latter use of the term.

Your answer should include the planning of the activities but also the likely communication problems and conflicts that might occur between people with differing priorities (marketing and production). It will be easier to answer this if you think of specific product developments.

STUDENT ACTIVITY 3.4

What kind of information does top management require from the product champion as the design project progresses?

FURTHER READING

Belbin R.M. (2003) *Management Teams: Why They Succeed or Fail.* Oxford: Butterworth-Heinemann.

Egan J. and Harker M. (eds) (2005) *Relationship Marketing,* vols 1, 2, 3. London: Sage.

Salaman G., Storey J. and Billsberry J. (eds) (2005) *Strategic Human Resource Management.* London, Sage.

PART 2

Developing New Services

4   The Product and Service Design process

This section addresses the broad spectrum of the Total Design management process. here it will be shown how it relates to both products and services. It includes analysis of why Total Design is important and reports our research findings showing that service design management is poor. Included in this chapter will be an analysis and evaluation of design strategies; of how the Total Design process can be used to manage money, time and concurrencies. Our recent research on simplifying the new product design process will be described as well as how blueprinting can be used in the design of services. The link with project management will also be shown.

5   Customer Identification

There is no point in developing or trying to improve services if there are insufficient customers who need these services. In this chapter we look at identifying customer needs and how to avoid the main reasons for product and service failure. We also look at why customers buy – advantages and benefits – as well as sources, types and analysis of information needed to ensure a viable operation.

6   Design Specifications – Controlling the Process

These are the controlling mechanism for the process. Although it has been appreciated for some time that specifications are important, it is only recently that serious consideration has been given to how these should be written, who should write them and what they should include. Here are identified the most important aspects of a product and service design, where managers should focus their services. The link between the Marketing mix and specifications is also discussed.

7   Creativity and Innovation

This chapter is about conceptual design – how to control the early stages. It includes the nature of creativity and the creative process. It describes where ideas come from and the tools and techniques for enhancing creativity. Also discussed is when to innovate and when to improve services and how too choose the best concept. Lifestyles are also discussed.

8 Learning from Product and Service Failures

Often, more can be learned from failures than successes. The failure of products and services is investigated: what is a failure, the types of failure and where they occur in the design process. The chapter looks at how failures can be minimized and where management should concentrate their emphasis.

4 THE PRODUCT AND SERVICE DESIGN MANAGEMENT PROCESSES

> Good design is good business.
>
> Tom Watson Jr, CEO of IBM

The purpose of this chapter is to introduce you to the processes through which design can be managed effectively in an organization. Initially, design management is explained and put in context. Some design models are introduced but the content of the various stages is described in later chapters. The chapter continues with a case study in which an attempt has been made to simplify a complicated and difficult-to-use process into something that is more likely to be adopted by practitioners. The chapter ends with a description of research that was undertaken by the authors into the effectiveness of some managers in service design management.

LEARNING OUTCOMES

When you have completed this chapter you should know:

- What design and design management mean in business today and what the design process looks like.
- How researchers have widened the use of 'design' and attempted to improve design management processes. The elements introduced in this section will be expanded upon in subsequent chapters.
- How to use blueprinting as an aid to designing services.

Getting the right product or service is never cheap. It is not surprising, therefore, that many companies hold back. But without a constant supply of new products or services the company's offerings soon become outdated, it loses customers and spirals into decline. An organization that develops no new products or services will slowly decline and fail. Once they develop failures they will go out of business far more quickly. This may seem to be pretty obvious, but our recent research on how people manage the development of their new services (described later in this chapter) shows that the majority do so inadequately. Their companies and their job security are therefore in peril. Developing the right services in the right way is probably the best means of keeping ahead of the competition.

The key here is 'design'. As Tom Peters (1996) wrote, 'Design, as I see it, is the number one determinant of whether a product – service – experience – brand stands out or doesn't. So … why do so few pay (obsessive) attention to it?' It is quite apparent that service design takes a back seat in the minds of senior managers and chief executives.

In a manufacturing company they may not do design well but they will know what it is. In the service sector, many people still believe that design is something not relevant to them. But several service organizations, such as Royal Mail, BA, BAA, already have well-developed processes for developing their new services.

WHAT IS DESIGN?

Have you seen the number of programmes on TV that have 'design' in the title? They are invariably about some amateurs 'making over' a kitchen or garden or whatever. Some years back the average man or woman in the street thought that 'design' was only about the look of the things they bought. Thanks to the media, things have gone from bad to worse and now people think decorators and gardeners are the determiners of what is 'design'. It is surprising that real designers have any 'street cred' left at all when graphic artists, hair stylists and the said decorators all not only call themselves designers but also have a higher profile than the worthy ones. Even the corporate identity (sorry, brand identity) brigade call themselves 'designers', even though they call upon almost none of the measures by which designers attempt to justify their work. And what you can't measure you can't manage.

So what is design?
Design, after all, is not just about producing effective and attractive objects – as worthy an end as that is.

Designers are trained to analyse and improve processes, exchanges and encounters – between customers and products, clients and services or, potentially, between citizens and States. (Design Council 2004).

The definition that we use is:

> **A multidisciplinary, iterative process that takes an idea and or market need forward into production/implementation and through to disposal.**

The important early stages

Identifying potential failures at the earliest possible time enables an organization to concentrate on those new product developments that are more likely to succeed. It

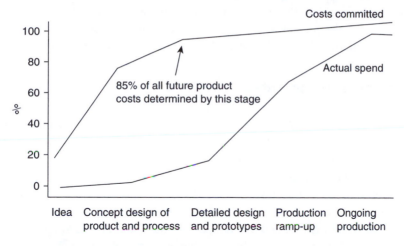

FIGURE 4.1   THE PRODUCT DEVELOPMENT CYCLE: 80% OF FINANCIAL COMMITMENT AND 80% OF MANAGEMENT DECISIONS ARE MADE AFTER 15% OF THE PROJECT EXPENDITURE (AFTER DESIGN COUNCIL, 1985)

was a long time ago that Starr (1963) said that it was not the cost of failures that was so bad, it was the *lost opportunity* of this time not being spent on developing successes.

One of the main reasons for new products failing is that the full requirements are not considered at an early stage in the process (Hollins and Pugh 1989). It is near the start that all the compromises (new products are all about compromises) need to be resolved. For example, can the company actually produce the new service? Can they market it? Can they afford to develop it? Can it be made to work? (Hollins and Hollins 1999).

All of these decisions need to be confronted in the early stages when (like in man-ufacturing) 80% of the management decisions are taken and 80% of the funds committed but only 15% of the actual expenditure made (Figure 4.1. Design Council 1985). It is this low cost, front end of the process where most product and service failures are rooted and yet this research shows that it is here that the service companies are most inadequate.

Most products and services without a profit are an exercise in futility (to para-phrase Gisser 1965). Determine at the start that the service *should* provide a profit (or be provided within a certain budget) by looking at the market and the company capabilities. In the specification stage identify the necessary return on investment (ROI). If it is inadequate, then do not pursue the project. Remember to include the cost of money – so consider the discounted cash flow (DCF). Either the develop-ment is to be funded on borrowed money – where interest has to be paid, or on income from the organization's other products – which means interest from invest-ing this money is lost. Also, do not demand an excessive ROI as this will kill many new, potentially good designs – as happened at Xerox many years back when they insisted on matching the profitability of all new products to those of photocopiers.

Look at the whole life of the service for potential profit points that can be gained for the service (e.g. delivery, fitting, warranty, spare parts and servicing, leasing and renting, disposal). All are opportunities for involvement and profit.

These steps occur at the front end of the process. It also is the easiest and only sensible part of the process at which to identify whether a service is likely to be a success or a failure – before a great deal has been spent on its development.

Design management?

There are lots of differing views on what should, or should not, be included in the design management process. There are few 'definites' in this subject and room for a wide range of proposals, and for that reason we have included what we have found through consultancy works best for us.

The key to this is **Total Design**. If the 'design' process is identified in full and early on, the whole management process can be more effectively organized and controlled from the start. Identifying the stages then allows the manager to allocate the time and identify the people needed in this cross-functional/multidisciplinary process. The budget can also be allocated between the stages and the stages that can be undertaken concurrently can also be identified. The manager is then more effectively in control. Shortages in people, time and finance can be identified and addressed long before they become a serious problem. If they cannot, then it is wise to abandon the whole venture and get on with something that is more worthwhile – before much money has been spent on it. Costly product failures can then be avoided.

Design management confronts these problems and aims to solve them. It is the way successful organizations are managing their products in a changing world and with more discriminating consumers. It can be seen that design and its management is much more than many think. We will now describe what it does involve.

The background

What constitutes the development of new products has 'grown' over the past 30 years. Design as undertaken by art school designers was once considered to be an end in itself, which resulted in products that were for an 'educated elite' (Walker 1989) but were invariably difficult to make, expensive to buy and had limited appeal. This type of design was a throwback to the Arts and Crafts movement pioneered by William Morris at the end of the ninteenth century but it fails to fulfil the needs of those operating in mass markets.

In the mid-1970s, as supply began to approach and then exceed demand in most product areas, companies considered design to start at the concept stage and also included consideration of ease of manufacture (e.g. Anderson 1975).

In the mid-1980s pioneers, starting with Stuart Pugh (1982), proposed 'Total Design' in which the market was given prior consideration and a thorough specification was developed all before the concept stage of design (Figure 4.2.) A written design process is often called a 'design model'. This still widely accepted model ends at the selling stage, but the scope of 'Total Design' has been extended to include everything up to and including 'disposal', such as servicing, marketing and redesigns (Andreasen 1994, BS 7000-1: 1989; Hollins and Pugh 1990).

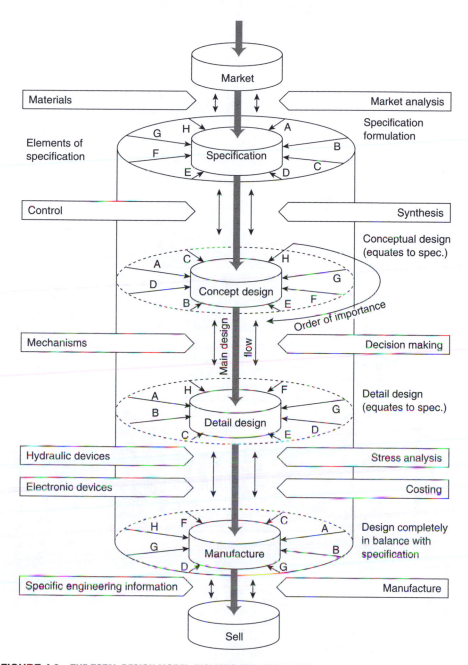

FIGURE 4.2   THE TOTAL DESIGN MODEL (HOLLINS AND PUGH 1990)

The application of Total Design has also been widened to include services (Figure 4.3) (BS 7000-3: 1994 – to be replaced by a later version; Hollins and Hollins 1991) and the British Standards Institution has published other sector standards on design management of manufactured products, and in the construction industry (BS 7000-2: 1997 and BS 7000-4: 1996).

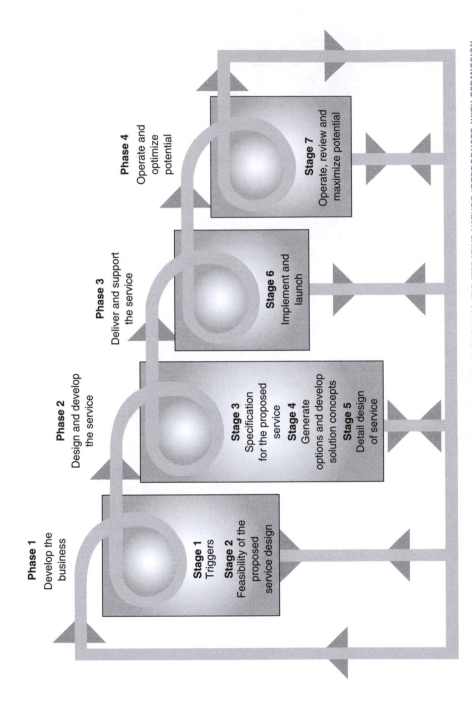

FIGURE 4.3 THE LATEST MODEL OF THE STAGES OF THE SERVICE DESIGN PROCESS SHOWING IT'S ITERATIVE NATURE (REPRODUCED WITH PERMISSION FROM GILL WILDMAN OF PLOT, www.plotsite.net)

The total process has been yet further expanded in recent research and publications to include a strategic viewpoint so that organizations can set themselves in the right direction for future developments. Such writings take the process to start earlier than an idea – more to identify and assess the capability of the organization in which the right products and services can be fitted.

Most recently, a longer-term consideration of design management has taken planning up to ten years into the future (BS 7000-1: 1999; Hollins and Hollins 1999) so that organizations can predict and make a strategic long-term plan to develop products and services well into the future (more of this in Chapter 14). So the spectrum covered by design management continues to grow.

> Good design is not just a matter of flair or an occasional flash of inspiration – it is an ongoing systematic process.
>
> George Cox, Former Director General, Institute of Directors

Design management can be defined as:

the totality of the design activity, its administration and contribution to an organization's performance. It includes the organization and implementation of the process for developing new products and services. (BS 7000-3: 2006)

Therefore, the process is the key.

Developing a design process

A well-managed design process will ensure that new services that reach the market will be competitive, safe, satisfy customers and be profitable. Furthermore, as markets change, continuing design ensures improved services that will lead to a greater chance of company survival. The approach to take when starting the new development is to follow a procedure that is a bit like peeling the various layers from an onion. Initially these layers are more strategic and set a series of parameters within which new product development must be managed (Figure 4.4).

These are generally independent of the particular new product under consideration and can be set down as a series of boundaries in which any new development must be positioned. As each layer is completed and the skin is peeled off a new set of 'problems' emerge that need to be resolved. After a few layers have been peeled away then the problems become more related to the actual new service under consideration.

It is necessary that each stage of the process be written down before any development starts and this process will need to be quite long and complicated. You cannot develop a new product or service with just a few boxes describing the broad stages that need to be undertaken. Certain stages will feature in any design process. It will be necessary to look at the market, write a specification, think of the various concepts for doing it, do the details and implement it. But there will need to be many more stages and there is no one process that is suitable for all services. Even with a full design process, in practice the activities taken will be iterative, that means

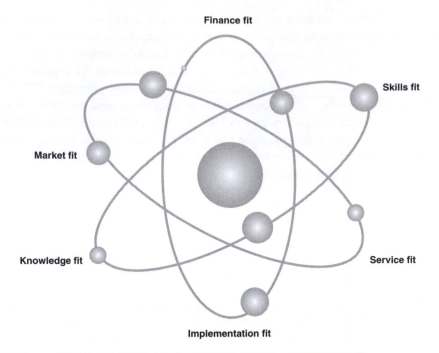

FIGURE 4.4   TYPICAL PARAMETERS TO BE SPECIFIED AROUND ANY NEW SERVICE

it will be necessary to backtrack on various stages, as your understanding increases and more information becomes known. This is normal and is not a sign that the original work was necessarily wrong, it is just that knowledge has grown.

Initially the design process will state what work has to be done. Knowing these stages it will then be possible to make a close estimate on the cost of each of these stages and, therefore, the total cost. Also, the time that each stage will take can be identified and, therefore, the total time for the project. This means that at the start of the project it is possible to estimate with some accuracy the total cost and the completion date. Of course, this is an estimate and there are likely to be inaccuracies within it, but the more experienced one becomes the better these estimations become.

> It is now more than forty years since Sidney Gregory wrote The Design Method *(1966)* and in this he showed an understanding of design and its management well beyond his contempories. In his book he states:
>
>> The process of design is the same whether it deals with the design of an oil refinery, construction of a cathedral or the writing of Dante's 'Divine Comedy'.
>
> Essentially, this is correct and a fundamental of good design management. Sidney Gregory was talking about design as a process then and many haven't got round to realizing that it is one even now!

The design management process is generally considered to start with an idea or 'trigger' (of which there are 30 sources for new products or services listed in the box. Regarding terminology, design begins with an **idea**. The word 'concept' is used by many designers to describe the start of the process, but you should avoid this otherwise there is some confusion with the concept stage that occurs later. For example, a service design **idea** may be to deliver parcels. After the specification has been written, in the **concept** stage, all the different ways for delivering the parcels are considered (helicopter, bus, walk, submarine, catapult etc.). The idea can be achieved by lots of different concepts.

TRIGGERS

From BS 7000-3 (2006)
Considerations that may lead to a new product include:

1 *an order or enquiry from a customer;*
2 *a response to a perceived market need;*
3 *government initiatives and charters;*
4 *a research finding, perhaps associated with the development of a new technology as appropriate;*
5 *a new way of applying existing technology that may result in an innovation;*
6 *a licence or franchise agreement;*
7 *a creative thought from any source;*
8 *a change of company facilities or assets that may provide an opportunity to redesign the product;*
9 *problems, failures or deficiencies with existing services;*
10 *loss of sales to competitors, success of competitor's services or a decline in orders;*
11 *improvement to existing services to reduce their cost, simplify, rationalize or to 'stretch' the design;*
12 *complaints and ideas from, or surveys of, customers, sales staff or dealers etc.;*
13 *published market research findings;*
14 *inventors, academics, scientists and consultants;*
15 *new regulations, legislation, standards and codes of practice;*
16 *economic trends;*
17 *quality circles and suggestion schemes (including customer suggestion schemes);*
18 *observation, imitation or improvement of competitors' services;*
19 *environmental issues;*
20 *a change in the organization's or a competitor's vision or image;*
21 *augmenting the product to get closer to the customer (for example, direct delivery);*
22 *community welfare need;*
23 *experience and intuition;*

(Continued)

(Continued)

24   *natural change (for example, ageing infrastructure needs replacing);*
25   *improvements to security;*
26   *improvements to existing services to make them easier to use;*
27   *a new way to apply existing design management skills, knowledge or experience;*
28   *to explore gaps in the market or in the current product/service range.*

These factors may initiate additional studies that might include specially commissioned market research reports, warranty and service reports and competitor activity reports completed by staff and agents.

The latest design models all end with 'termination' and 'disposal'

Plastic Bags

And just when you thought all the hype had passed about the Millennium Dome, one thing they should have contemplated but have not and that is how are we going to dispose of it? The monstrosity has a life…

The cost of the stages of product development

Finance is important. The first and most important aspect is to determine the maximum financial outlay that the company is prepared to 'invest' in any new development. It may also be related to the anticipated rate of return but there will be a maximum beyond which it would be potentially dangerous for the organization to risk such expenditure.

When you start developing new products you start spending money. These costs keep mounting until after the product appears on the market. If the product is a success, eventually all the 'up front' expenses should have been covered and the project will then go into profit. But it is not just the cost of the development that must be considered, but also the cost of borrowing the money.

The minority of new products that are a success must not only repay the investment made in them, but also the investment made in all the other items that have been failures. This, of course, will be easier if the potential failures are identified earlier and the investment in them is, therefore, low.

This can be taken further: The investment made in a product that fails in the market place not only loses most of that investment, it also incurs the lost opportunity cost of not using that time and investment another way, either through not borrowing the money (or leaving the money in the bank to gain interest), or more wisely, developing a more profitable product.

Consider the cost of the various stages of developing a new product. Initially these are relatively low as there are not many people involved, no investment in capital equipment or materials and most of the work (market research etc.) is still only on paper. As the project progresses through the process the costs increase dramatically, especially during the implementation stage.

Once a design has reached beyond the specification stage it is, usually, possible to think of some concept that will fulfil it. Having done this, it is, usually, possible to provide detailed drawings and to implement and sell the product. Therefore, if the decision has not been taken to abandon the design before it gets beyond the specification stage then it is more than likely that a product will appear on the market.

A service failing at the market research end of the process is much less expensive and therefore far less dangerous to the company than one failing after it has been put on to the market. So a manager should emphasize the effort at the front end of design to identify and eliminate potential new product failures before they become a heavy investment. The costs for the various stages of the process are shown in Chapter 3.

Up to a point, this already happens, with nearly 80% of product ideas being abandoned at the early stages. This is not good enough, as the majority of those remaining 20% are taken forward to the market and the organization is likely to be lumbered with an expensive failure on their hands.

When one reads that various projects, often architectural projects, are hopelessly over budget and ridiculously late, for example the Scottish Parliament Building, the new British Library, Wembley Stadium and others mentioned in Chapter 8, it just shows how desperately poor those heading up such projects are at their design management. Such incompetence should be avoidable through a well-developed design process. The reason why many people fail to do this properly is that it is difficult and time-consuming. Certainly, it will take some time – but this is far less expensive and time-consuming than blundering along, as so many incompetents appear to do, being forced to throw vast sums of money at an out-of-control project at the implementation stage of the process.

ARE BUILDINGS ALWAYS OVER THE TOP?

You may have noticed that the quoted price for building things rarely seems to count for much. The escalating cost for the Commonwealth Games in Manchester was met by a government minister defending the blunder with 'the cost for these type of things always escalates in the final year'.

In a chat with a project manager in construction, he said 'It is normal for costs to go up by 40%.' When the author asked 'Why?', the answer was, 'The customer knows that it will cost about this much more than the original quote.'

The suggestion was then made that the original quote should be a realistic price but the response was this would make their quotes higher than the competition by – about 40%!

The next suggestion was that they offer a realistic price and stick to it and let the customer know that they would. The project manager then said that customers don't like that because it implies that the original quote is deliberately high to cover eventualities that might not actually occur.

So, strange as it may seem, that, apparently, is custom and practice for you!

When one has developed the design process in full, the next stage is to identify the actions, which can be done in parallel. This is known as simultaneous processing or concurrent working and has the effect of reducing the overall time scale of the project, but there will be certain logistic and communication problems that will arise and these need to be sorted out before proceeding further.

The next stage of this planning is to identify the people who will be needed at each stage of the process. This was covered in Chapter 3.

There is one other stage that needs to be considered. It is unlikely that this is the only project taking place in the organization at that time. Compare each design process and identify where there is likely to be a clash in the need for resources. Then identify which projects have greater priority. The more important projects will have first choice for facilities. If projects of equal importance require the same resources at the same time then it will be necessary to plan for additional people or resources to be made available. Generally, potential delays in a project are significantly less of a problem if they are identified right near the start.

All that has been said above is very difficult to achieve, and even in the best-planned projects, there will be some things that are unexpected and these will cause delays, typically when the organization is embarking on something new – which will eventually lead to an innovation (see Chapter 7). In many projects contingencies are inbuilt, which allows some slack to be taken up in the event of the unexpected. This may just be in the form of 'float' on any non-critical path route through any design project. If a 'critical path' is identified for a design project, that is, the route through any project where a delay on this path will delay the entire project, extra management focus on the activities on this path can minimize likely delay problems. Again, an excessive allowance for contingency is often an example of an inexperienced project manager or an experienced project manager who lacks competence. Clearly, the most inexperienced project managers should cut their teeth on smaller projects, and having proved themselves on these, they can then move up to something more substantial.

Blueprinting

The original use of the word 'blueprint' was to describe a technical drawing showing a general arrangement of all the components. Because of the copying process involved, they were actually blue. This use of the term has fallen into disuse and has now taken on a whole new meaning in the identification and improvement of quality, usually of services. A blueprint is defined as a 'process broken down chronologically into sequential constituent stages' (BS 7000-1: 1999). The process involves describing, in small detail, the various stages of the delivery of a service. In other disciplines it is sometimes called a **project schedule, project** or **process plan**, or a **process map**.

Blueprinting is a simple but effective way of identifying areas for improvement in products and (mainly) services. Look at the process. Look at the customer chain and understand how customers relate to the process. This is shown when the process is mapped out, and this will identify bottlenecks and areas where the service quality may be improved. One can then design the problems out of the process. This also has the affect that service quality, which tends to be mainly qualitative (and therefore difficult to measure), can be made more quantitative by giving the service process the appearance of a production line.

The process was described in a paper published by Shostack in 1984, although it had probably been around for many years. Blueprints were later developed by De Brentani (1991), and Meyer and De Tore (2001) have linked its use in the improvement of the quality of services (Kingman-Brundage 1993; Randall 1993). Blueprints should always be presented with a base of time for determining the parallel stages, the concurrencies, the total time and therefore cost. The production tools that can be applied in this new context will include value analysis, TQM, and line of balance, queuing techniques and JIT.

Randall (1993) showed how the application of blueprinting in the Exeter Wonford hospital improved the overall throughput of patients in the outpatients department, which was the aim of the project. This had the added benefit that the hospital car park (which had previously been full) then had spare capacity. Apparently, the previous congestion was due largely to the people waiting in outpatients. When one problem was cured, the second became less of a problem.

The more enveloping the blueprint of the customer journey, the longer it will take to do but the wider will be the potential improvements, benefits and perhaps savings. In the case mentioned above, the potential saving at that time exceeded £1 million.

Blueprints have been used much more widely (Heskett et al. 1997), but it is believed that further extending use of a service blueprint could allow it to greatly advance service design management.

Initially we will describe how the blueprint fits in with the development of a service. A service cannot be effectively designed by the isolated use of just a blueprint without a design model as this will ignore the existing competencies available to, or needed by, the designing organization. To a lesser extent, it is unlikely that an effective service could be designed without the use of a blueprint. To date, the link has not been made between these two and it will now be shown that blueprinting fits neatly into the stages of the service design process.

Design models are often presented as a vertical sequence whereas the presentation of the service blueprint is normally presented horizontally. So where on the design model does the blueprint cross?

The link between a blueprint and the design process

The design process starts from an idea or trigger (fitting in with the corporate strategy) and goes right through to the termination and disposal of the product. Part of this is the product design and the process design (the method of manufacture or implementation) and it is on these that this section will focus.

The detail stage of the product design and the process design (design for production or implementation) must occur together if the eventual product is to be easy to produce, and therefore inherently of higher quality and lower price. In the design of

- MARKET

- SPECIFICATION

- CONCEPT DESIGN

(the blueprint DETAIL DESIGN + PROCESS DESIGN comes here)

- IMPLEMENT

- through to 'DISPOSAL'

FIGURE 4.5   BLUEPRINTING AT THE DETAIL STAGE OF DESIGN

a car this would be the actual design of the car model and the design of the production methods, machinery and tools to produce that model. In a service it would be the design of the service itself and the infrastructure that supports and delivers the service.

In a service the delineation may not be so clear-cut between product and process. In many cases the production and consumption may occur together (which is part of the definition of a service) so customers and suppliers (together) are part of that process. The product itself may be intangible, like legal advice, but the process can be clearly specified and could be shown in a blueprint.

Most services ride on the back of products. In the supply of car spare parts it could be that the manufactured part and the service part (and blueprint) almost occur in sequence. In another service the product could be a hamburger and the production process would partly be the production of that hamburger (or a better class of meal in a restaurant). In parallel with this would be the stages that the customer would pass through as part of the total process. So one of the main delineations of a blueprint is between the customer involvement and what goes on in parallel but without the customer directly being involved, called the line of involvement.

So it is clear from this that a service blueprint is really a demonstration of service process design and this fixes its position firmly in the total design process from the detail stage through to implementation and subsequent product and process improvement. This is shown in Figure 4.5.

How the two can be used together to improve service design

So, the blueprint will show the stages that the customer passes through when they use the service and the parallel activities that occur at the same time (if sufficiently well constructed). It will also identify bottlenecks that may slow or reduce the quality of the process and may show who will be involved in the delivery of the service (and therefore potential skill shortages). From this can be identified the timescale for the service delivery and the potential costs. It will also show the critical path upon which any delay will result in a delay in the total process.

This being the case, many of the production process techniques such as TQM, benchmarking, total production planning techniques and process layout can be applied to improve the blueprint. After all, it was the linking of product and process design in manufactured products in Japan which was one of the keys to improving quality and lowering costs that first enabled them to win world markets. Blueprints tend to omit many of the more important qualitative measures such as mystery shoppers (the measures from these can also be quantitative). In this the measurement of the quality of a service is through getting 'customers' to use the service and judge the effectiveness of each stage. Mystery shoppers are now widely used in the service sector, for example in pubs, and in the airline and rail systems, and before it can be applied some form of interaction of the customer with the service supplier needs to be identified, typically, through a blueprint. Of this, Shostack (1984) would not approve. To quote:

> The operations side of services often use work flow design and control methods such as time-motion engineering, PERT/Gantt charting, and quality control methods derived from the work of W. Edwards Deming. These procedures provide managers with a way to visualize a process and to define and manipulate it at arm's length. What they miss is the consumer's relationship to, and interaction with services. They make no provision for people-rendered services that require judgement and a less mechanical approach. (p. 134)

All true, but one should not lose sight that improvements can be brought about by the 'mechanical approach' and by using developments in production engineering which can often also be applied to services. By applying these, efficiencies can be achieved that benefit both the supplier and the customer without damaging 'customer relationships'. Therefore, the blueprint should be analysed using production tools, and this was entirely what Shostack was against.

In Shostack's original article a time study element was included and in the subsequent 20 years – although actually earlier if one includes the earlier work of Herzberg et al. (1957) – such an approach of payment by quantity is now discredited and is 'anti TQM'. On the other hand, improvement through reduction in time for the service can benefit all concerned and allow more time 'for making people feel special'.

It is also possible to 'stretch' the blueprint, often at the completion end, to include more of the service aspects of the offering: for example, include selling as part of production, and servicing, and even down to taking responsibility for reclaiming and recycling old cars at the end of their life (a type of vertical integration). In a service this could mean a supermarket delivering shopping and then collecting the waste, whilst taking more orders. Look at either ends of a blueprint in order to identify extra potential markets. London Underground has done this when it identified that some passengers would like transport from the station to their home. A scheme was introduced at some stations to provide a bookable minicab pick-up service.

TROUBLE-FREE MOTORING SCHEME: DAEWOO 1999–2002 – STRETCHING THE BLUEPRINT

Daewoo was able to make a serious impact on the British car market despite having an undistinguished product range, through innovative marketing. Initiated in the UK marketing department in Watford, the scheme provided a 'no pressure' sales service and three years of free servicing for the car. When the service was due the car was collected and a service car loaned while the owner's car was off the road. On the completion of the service the car was returned.

In effect, this gave three year's trouble-free motoring. This answered the needs of a particular market segment. The downside was that the whole life design of this service had not been considered as far as when the customer eventually wished to change their car. Furthermore, problems in the country of origin destroyed the market for their cars and this innovative scheme.

A 'tip' when doing a blueprint is to do it, then do it again. First describe all the boxes, then subdivide these into twice as much detail and twice as many boxes. This system works better with greater detail.

In a service, match the length of time of one stage of the process with the next, so that as a customer finishes one stage they go straight on to the next without having to wait (called 'line of balance'). This promotes a much higher quality service. (See Chapter 11 on Capacity Planning.)

The link between design management and project management

There is also a link between design management and project management. It used to be thought that project management started with a product specification being supplied and the activity finished when the product was handed over to the customer. This certainly suggests that one fits inside the other. But BS 6079 (1996) and later (2000) *Guide to Project Management* shows the four main phases of the process sequence as being 'conception, feasibility, implementation realization, and termination', which implies a broader view. These four broad stages are also included in the design model of BS 7000-2 (1997) *Guide to Managing the Design of Manufactured Products*. When looking at a table in the standard BS 4335 (1999) *Vocabulary of Terms Used in Project Management* it can be seen that there is a much larger model of the process starting with 'conception' and finishing with 'final report', which occurs after 'termination' and 'disposal'.

The scope taken by these two standards (and BS 7000-3 (2006) *Guide to Managing the Design of Services*) is now very close, as these standards start by looking at the corporate objectives and continue through to project/product/service termination and disposal. This implies that perhaps project management and design management are the same thing – that is until certain definitions are sought in the standard of project management vocabulary. There are two clear omissions: there is no mention of the 'market' nor of 'innovation'. Both of these are mentioned in BS 7000-10 (1995) *Glossary of Terms Used in Design Management*. Perhaps design management does indeed take a broader perspective of the wider environment in which the work is positioned. So design management continues to 'expand'. So does project management – but a little way behind.

There is also a greater and growing emphasis on leadership in design management, towards much more of a strategic long-term view of a company's products as well as providing the inspiration to get these visions implemented. Alan Topalian of Alto Design Management (who wrote one of the earliest books on design management) and Raymond Turner (who led the design of the Heathrow Express) are at the forefront of this new area of **design leadership**.

Pause for Thought

If the project management's tomorrow is design management's today, then, perhaps, there is a market out there for design management skills and standards for those who see their future occupation in project management.

Complexity

In 1990 Wikstrom and Erichsen (1990) presented the results of a study of North Sea oil installations in which they concluded that none of the academic models of the design process worked in practice as they were all too shallow to be of practical use. Rohatynski (1990) deduced that it was the attempt to make these models universal that made them impractical.

As described, over these intervening years the understanding of design and its management has grown. Today, design management has a higher profile as people in business and government realized that through effective management of new products and services, companies could demonstrate faster growth and become more profitable. This has been confirmed in two recent studies from the UK and Denmark (Rich 2004) which have shown that companies that invest in design have a faster growth in their share value.

The author developed some design management processes for some companies, which were later revisited to see how these processes were working. A typical comment was that the processes appeared to work all right, but on further questioning it was revealed that they were not always (sometimes rarely) used because they were difficult, often slow and this directly impinged on the product 'time to market'. It is important to reduce the time that a product takes in its design, as shown in the Box.

REDUCING TIME TO MARKET IS IMPORTANT BECAUSE

- *It means that the product reaches the market earlier.*
- *This gives the company a lead over the competition.*
- *This allows the company to charge higher prices (skimming) and/or achieves higher sales (you are on the market ahead of the competition).*
- *The money 'borrowed' for the product development can be paid back earlier so interest charges are lower.*
- *The company can then start the next product development earlier to get further ahead of the competition.*
- *The company will start to get a reputation for being 'fast on its feet' in developing new products and services.*
- *The morale in the organization will improve.*

It is believed by some researchers that the theoretical models, design techniques and recommended activities in design management have now moved from being too shallow to being too complex and thus are still impractical for the skilled practitioner to use. As a result, it would appear that academics and researchers are losing touch with their real market (McAloone 2004).

Also, such developments in models tools and techniques do not include an appreciation that people who are experienced, or expert, in a particular field may not need to pass the design through every stage of the development process. In some cases, their experience of the market or of certain aspects of design will allow certain stages to be by-passed.

On the other hand, proposing 'fast-track' processes can also be 'dangerous'. The problem with these is that they can be written for one set of people and then used by a different set of people with different experience within an organization. This could result in the omission of important stages in the process.

Design processes must be simple to use or they won't be used. Therefore, some of the recent work has been devoted towards simplifying these processes without losing accuracy.

It is a simple task to make things complex, but a complex task to make them simple.

Meyer's Law

Using experience in design – a practical attempt to simplify the design process

Here we introduce an attempt to simplify the design process based on the belief that many competent design managers will have a great deal of experience with the particular product or service type that is being developed. This process will work better in business–to–business product and service provision, as with such products and services the customer base tends to be smaller, more finite, more easily identified and their purchase decisions tend to be made on more logical grounds and less by emotion, whim or impulse.

The emphasis is on the needs of the market in an attempt to avoid the main reason for product failure, which is market failure. The three directors in this example, had more than 25 years of experience in the market and the new product was aimed at particular known customer needs.

Case Study

The project
The main method for cool distribution is still to package the product into well-insulated containers and keep the insides cool through the use of ice packs. The trick has been in the testing of the systems for the certification to ensure that pharmaceuticals etc. can be sent throughout the world with the confidence that the contents will arrive in good condition.

Of course, all this works well, which is why the systems have remained virtually unaltered for such a period. But there are drawbacks to the existing methods. Pharmaceutical distributors need to keep ice packs frozen in a refrigerator until it is time for them to be used. The problem can be overcome with the use of refrigerated transportation but this is expensive, typically 50% more than the price of non-refrigerated trucks and there is no reliable aircraft equivalent. Then a new concept was discovered.

A new product
An innovative new cooling device was designed that is built into the lid of an insulated container. The cooling process is actuated by the press of a button on the pack and can provide up to several days of product cooling without the need for any form of electric power or pre-cooling. This means that a delivery company could collect temperature-sensitive products from their customers (such as blood samples for analysis) and the cooling process can be initiated just as the product is put into the box.

Product advantages
One of the main advantages of the development is that it is much smaller and lighter than the equivalent ice pack. This means that a larger amount of pharmaceutical product can be put into the same-sized box or a smaller container can be used for the same quantity of product to be shipped. With a smaller container there is less

surface area to be kept cool, and therefore, even smaller devices can be used, which means a further reduction in courier costs.

As transport costs, usually by air freight, are one of the major costs in transporting pharmaceuticals, the overall saving in volume significantly reduces the overall costs. Because of this, an apparently more expensive new product can actually operate competitively on price compared with using ice packs. Another advantage is the saving through not having to pre-freeze ice packs which makes the freezer redundant, thus saving its cost and running and the space that it takes up in the warehouse.

A 'green' advantage lost

Links were also made to the whole life benefit for the company through the various stages of the design model (Bush and Sheldon 1993). One aspect of this was the prospect of developing the product so that the cooling system could be reversible, making it worthwhile for the product to be returned to the company. It is perhaps disappointing in this time of concern about the environment that market research has indicated that major customers do not want the bother of returning the used devices even if there were a financial incentive to do so. This indicates that perhaps much of the discussion emanating from the top of being a 'green' organization has not permeated down to the 'doers' in these companies (BS 7750: 1994; EMAS 1995).

Lateral thinking

An interesting piece of lateral thinking (de Bono 1993) was brought into play whilst developing the new product. When operating correctly, the temperature curve drops to the required temperature and then stays flat until the process ends and then the temperature begins to rise. Quite often, the temperature inside the container, when in use, would drift down to zero causing freezing and the device would stop working. The temperature would then rise and the device would start to work again, whereupon the temperature inside the container would again drift down towards zero starting the cycle again. This 'saw-tooth' freezing effect was initially considered unacceptable.

Then, during one of the many brainstorming sessions that occurred in all stages of this product development, somebody mentioned that it should be possible to control the freezing effect and to allow the temperature of the device to 'saw-tooth' within controlled parameters whilst keeping the product in a slightly warmer part of the container. This saw-tooth effect is exactly what occurs with the temperature output of a domestic fridge or freezer.

Implications for the design process

The development of the new product described in this case study provided the opportunity to 'test' some of the latest theoretical design management models and principles in a practical application. Much of the existing doctrine regarding design management was found to hold true. This shows that we, as academics, have progressed in our useful understanding and aid to the practitioner in recent years.

The findings were as follows:

1   The results confirmed the effectiveness of the 'stepped' approach for specification compilation (see Chapter 6) where a small amount of information is identified and from this it is possible to make the decision as to whether it is worth making the investment to take the project to the next stage of product development. Thus the information grows in a series of steps. In effect, this gives a front-end loading to product development and causes more projects to be (rightly) abandoned without much having been spent on them.

2   Prescribing an initial set of parameters on which an organization should base future developments, as described earlier in the chapter and in BS 7000-1 (1999) and Hollins and Hollins (1999), focused a potentially good product towards specified market niches that the company could usefully exploit. In this case, a sequence of different markets was identified, starting with the high value markets and down through to the low value, high demand commodity markets. The sequence of proposed whole life planning for market penetration has been projected for a significant number of years. This was also similar to the mapping of both the length and width of the 'innovation highway', described in Chapter 14.

3   Another aspect that was prevalent throughout the design process was concurrency. It has been accepted that concurrency in developing new products tends to occur within certain stages of an overall design management process (Hollins and Hollins 1991). That is, concurrency cannot (logically) occur in between, say, the market research stage and the detail stage of the design process.

    The design process of this highly innovative product was so iterative that aspects of all stages of the design process were occurring at the same time. The degree of innovation involved in this project meant that it was necessary to undertake some planning of the later stages (selling and manufacturing) as early as the market research stage. This indicates that iteration is far more extensive and detailed than is generally acknowledged.

4   Innovation can occur throughout the value chain (Topalian and Hollins 1998), including the marketing end of the process, and all such opportunities need to be confronted and resolved at an early stage. In this particular case, the marketing side would not require a significant degree of innovation and so the existing knowledge that the directors held of the market could be used.

5   Communication has been identified as being a key difficulty in concurrent engineering. This was found not to be the case in this project as the company was sufficiently small to get all the project participants around a large table. The project did benefit from having the active involvement of a director who acted as product champion (in both definitions of the term, i.e. actively involved in the process and by giving support to the project – see Chapter 3) (BS 7000-10: 1995; Hollins and Hollins 1991).

6   It was found to be advantageous to break down the project into those parts that were known from experience to work and the 'new to the company' parts to be considered 'sub-innovations'. Each could then be approached as a separate target and prototypes and testing developed to prove each of these sub-innovations in turn (whilst not losing sight of the 'whole').

7   Design models imply one concept stage but practice showed that many beneficial 'off-hand brainstorming sessions' (Lockwood 2000) took place throughout the design process to 'sort out' small difficulties as they occurred. These concerned marketing and operations as well as design. This is a confirmation, or rather, an expansion of, that proposed by Hollins and Hollins (1995), that a design process consists of many concept stages within the overall design process. A gestation period was in-built into the brainstorming sessions by revisiting various themes after a period of a few weeks (BS 7000-2: 1997) (see Chapter 7).

A new way of using experience?

As a result of this research, it is suggested that existing experience might be incorporated into a simplified process for developing other products and services through the identification of areas where development is actually needed. Planning this new product should be viewed mainly as an exercise in satisfying the market at all stages of the customer experience (at a profit). This means that customer needs throughout the life cycle of the new design should be paramount in its design.

> *Products appear on the market with many features that customers neither want nor subsequently use. For example, a pneumatic product was promoted as 'an idea looking for a solution'. What the company really meant was 'we have developed this new product and haven't a clue who wants it or what we should do with it'.*

In the case study above it was anticipated that the new product development would be closely related to the company strategic plan, but this plan did not allow for the serendipityous manner in which this new high-potential product came about. It was found that the product development programme tended to inform and alter the strategic plan. If this is a common occurrence it would appear that:

1   Product (and service) development, especially in very small companies, leads the company strategy rather that following it. This is fundamentally different from most writing on strategic management. It appears that the importance of strategic design management has been understated in management literature.
2   Furthermore, the common practice of considering strategic management without giving thought to product design may actually be wrong in all but large multi-product enterprises.

Conclusions

The spotlight was focused on developing those areas that were particularly needed to make the product competitive, fully utilizing the existing knowledge/skills of the particular design team − which would be different in any new design project for a new market or new design team. Furthermore, this quickly showed whether the potential product was possible and could be achieved through concentrating on specific design areas. This would encourage potential failures to be abandoned early in the process.

The focus here is the product idea, the market, the competition, but not necessarily the company business plan.

A simplified design process

Resulting from the research described above, the following outline of a design process is proposed.

1   Understand the existing products (competition) that serve the market you are trying to reach (some may be your own products). Beware of Levitt's (1960) marketing myopia as this may indicate that the competition is likely to be wider than initially thought. Experienced product developers often know this competition if the new product is to meet their existing markets. As said, this is easier for products and services that are not aimed at a consumer market as there tends to be less 'emotion' involved in the purchasing decisions.

2   Then identify the advantages and disadvantages of the potential new product against that which already exists on the market. This stage is not new (Hollins and Hollins 1991). Parametric analysis can help here if it is a manufactured product (Hollins and Pugh 1989). This tends to be less useful when appraising a service.

3   Specify the *minimum* performance standards in each case for the new product to be able to compete with the competition in every case. Some will not be very important and some will be essential and this must also be indicated. This reasoning is made on the realization that people do not buy technology, they buy the benefits that can be derived from that technology (Hollins and Hollins 1999). As a result, it is also necessary to identify the technology that will provide the performance standard that customers require for the various design parameters. This stage is quite difficult in practice and although experience helps, it needs to be confirmed by customers through market research.

4   Specify the *maximum* performance in each case that is required by the potential customers. Deming's (1986) phrase that we should endeavour to 'delight the customer' is now common as a basis around which Total Quality programmes are built. Parasuraman, Zeithaml and Berry (1988) applied this thinking when developing their SERVQUAL and the gap analysis to demonstrate at which points to improve the quality of services. But Huda (1997) has proposed that there is a service level beyond which customers do not require (or notice) a greater level of service. Over time, expectations rise but this can be anticipated and accommodated within subsequent design improvements.

If it is accepted that there is a maximum (and therefore optimum) performance level for a service, then providing a product that exceeds these performance levels (usually at a higher development cost) is a waste of time, effort and money. This requires a well-focused understanding of the market that may come through

Performance function \ Design Parameter	1	2	3	4	5	6	7
			X				
Maximum customer performance required	—	—	—	—	—	—	—
	X						
		X					
							X
				X			
Minimum customer performance required	—	—	—	—	—	—	—
				X		X	

FIGURE 4.6   MINIMUM OR MAXIMUM STANDARDS/PERFORMANCE THAT THE CUSTOMER WANTS FROM EACH USP OR PRODUCT BENEFIT. IN THIS EXAMPLE PERFORMANCE FUNCTION 3 IS OVER-DESIGNED. PERFORMANCE FUNCTIONS 4 AND 6 ARE UNACCEPTABLE TO THE CUSTOMER. THE PERFORMANCE THAT IS REQUIRED CAN ONLY BE IDENTIFIED BY UNDERSTANDING THE NEEDS OF POTENTIAL CUSTOMERS

experience. Parallels can be drawn here with Quality Function Deployment (Akao 1990; Hauser and Clausing 1988), where the 'voice of the customer' defines the subsequent design work that is to be undertaken. In practice, what is being proposed here is less structured and is configured around the identified important elements in the product design specification.

5   Identify the unique selling propositions (or benefits) that the new product idea could provide, over and above the competition, and identify whether customers really want these benefits.

6   Identify the *minimum* standards/performance that the customer wants from each of these benefits. The effect of this is shown in Figure 4.6.

7   Identify what needs to be done to compete in each (important) area – to reach the minimum standard. Some of these may be achieved by engineering or product design. Others may be achieved through the design of the service.

8   Develop each of these sectors using stepped specifications (Hurst and Hollins, 1995 and Chapter 6). Know the important design problems, which must have

greater resources devoted to them. If any one of these important features cannot be achieved, then the project can be put on hold until a technical breakthrough is made (archived) or abandoned. In practice, most of these problems can be identified early in the process and thus do not appear after much time or money has been spent on the project.

As can be seen, the ease with which a design team will be able to achieve the above depends a great deal on their experience and understanding of the product market. Less experience will indicate more work.

At first glance what is being proposed seems fairly obvious but it is not the way that many operations plan their new product development. It could be called 'Design Management by Objectives' and mirrors aspects of Management by Objectives as first prescribed by Drucker in 1955. Particular objectives can be identified and the design team can concentrate on fulfilling these. Other areas are of less importance and, in some cases, can be ignored. Of course, all of this is highly iterative, more so than would be expected, but most of this iteration will take place before the detail stage of design.

Our research into service design management in the UK

Recently our theoretical understanding of design and its management has grown, especially with regard to design in the service sector, so research was undertaken to see the 'level' at which service organizations were operating. The results of this were then used to set the 'level' in the update of the standard BS 7000-3 (2006) *Guide to Managing the Design of Services*.

The research

Starting in October 2002, 250 questionnaires were distributed to managers and senior managers working in the service sector in and around London. Twenty-five per cent of the questionnaires were returned. Most respondents (68%) stated that they were actively involved in the development of new services for their organizations.

The results

The results of this research reveal that there are aspects of service design that are now consciously being undertaken within a few organizations but these results also show that in most organizations there is still little realization that services can be designed or this design managed. This was a slightly surprising finding as there has been a British Standard on how to manage the design of services available since 1994 (BS 7000-3).

The overwhelming finding was that managers in service design are operating at a very basic level and are not in control of the future of their organizations.

Only 28% of those who responded use any British Standards in the development of their new services and even more surprising is that none use the Design Council. This could suggest that the potential users may not know of the output from these bodies or find it too difficult, or unsuitable for their needs.

Only about half the respondents had a reasonable idea or definition of design or innovation. One-third of the companies questioned do not have a product strategy document and only one-fifth have a written process for the delivery of new services. If the way to manage services is through the organization of the process for developing these services – then why do they not have a process? How do the managers given this responsibility know how to start? Those few that do, at least review it on a regular basis to keep it updated.

Take some other 'strange' findings. It has been known for many years that market failure is the main reason for failure of products and services – not enough customers want it. Yet 48% do *no* research for new services prior to their development. It is here that the most obvious failures should be detected and eliminated; it should not be after these services have had all the development costs pumped into them only to be shown up as failures when in the full view of the market (see Chapter 8). So their designers are working in the dark when it comes to satisfying the potential customer's wants and needs. Furthermore, what some companies state as being market research can hardly be considered as adequate. One respondent's only apparent market research activity was quoted as 'cocktail parties' – fun but not effective.

Regarding seeking new ideas, several respondents stated that they look at their competition or the market leaders. This 'me-too' attitude has been shown to be an unsuccessful route to new product success. You cannot overtake the competition just by copying what they do. Quite a few companies seek ideas only from inside their organization, such as ideas from directors, senior managers and even suggestion boxes. This is allright as long as it is backed up by some market research to show the customers who might want them, the benefits that these new ideas may provide. Sadly, the research results indicate that this is generally not the case.

Another surprising response in these times of Total Quality Management and ISO 9000 was that 'customer complaints' is still quoted as a source of new ideas. One wonders whether those customers will still be around for these companies' products when they have sorted out these complaints.

Unlike most manufacturing organizations, in service design, specifications (the controlling documents) tend not to be written. Those who said they do produce specifications tended to describe an inadequate set of documents. In fact, 48% of respondents said they have not seen a specification for the development of a new service in the past seven years (remembering that most were actually involved in the development of new services). Of those who have seen a specification, in only 16% of the companies did this appear to be adequate. (A British Standards guide for writing specifications for the service sector is available, BS 7373-3: 2005).

It would appear that service companies tend to start the process at the concept stage thus missing out altogether the vital first 15% of the design process (the 'that's a good idea, let's do it!' syndrome).

Innovation, being an important subset of the design process, is poorly applied in the service sector. Innovation can occur in all stages of the whole life of a product, especially (and increasingly) at the service end when customers are more likely to be directly involved with the delivery of the service. Innovation is generally easier with services as there is less of an existing infrastructure to be replaced by the new. As such, customers more readily accept changes brought about through innovation.

Only about one in six manage the process in a logical and effective manner. What the research did show was that the few companies that did appear to be effective (about 17%) were very good. This was further shown in the fact that these generally included the 16% that generated greater than 30% of their turnover from services developed in the past three years.

Our conclusions

It would appear from this research that the majority of service organizations in and around London are not effectively managing their new services. Therefore, they are vulnerable. It has been said that 'the analysis of successful and unsuccessful new services indicates that a formal and planned approach to NSD [new service development] leads to better performance ... Aside from using a detailed NSD process, the success in new service development depends on getting the necessary commitment and interaction from management and from their different functional specialities within the firm' (de Brentani 1991).

Many senior managers involved in the service sector are still unaware of the benefits that design can bring to their offerings and, as a result, their organizations are operating at a sub-optimum level. As service design and its management tend to be poorly planned, it is quite easy for a company to gain a competitive advantage through the application of some quite simple design techniques. If an organization is not designing its new services, how much longer will it be before they start to lose market share to those who are more design conscious? Nothing stands still forever and very few things stay the same for long. Sooner rather than later they are going to have to develop some new services to replace the ones they currently sell. But do they know how to do it? They need a new service development organized, formalized and communicated to all in the organization. On the other hand, about one service company in six is very effective in this area and seems likely to thrive.

This implies two requirements. First, that the personnel in such companies need to be educated not only about the importance of design, but also how to do it. Secondly, design projects require well-trained leadership and a strong product champion to encourage those involved as to the realities and benefits of using design. The main differences in the management of the design of services and manufactured products tend to be in the later stages of the process, so the similarities at the important front end of design mean that those currently applying their skills in manufacturing can apply their knowledge in this much larger sector.

Postscript

Recently, there has been speculation that the latest tools and techniques 'have not had the expected impact' (e.g. Lopez–Mesa et al. 2004). The academic advances seem to be moving further beyond the reach of users and are not being taken up by practitioners. An advantage of the approach stated in this chapter is that tried, tested and accepted tools are shown to be usable in a wider context than that in which they are currently used. This means that these workable tools are more likely to be adopted in these wider contexts.

Furthermore, a successful product often hinges on more than just the 'mechanics' of design and development. There is often the 'big picture' that needs to be considered.

SUMMARY OF KEY POINTS

- It is the products (and services) that companies sell that bring in the money.
- These products and services must be designed and this design must be managed.
- Design is Total Design and design management is the organization of the process for developing new services.
- It is necessary to identify a detailed process for any product or service that is being developed.
- The design process can be used to organize activities, concurrencies, people, finance and time. It can also be used to identify priorities between various projects being undertaken within an organization.
- The design process must take into account the strategic implications of the organization, the whole life costs and benefits, and should be taken right through to the eventual termination and disposal stages of the project.
- The early stages of the design process are low cost and this is where design managers should concentrate their effort.
- The main measure of product and service success must be financial.
- Blueprinting is an effective way to develop a service.
- Project management is very similar to design management.

STUDENT ACTIVITY 4.1   INCREASING COMPETITION

With national barriers being broken down companies must operate on a world market and competition is fierce. As more developing countries and the Eastern bloc start manufacturing competitive products, their low wage economies will increase the supply of low cost goods. The more successful countries are not trying to compete only on price, but also on 'non-price' factors that give added value as perceived by the customer.

You are consumers. When you go to buy something you generally decide how much you are prepared to pay, then select the product that gives you the most for your money in that price bracket. You can almost be certain to get 'value for money', because there is nearly always a wide choice.

1 Write down why you bought your car.
   Almost any car will get you from A to B but there are other reasons, many reasons, why you chose that particular make and model.
2 Now write down all the reasons why you bought your particular jug kettle, your computer, your DVD player or your last holiday.
      People buy services for design reasons. Services and products must be designed and this design must be managed.
3 Write down all the products and services for which there is no competition in the UK.
      Only a few years ago most utilities were monopolies but now you can even choose whose electricity will flow into your three-pin plugs. This trend is growing. The best from everywhere is now available and if a company does not supply the best, then its days are numbered.

STUDENT ACTIVITY 4.2

1 Write down where design ends.
2 Write down for how long you expect to get spares for the following products:

   - A car?
   - A vacuum cleaner?
   - A washing machine?

   On the other hand, it is possible to make the product service-free.

3 List ten services that are maintenance-free.

STUDENT ACTIVITY 4.3

Write down seven broad stages of the design process for a product or a service.
   This will give an overall picture of Total Design, but it is far too brief to be of any practical use. In practice, you will need something far more detailed. The sequence and content of the model will change depending on what is the product or service. It is vital that the model is constructed for each new venture. You need to identify the process before you can organize it.
   This should be in many stages, some of which are more important than others. If you have fewer than 50 stages then it is probably insufficiently detailed.
   Suggest why you need so much detail.

STUDENT ACTIVITY 4.4

Dyson is quoted as saying:

   I don't aim to be clever: I aim to be dogged. The research process was painstaking because one of the golden rules of development is that you only make one change at a time between tests. It's the Edison approach.

   Up to a point, this is correct, but reflecting on what has been covered in this chapter and other relevant literature, how could this design process possibly have been reduced?

FURTHER READING

Baxter M.R. (1997) *Product Design. Practical Methods for the Systematic Development of New Products.* London: Chapman and Hall.

BS 7000 Part 3 (2006) *Guide to Managing the Design of Services.* London: British Standards Institution.

Design Council (1998) *Designed to Compete. How Design Can Make Companies More Competitive.* Red Paper 1. London: Design Council.

Design Council (2004) *Touching the State. What Does It Mean to be a Citizen in the 21st century?* London: Design Council.

Hollins G. and Hollins B. (1991) *Total Design: Managing the Design Process in the Service Sector.* London: Pitman.

Rich H. (2004) 'Proving the practical power of design'. *Design Management Review,* Fall.

5 CUSTOMER IDENTIFICATION

Even if you're on the right track, you'll get run over if you just sit there.

Will Rogers, American Political Humourist

In broad terms, all services need customers and this chapter will focus on market research. This is just a brief introduction to the topic. It will show some simple tools for data collection, which very early in the process and with very little effort, can identify potential failures and eliminate them. This will enable those managing operations to focus on products and services, which will be potentially more successful.

LEARNING OUTCOMES

When you have completed this chapter you should be able to:

- Realize the importance of market research.
- Know how to use the experts within an organization.
- Identify what services are not right for an organization.
- Identify advantages, benefits and USPs for a service.
- Know the difference between and application of primary and secondary market research data.

In simple terms, don't attempt to introduce a new service or significantly improve an old one without first having undertaken some market research. There are exceptions to this, but only when the product is so insignificant or it is quicker and cheaper simply to introduce it than to undertake the complex processes described in this book. These are exceptions and you are not going to change the world, even the fortunes of a company, with such trivia. These are the exceptions – for everything else the rule holds true.

However, market research has its problems. For example, people may say that they will buy the item, but then do not when it comes to putting their hand in their pocket. A good example of this is to play a record to a large group of people (say, a lecture theatre with 300 students present) and then ask if anyone would buy that record. If *just* one person says that they would then (statistically) the research would indicate that this record would be a chart-topper. But was the lecture theatre filled with a cross-section of the population? And will the one who said they would buy the record actually go out and do so? Such is the problem of market research. The moral is, if it is quick and easy to try then do so. Unfortunately, it is usually very expensive to 'suck it and see' and therefore market research is necessary on all but a few occasions. Remember that market research is an inaccurate science.

> *The overwhelming cause of new product failure has been, and continues to be, due to companies not providing what the customer wants, in short, not understanding the market (Cooper 1988). Market research is very poorly undertaken by most companies. They drift into developing products on a mere whim or 'gut feeling'. By all means be inspirational, but then do the market research to back up these 'hunches'.*

Market research covers:

1   The description of channels through which products and services reach customers, the way these products and services are used, and the perceptions and attitudes that lead to customer choice.
2   The explanation of these attitudes, perceptions and behaviour.
3   Evaluation in which the cost-effectiveness of new products and processes is assessed.
4   Prediction of the trends and specification of the proposed direction for future plans.

The most important first step is to be clear as to what you are trying to find out. What you are researching are the needs of potential customers. Focus on the benefits that the new service will provide over the competition, then determine if enough people want these benefits. Remember, people buy **'benefits'** which are expressed as 'advantages', which may also be 'USP's (unique selling propositions) when compared to the competition. Customers' behaviour and buying activities are also affected by emotion. Not all people want the same type of car or pizza. Identify and build these into the service, and feature these in the service promotional activity.

Furthermore, customers may make their purchase decisions on the 'fringe' things that differentiate between one product and another. It is up to the marketing department to say what they want but also up to operations to determine the cost for providing each of these. There is a penalty for all additions.

To find out wants and needs, somebody has to ask potential customers, (it isn't quite that simple, but still the best way of finding out what people want depends on asking them questions.) This may seem pretty obvious, but many marketing people consider themselves mind readers and clairvoyants, able to gauge information coming through the ether. This can sometimes be seen in action in various meetings. For example, in Quality Function Deployment meetings the 'voice of the customer' seems to become audible to them without any apparent real research.

Primary and secondary data

Market research can be divided into two broad categories: secondary data collection, which includes desk research, the collection of existing documentation and expert estimation, and primary data collection, which includes interviewing, observation and experimentation.

Secondary data

Secondary data collection should nearly always be undertaken first: carry out some exploratory research, but keep revising the research objectives in the light of the results and information obtained. Such collection is the principal source of marketing information. It is inexpensive and gathered quickly. A person with well-focused objectives can usually gain all the necessary information regarding a product in, typically, one full week's work.

Desk research is particularly important if you are considering export markets. It is far quicker and cheaper to find out local differences in legislation, customs, distribution methods etc. from your home base than after arriving on foreign soil.

This initial market research need not be arduous and can all be desk (secondary) research. All that needs to be researched are products that are likely to compete with the 'idea'. List the advantages, benefits or USPs of these competing products over the new product idea being considered. Only develop things that people are likely to want. By knowing why the product is better than the competition, these benefits can be maintained throughout the process and eventually used in the promotion of the marketed product. Also, by knowing why a competitor's product is better (including the service side), improvements may be possible to minimize or eliminate these disadvantages.

Not all benefits are of equal value and in some cases disadvantages can outweigh all the apparent advantages of a potential new product and, sometimes, vice versa. For example, an electrical product manufacturer developed a more reliable and longer-lasting lighting system for cars. This was a failure because the initial purchase price was increased. The main group of customers, being the car manufacturers, expressed no interest in any product that increased the initial purchase price as they did not value highly the whole-life costs to the eventual car owner. The initial price to the car manufacturer was their over-riding consideration.

Primary data

Primary data is that which you have collected yourself. It is 'primary' because you are the first person to get it. Small group interviews generally come first and these are 'attitude forming'. The psychologist leading these discussions is trying to find out people's perceptions and attitudes. From this the questionnaire can be compiled, using (generally unskilled) people to find out how many hold these attitudes and perceptions.

When planning your marketing research follow this sequence:

1   Decide what your problem is.
2   Set preliminary research objectives.
3   Carry out exploratory research.
4   Revise research objectives.
5   Design the research method.
6   Undertake a pilot survey.
7   Estimate the time taken and the cost to obtain the data.
8   Survey the data collection.
9   Analyse and present findings.
10 Make marketing, design then operations decisions.

Organizations should use their experts

Many small organizations are remiss in doing proficient market research because they believe that it is expensive. This is a myth. It should come in at no more than 12% of the total cost of bringing a new service to the market, although most organizations spend less than half that amount. By spending that money up front, in many cases it is possible to avoid spending the rest later, by identifying the potential failures and getting rid of them – which means time and effort can then be directed into the right product.

Many small organizations do not have the resources to conduct extensive market research themselves or to freelance it out. This need not be a problem. Organizations are full of 'experts' who can provide you with estimates on your market. For example, the sales personnel will have a knowledge of what they sell and to whom, where they sell it and how it is delivered. They will also know where they fail to sell and why, what complaints there are about your existing range, who their competitors are and in what ways the competitors are better or worse than your organization. Each department will have experts, who can provide 'free' information or data, which should be gleaned before seeking outside advice. This will include customer service (e.g. customer complaints and returns) to production (e.g. what is difficult to make) to finished stock inventory (e.g. what are slow and fast movers). Outside the organization it is possible to obtain information, often at almost no cost, covering many aspects of products and organizations.

The key here is to provide your sales personnel and these other experts with questionnaires covering areas of information that you wish to find out about. Make this a formal procedure, whereby this data is collected and analysed on a regular basis.

It is important to gather ideas from all, and it is also important to keep asking 'Why?' when a new product is requested – from wherever the request emanates

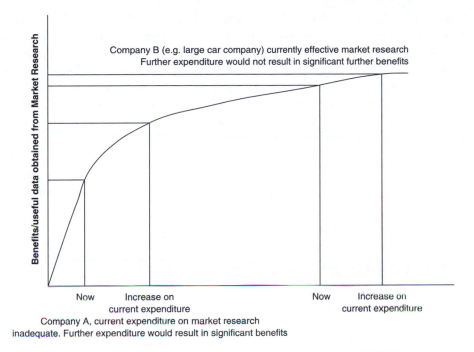

Company B (e.g. large car company) currently effective market research
Further expenditure would not result in significant further benefits

Benefits/useful data obtained from Market Research

Now   Increase on
current expenditure

Now   Increase on
current expenditure

Company A, current expenditure on market research
inadequate. Further expenditure would result in significant benefits

FIGURE 5.1   THE AFFECT OF INCREASING THE EXPENDITURE ON MARKETING RESEARCH

(Research has shown that the worst ideas often came from the most senior people – those furthest from the actual market.)

Initial market research

In simple terms, it is possible to recommend to most organizations that whatever they spend on market research they should double it. This is shown in Figure 5.1. The curve shown follows the law of diminishing returns. The greater the expenditure, the less significant the benefit that can be achieved. Car companies, amongst others that operate in highly competitive environments and invest a great deal on market research, tend to be near the top of the curve. If they spent much more they would not benefit from a significant increase in return for their investment. On the other hand, most companies that are inept at market research operate very much at the lower end, the linear part of the curve. An investment here will bring significant returns for that investment.

The initial purpose of market research is to determine whether, at first look, the idea (that is all it is at this stage) is likely to be wanted by the market and can compete against the potential competition. If it can't, then work on it should stop at this stage. This information then feeds into the product design specification.

The next stage is to consider that most new products are similar to, or a replacement for, existing products on the market. The new product must be demonstrably better than what is on the market – or why should people change their buying habits? At this stage of the process the product is still often an idea, without form, so it is difficult to state precisely why it is different/better. But the idea is at a sufficiently early stage to enable improvements to be suggested, considered and built into the proposal to offset or overcome potential 'flaws' or limitations when compared to the competition. So it is here that the first rudimentary market research is undertaken. Look at all the competing products and remember Levitt was right when he wrote, back in 1960, about marketing myopia. Most people still tend to think of the competition as those who make very similar products to themselves. When asked how they do 'competition analysis' people often talk of reading their trade journals and going to trade exhibitions. The competition is probably far wider than first considered and one needs to think much further than the obvious competition.

IS A NEW PRODUCT GOING TO BE COMPETITIVE?

Answer the following:

- *State the competition.*
- *State the advantages and disadvantages of the product over the competition in each of these market segments.*
- *Can the disadvantages be turned into advantages with design?*

(If the disadvantages exceed the advantages, allowing for the fact that they need not be of equal value, then compare it with the competition in another market niche until the niche with the most advantages over the competition has been discovered.)

- *State the approximate size of the market niche.*
- *State the approximate share of the market niche that can be expected.*
- *Estimate the selling price.*
- *Estimate turnover in each market segment.*
- *What is the sensible amount that can be spent on developing/modifying the machine for that market?*
- *Is it possible? Is it worth pursuing?*

NO – abandon that market segment.
YES – Do market research (you haven't done any yet).

The simple procedure set out in the Box easily shows that a product such as most electric cars would only ever have a small market. Those who remember the Sinclair C5 (essentially a form of transport for those too lazy to ride a push bike), which had a potential market of about a thousand sales a year, will realize that this procedure could have saved the organization £8 million by showing that the project wasn't worth starting. Perhaps it could even have saved the organization! It might also have highlighted aspects of the design that would have made the product better (e.g. weather protection). The moral is to define your product and then it is easier to identify your market. By following through this procedure with all new product ideas and one can learn a lot about the market potential with very little effort.

One can easily check a product and service range periodically against any new competitor product that appears on the market by listing the advantages and disadvantages of any potential threat. One can then direct the necessary action to defend the company. This may mean just copying the threatening features of the new competitor, or in some cases even planning to extricate the company from that product market, if the threat is insurmountable, and focusing more on another product, service or market.

Even when not investigating a particular market for a particular product or service, keep looking at the competition or looking at new technology. This ensures that existing products remain competitive, or where they are not, this shortfall can be identified and improvements made.

Can the company afford to provide the service at a price the market can stand?

Identifying potential financial failures is quite difficult at this 'idea stage', as the work that has to be undertaken to bring the idea into fruition isn't even known. This is where the initial financial parameters can first be used. It is often obvious right at the start whether most ideas can or cannot be produced within the financial boundary specified for the organization. There may be some decisions at this stage as to whether the parameters should be breached if the idea looks particularly 'exciting'. This should be the exception rather than the rule if the maximum investment parameter has been set with due consideration. In any case, the decision to spend more than the maximum specified is something that must be made at the director level and, in large organizations, needs to be passed up to a management level higher than those actively involved in the product or service development.

Time and money are closely related and an estimate must be made as to whether the idea can be completed within the maximum time allowed for any development. Usually it is possible to know from experience whether these parameters can be achieved. If the product is to be manufactured many companies have a rough 'factor' that indicates the *minimum* selling price from the anticipated actual manufactured cost. Typically a factor of five will cover all other costs, such as selling, promotion, product development and other non-productive but necessary cost centres within a company, and this also includes the profit margin. If this factor is set too high it can stifle new product development.

This 'cost-plus' thinking is bad marketing practice. The selling price should always be pitched as high as the market will stand. 'Cost-plus' does indicate a minimum selling price, to help determine the potential viability of a new product and help avoid many subsequent financial failures, as the picture becomes clearer and more information has been collected. Of course, these figures are revisited at various stages throughout the development as part of the normal iterative process of design. They will continue to be a basis on which most product developments will be abandoned. It is not possible, at this stage, to determine the likely return on investment, although, again, this will become more apparent at a later stage. The above works quite easily if a company is developing its own products. Where consultants are used (which is increasingly the case) these boundaries and limits must be clearly submitted to the consultants, *in writing,* in the form of an initial brief. If the consultants do not keep to them, then they haven't done their job properly.

Another aspect that should be considered at the start of any new development is its potential effect on other products and (increasingly important) services in the organization's portfolio. This may be fairly obvious where a new product could be subdividing the market between two other existing products but not increasing the overall total market, thus losing economies of scale. Less obvious are those new products that could damage profitable sectors of the organization. For example, a longer-lasting car battery may make for better initial sales but a reduction in the replacement market. Products that do not require servicing mean that the market for spare parts will be destroyed. Over-confidence in the spare parts market is one reason given as to why the large vacuum cleaner companies ignored Dyson's offer of collaboration with his bagless vacuum cleaner design. The market for replacement bags was £100 million a year. This was quite a big market to throw away. But, as things turned out, the fact that the big companies turned the idea down wasn't sufficient to kill it and they were the eventual losers.

It is only possible to delay the onset of a breakthrough technological advance if a company is very big or owns the patents, but one cannot patent a service so this option is not open to many. There is a lesson to be learned here. If a new idea is sufficiently good it will get on to the market – and it is far better that a company should make a potential profit than lose out altogether to the competitor. In short, at the start, it is necessary to consider all the potential ramifications of any new development – both positive and negative. An example could be the delay in the introduction of disc brakes in the 1950s, because the large United States car companies had just invested in machinery for making drum brakes and had to wait until this was paid off and worn out.

The above is not a case for building in obsolescence in order to keep up the market for spare parts. If a company's products do not last as long as the competitors then, when it fails, customers will seek a supplier with both better products and a better reputation for better products. This has a lot to do with quality – fitness for the purpose. It also demonstrates why reliability is considered to be the one most important design aspect of a product or service. Customers will soon forget how much a product costs but will remember if it causes problems, and will avoid that make in the future. They may also tell their friends, and they may avoid that company's products.

Ethnography

The plural of anecdote is not data.

Anon

One of the more 'fashionable' aspects of market research that works well for services is for organizations to send 'observers' to see how we spend our lives. Having seen how we do – or struggle to do – everyday things, the company designers can develop new services to make our lives just a little easier, or so the theory goes. . Through such observations multinational companies can be aware of particular cultural differences and these can be accommodated by fine tuning their product offerings. Paula Zuccotti described these multinationals as 'chameleons that reflect local colour but retain their form'.

For this ethnography to work people must volunteer to be observed or filmed going about their daily lives. This probably appeals only to a certain type of person who doesn't mind being observed and so skews the results in the favour of 'exhibitionists'.

HOW HAS ETHNOGRAPHY ENRICHED OUR DAILY LIVES?

Apparently, we all put our own specific length of toothpaste on our toothbrushes. You may put on one centimetre or half that amount – but you will be consistent. Toothpaste manufacturers have built this wisdom into their toothpaste tube design. They made the hole in the tube bigger! Now when you squirt your one centimetre of toothpaste onto your brush you are, in fact, using more toothpaste and the tube will run out more quickly and you will have to replace it earlier thus, over time, buying more. Isn't ethnography wonderful?

Conclusion

Market research is not a panacea. It will not solve all problems, and even if done well, the results can be misinterpreted. Good market research will not guarantee the product will be a success, but it will eliminate the most obvious failures and therefore increase the chances of success. Furthermore, although market research is not as expensive as many people believe, it still uses finance that may be better spent elsewhere. Before embarking on market research always consider if the return from the project is worth the financial outlay on the research. In some cases it may be cheaper and quicker to just try the idea and see if anybody wants it.

SUMMARY OF KEY POINTS
- An organization is full of experts. Learn to use their knowledge.
- People buy what they perceive to be benefits though they are affected by emotion.

- Secondary research generally precedes primary research.
- Data needs to be qualitative and quantitative. Qualitative market research generally comes first.
- Just looking at advantages and disadvantages when compared to the competition can eliminate most unsuitable ideas near the start of the process.
- Market research is not a panacea. It can often be wrong or misinterpreted.

STUDENT ACTIVITY 5.1

1   Describe, in one paragraph, a product or service that was introduced by a company that you know well.
2   How was the market research undertaken for this?
    How did this compare with what was described in the literature?
    How could the market research undertaken in this organization be improved?
3   How long did the total market research take and how many people were involved? From this, determine the cost of the market research stage of the process. Can students discover this?

FURTHER READING

Dibb S., Simkin L., Pride W.M. and Ferrell O.C. (2006) *Marketing Concepts and Strategies,* 5th edn. New York: McGraw-Hill.
Hague P. (2004) *Do Your Own Marketing Research.* London: Kogan Page.
Madanayake R. (2002) *Strategic Marketing Plan: The 12 'P' Model.* Sri Lanka. Vishva Lekha.
McQuarrie E.F. (2005) *The Market Research Toolbox.* London: Sage.

6 DESIGN SPECIFICATIONS – CONTROLLING THE PROCESS

Businesses today face an increasingly stark choice. They can aim simply to be the cheapest – and leave themselves vulnerable to being beaten on price. Or they can achieve secure growth with design at the heart of their strategy, acting as a catalyst to completely new offerings.

Digby Jones, Director General CBI, 2002

The product design specifications are the most important documents pertaining to any new product. Generally, they are badly written. Writing a good specification is not easy; several elements are dependent on others or are interrelated. The processes adopted, such as automation, depend on the potential number of customers, the technology available, the costs involved, as well as the facilities available and the actions of the competition.

LEARNING OUTCOMES

When you have completed this chapter you should be able to:

- Develop a specification for a new service.
- Know which are the most important elements of a specification.
- Understand the link between the Marketing Mix and specifications.

Terminology

Pause for Thought

What is the difference between the 'brief' and the 'specification'?

Often the words 'brief' and 'specification' seem to be interchangeable and can cause confusion. On the 'soft' side of design – the aesthetic side, including graphics and industrial design – the specification is known as the brief. In the various branches of engineering design the brief is the word that describes the initial set of requirements and this is subsequently built into the specification. Specification embodies sufficient information, often obtained from market research, from which the product can actually be designed. The brief and specification have both been defined in the British Standard *Guide to Definitions in Design Management* (1995), which offers a more 'workable' use of the terminology.

British Standard definition of 'design brief'

Statement that describes the purpose and required performance of a *product* or *service*.

Note 1: With the exception of the construction industry, the statement includes the time and cost to complete the *design*. Product cost and investment cost targets are also included.

Note 2: In the construction industry, the *design brief* would not normally include the time and cost of design. These would be included in the design contract/*commission*.

British Standard definition of 'design specification'

A document that defines the requirements and restraints of the product design to those responsible for *design*.

Note: A design specification differs from a *design brief* in that it contains only definitive design requirements whereas a design brief also contains project requirements, e.g. time scale, and is usually less prescriptive.

POTENTIAL FAILURES

The problem with the brief is that it is often too brief to be meaningful or not focused enough to be altogether achievable. How many of us have seen a daft idea running helter-skelter towards an expensive disaster because of poorly described criteria at the start.

The specification should include all the elements that contribute to the product being a success or failure. We should question all of these to ensure that we are not wasting our valuable time, and if we are, we should make sure people know about it so we can then get on with something more useful.

Specifications

The specification document is important as it is one of the main places where product failure is rooted. The main reasons for a new service failing are **market failure** – it does not meet the customer requirements (and thus, it doesn't sell); **technical failure** – the service does not work; or **financial failure** – the budget is not sufficient to complete the design profitably. Two out of three of these reasons are rooted in poor specification – market and financial failure.

In design, everything matters.

Bob Feilden (1963)

Furthermore, the specification is one of those aspects of design that is poorly done in both the manufacturing and service sectors. It is believed that specifications are poorly written for several reasons:

1   Managers do not realize how fundamental these documents are to the eventual success of the product.
2   They do not see anything 'tangible' from the specification stage and therefore do not believe that the development is proceeding. The time taken compiling the specification gives the impression that 'nothing is happening'.

Another difficulty with the specification stage is that a lot of work may be undertaken only for the outcome to show that the product is unlikely to fulfil the organization's requirements and that the whole project should cease. This, of course, is a 'victory' in itself as resources (mainly time, money and people) can be diverted to something more worthwhile. In spite of this, there is a feeling that a great deal of time has been wasted with nothing to show for it.

A specification contains all the facts relating to the product or service outcome. It should try to avoid 'leading' the design and predicting this outcome, but, nevertheless, it should also contain the realistic constraints to be imposed upon the design by either the company or the market. The specification is the fundamental control mechanism that helps success to be achieved.

The specification is the basic reference source – it is the main control for the subsequent stages of the product or service design activity. It should be borne in mind that the specification is evolutionary and that it is a dynamic not a static document. A specification evolves and changes with the emergence of the design; if, during the design of a particular artefact or service there is a good reason for changing the basic specification, then change it.

The specification must be comprehensive and written in terms understandable to all departments of a business. All businesses are primarily about products or services for markets. If this primary criterion is not continually satisfied, profits either never materialize or are, at best, not maintained.

The number of elements

The headings of a specification represent the primary 'elements' to bring about the formulation of a comprehensive specification. In using them, the reader will find that, progressively, they start to overlap and integrate.

The preparation of a specification is a discipline in itself, which must be considered prior to the commencement or as part of the design. The specification forms the main design control, and the collective elements represent the design boundary. Incidentally, they also remove the necessity for a preponderance of 'gut feeling', which still looms large in product or service designs.

Specification formulation is included in BS 7000-1 (1989), with 21 elements. Then there followed a large increase to perhaps the most comprehensive listing of what elements should be included in BS 7000-2 (1997), with 125 elements! The number of elements has now become unmanageable in its simple form. We propose that the one shown in Figure 6.1 shows a thorough but useable list of elements.

It could be argued that all these elements need to be considered with all designs (although each may not be relevant in every case), and here lies the main problem. Full specifications are difficult and time-consuming to compile.

All of these elements needed to be considered before it could be decided whether they were each important or unimportant and, invariably, there were compromises that needed to be reached between these various elements. These larger lists of elements tended to include all the marketing mix – especially as product design research acknowledged the greater importance of the marketing/selling end of the process.

There are usually several specifications and these should be compiled by all the experts within the organization. There will be contradictions and these will be resolved by the product champion early in the process (see Chapter 3). There are a lot of useful check-lists to guide those writing a specification.

The eventual document that will result will contain sufficient information for top management to make the decision to develop the product or abandon the exercise (or to hold the project until further information has been obtained). This is often described as 'Go', 'Hold', or 'Stop' in the Gate Theory developed by R.J. Cooper (1988).

With the advent of Total Design (Pugh 1982) the specification compilation followed an investigation of the market and it then forms a 'boundary' around the subsequent stages of the process. This is an oversimplification as it is acknowledged that the process is highly iterative with much backtracking as more information becomes available.

Briefs, specifications and the Marketing Mix

One of the purposes of this book is to show how the barriers between the various disciplines of marketing, design and operations management can be broken down. This is one area where there is confusion that can perhaps be clarified.

How many Ps in the Marketing Mix?

The Marketing Mix was first proposed in 1948 and was based around the now very familiar '4Ps' of Product, Price, Place and Promotion. Subsequently this was increased by Cowell (1985) with the addition of People and (the rather contrived) Physical Evidence, which were considered to be necessary when marketing services. More recently several authors have included Process (for example Dibb et al. 2001). Other publications list as many as ten Ps (including such as Psychology) and when visiting the Aquinas University College in Colombo, Sri Lanka, one of the authors was told of an Indian academic who gives talks on the 30Ps of marketing'. These 'extras' have

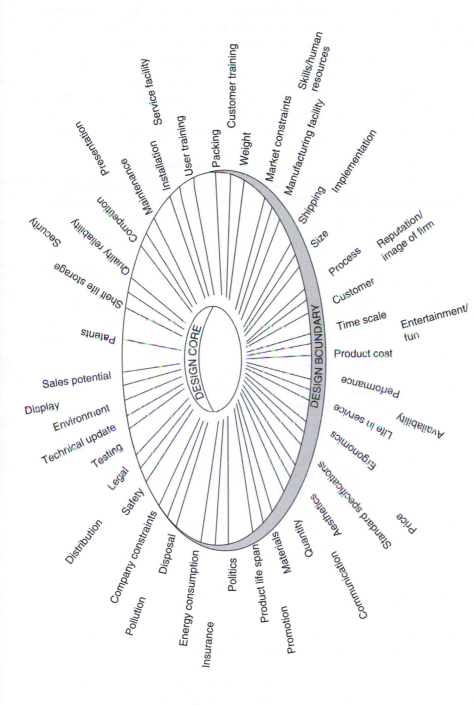

FIGURE 6.1 A SERVICE SPECIFICATION WITH 53 ELEMENTS BASED ON ONE CALLED 'PUGH'S PLATES' AFTER STUART PUGH (REPRODUCED FROM HOLLINS AND HOLLINS 1991, WITH PERMISSION)

not been generally adopted, however, and the 7Ps forms the basis for most consideration of the Marketing Mix.

At the start of a new product or service there is an idea. This is then presented as a brief and in this the broad parameters of the product are outlined. These are compared to the organizational parameters and if they fall outside these requirements then it is reason enough not to pursue the idea further. In much of the marketing literature the Marketing Mix is a strategic consideration at the start of the process and is also used to develop the marketing plan, often towards the 'selling' end of the process.

The initial Marketing Mix shows the broad area in which the new product is likely to be directed. It is likely to be more thorough than is normally found in a design brief with, not surprisingly, a greater emphasis on the needs of the market rather than the profile of the potential product.

The obvious starting point is to categorize under the heading of each of the 7Ps of the service Marketing Mix all those elements that appear in the literature on specifications. Then by linking each of these to where the marketing and design management literature states that each should occur, or be considered in the process, a greater understanding should emerge. This will give more clarity in both disciplines: to design managers at either end of the process and to marketing managers in the centre of the total process – where each group currently emphasizes their main efforts. The brief is later expanded into the specification.

Before any new product development is undertaken a series of parameters need to be specified around the organization's activities. These will be described by the top management and will (rightly) prescribe limitations on any products in which the organization will be involved. These may include the following:

- The maximum financial commitment to any one project.
- The maximum time scale for the development of any service before it reaches the market.
- The facilities that must be used, or that can be subcontracted or outsourced.
- The 'skills' that can be used.
- The markets at which any new service must be aimed.

There may even be a specified 'direction' for future services based on the company long-term strategy. All these give a 'focus' on the area and type of service that is considered 'right' for any organization.

Stepped specifications

In an attempt to simplify the compilation of specifications Hurst and Hollins, first independently and then together (Hollins and Hurst 1995; Hurst and Hollins 1995), developed a 'step' process. In this, aspects of the specification are stated and when these are completed the decision is then taken either to proceed to the next stage of the specification and the next stage of financial investment or to decide whether to 'bail out' of the project at that stage. This makes the overall compilation of any one

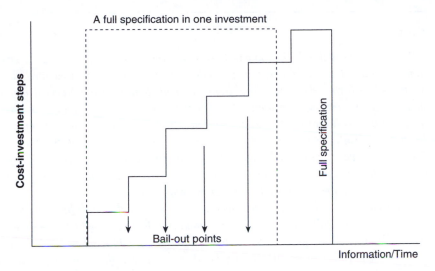

FIGURE 6.2   A STEPPED SPECIFICATION

specification a longer process but when all the programmes in an organization are considered, with the time saved in abandoning projects early, there is a saving in total time and investment (see Figure 6.2)

This results in a presentation of stages that will enable the user to investigate a potential design in increasingly complex steps. These will allow plenty of 'bail out' points where the project may be identified as being unsuitable without a significant degree of work.

The series of frameworks specified place a management and strategic boundary around the process that will define types of product idea that should be progressed further. These can be used to decide if the proposed product is possible/viable or should be abandoned at this stage. This framework will then be constantly assessed to ensure that the needs of the customer are still paramount and that the eventual product will also meet the requirements of your organization. If the profile of the potential product and market are still suitable for the organization, and this is a senior management decision, then the process is taken to the next stage and a full specification should be written.

FAILING FACULTIES

Much has been written and researched on Industrial Gerontology, but the general message seems to be that if you design something considering that it will be used by the elderly then it will probably be better for everybody.

(Continued)

(Continued)

The eyes are usually the first to go. This makes the instructions on almost every-thing an impossible blur. Generally, the older we get the more we need spectacles. A little while back a painting dating from the 14th century was uncovered which showed a monk wearing spectacles. This was the earliest recorded example of spectacles. So why is it that the lenses so often fall out of the frames of so many spectacles bought? Isn't nearly seven hundred years enough time to get them right? Furthermore, when the lens falls out the solution is to screw those silly little screws back in – which is almost an impossible job to do because you can't see what you are doing because the lens has fallen out of your spectacles!

The ergonomics of many devices leaves a lot to be desired. Much has been written about how difficult it is to open many products, though thought has gone into some packaging. To mimic the effect of trying to open something when old or infirm you can smear your hands with a greasy hand cream. If you then struggle to turn a top, that's what it's like all the time for an old person. Packaging designers should have permanently greasy hands.

Look at many gas cookers. The numbers on the dials are far too small to be read by anyone without 20-20 vision and the oven door often requires the strength of ten to open it. Of course, it all becomes easier when one becomes familiar with how to use things. Surely the art of good ergonomics is that one can use things without having to be shown. If you can't manage to use something it is not your fault – it is the fault of the designer.

(See BS 7000-6 (2004) Guide to Managing Inclusive Design)

How to write a specification

People involved in getting the right products have realized the importance of a properly written product specification. This must cover all the aspects of the product to be developed and provides a mantle around the subsequent stages of the development process.

Guidelines for preparing a specification

1 Remember that the specification is a control document; it represents what you are trying to achieve – not the achievement itself.
2 The specification is a user document – make it concise, putting down only information in a form that can be used by others. There is no contradiction between asking for a concise specification and stating that it will be long. If all the points are covered in sufficient depth, no matter how concise the writers have been, the document will be long.
3 An over-restrictive brief can limit 'flair'. Those involved in design should be given enough freedom to provide some intuitive or innovative design, if at all

possible. The brief ensures that the overall design will still satisfy the findings of the market research. If, whilst doing this, the eventual design performs in a different manner to the competition, so much the better. An over-tight brief can also make the final product or service more expensive to produce or implement.

4   Never write a specification in essay form. Use short definitive statements under headings. It is useful in practice to allow space for amendments and additions. Therefore, do not crowd the page: two to four headings per page are usually adequate.

5   Be quantitative (e.g. weight, size, cost, temperature etc.) rather than qualitative.

6   Always put a tolerance on a specified parameter. For example, if you state that the temperature in a room must be 20 degrees Celsius the person that eventually does the work may include a lot of heating and ventilation equipment to keep the temperature exactly that specified. If the temperature is given as 20 ± 4 degrees, then the system will be less complicated and hence less expensive.

Pause for Thought

If you specify that the temperature in a room is to be 'ambient' what does it mean?

If you specify that something should 'look nice' what does that mean?

---

7   Since a specification is always unique in a new design (i.e. dynamic), the relationship between the elements always varies. It is recommended that in preparing a specification you also vary your starting point. For example, you may start one specification with performance and another with environment or politics. Varying the starting point will aid the acquisition of flexibility of thinking required to prepare good specifications.

8   Total Design is a multidisciplinary activity and it is no longer the case that one person will have the necessary knowledge to enable them to provide all the inputs. Furthermore, research undertaken at IBM has shown that when people write specifications they tend to put too much emphasis on areas of their own expertise.

9   Always date the document and put an issue number on it. Whenever there is a change put a date and issue number on it. (e.g. 15.1.2007 Issue 2).

10   The iterative nature of the design process allows for the brief to be changed and updated as markets and circumstances change. This may even lead to abandonment of the idea if the competition brings out an identical or superior service with which your company cannot compete. Alternatively, you may be unsure about aspects of a particular element and in this case you may need to do some more market research.

11   Although changing the specification is allowed, there is a point beyond which it is unwise unless it is absolutely necessary. This is where good management

comes in, to know when to change and when to fix it to give some stability to the subsequent process. There is no simple answer to this. Aim to minimize disruption, but, at the same time, keep on target towards a successful product.

When to change the specification

At the start of the process people should be encouraged to propose and make changes as this is low cost and quick to do. Late in the process the reverse is true. Updating and changing a specification naturally causes disruption, and the later in the design process that the changes are made, the greater will be the disruption and its associated cost.

Sub-specifications: the most important elements

Not all elements in the brief are of equal weight. The important elements depend partly on the particular product, but there appear to be some that are more important with almost all products and these are:

- Reliability
- Safety
- Price
- Ergonomics
- Maintainability (because you cannot store a service) and
- Aesthetics.

It is, however, possible to grade the elements in your specification for importance and the easiest way to determine these important elements, having identified your market need, is to focus your market research to answer the question: 'Why will customers buy this product or service?' The brief will highlight inter-relationships and compromises between elements. Do not compromise on the most important elements.

*As **reliability** has been found to be so important, it is surprising how easy it is to specify unreliable products and services and often how difficult it is to specify reliable ones.*

For example, the postal service in our area used to be considered as very reliable. Recently a very small number of letters seemed to be going astray. The problem was that we never knew which letters were not getting delivered. Therefore, we never knew if there was somebody awaiting a reply. A very small degree of unreliability can throw into question the reliability of the whole.

As another example, you want your car to start first thing in the morning but how many times will the car not start before you consider it to be unreliable? Generally, this is very few and may be as little as one start in ten, but the disruption caused by that number of failures could cause you to worry every time you go out to start your car.

When writing your specification you will find that you must **compromise** between the various elements. When you have identified the most important elements in your specification, through market research, you should not compromise on these. 'De-rate' some other aspect of your design instead. Also, remember to take account of the whole life of the product when writing a specification.

Case Study: Twingo, Twingo, little car

The Renault Twingo was one of the best-selling cars in Europe throughout much of the 1990s. It even won design awards, yet almost none were sold in the UK. It was a fanciable car, small, cheap to run, big inside and ideal for a city dweller, but it was not available in right-hand drive.

After Renault's Directeur du Design Industriel, Patrick Le Quement, gave a paper at a conference in Paris about how great the design of this car was, one of the authors wrote to him asking why he didn't make the car available with right-hand drive. The gist of his reply was this. When Renault started to design the Twingo they were very short of money. Having designed the car, it was then decided that there needed to be a right-hand drive version as well as the product left-hand drive. It was estimated that the cost of this change could be £9 million – more than Renault could afford at that time – so the design exercise was never carried out and this best-selling car was never offered to the British market, in spite of being held up as a paragon of good design and having won design awards.

What does this tell us about Total Design management in Renault in the early 1990s? If Renault had written their design specification properly in the first place, they would have included the need to make both a left-hand and right-hand drive version. The information fed into the specification should have been determined from an investigation of the market and potential customers not only in France but also in the rest of Europe, including the UK.

This 'problem' could have been sorted out whilst the design was still in the form of 'bits of paper'. The costs to have solved this problem early in the design process would have been small, perhaps negligible. The costs early on in any product or service are usually small, the costs later on in the process tend to be high – £9 million high as it transpired in this case. It also meant that Renault missed out in the many lucrative markets for a small right-hand drive car, of which the UK is only one.

Product development is an honourable profession, so lets honour it by doing it well.

Clausing (1998)

SUMMARY OF KEY POINTS

- Effective product design specifications are one of the keys to successful product design but companies have been found to be ineffective in this area.

- The full specification embraces many factors and is a dynamic document, changing and evolving as the design proceeds. Check-lists of those aspects that should be covered within these categories are still relatively new.
- The staged specification process simplifies the design of products.
- Necessary compromises are confronted early on and there are plenty of 'bail-out' points as the result of a design review at each sub-specification of the process.

STUDENT ACTIVITY 6.1

Think of two products that you currently use in your home that you consider are difficult to use because they are poorly designed. Also, think of two products from your home that you consider are easy to use because they are well designed. State why each of the poor ones is poorly designed and how it could be improved and what makes the other two products so pleasant and easy to use.

STUDENT ACTIVITY 6.2

List five products or services that you consider to be reliable and five products or services that you consider to be unreliable.

STUDENT ACTIVITY 6.3

Think of any particular product that you have recently purchased, or are about to purchase, that cost more than £100. Write down the ten most important things that you want from that product.

STUDENT ACTIVITY 6.4

There are many lists of elements that can be used as a check-list when compiling a specification. Look at these examples then answer the two questions for each.

Furry Friends Cats Home

Furry Friends Cats Home wishes to introduce weekend boarding for cats. The cat will be collected from the owner on Friday evening between 5 and 7pm, fed and housed until Sunday night, when it will be returned to the owner between 6 and 8pm.

All the elements of the specification list shown in Figure 6.1. (which was derived for use in manufacturing) will need to be considered, but:

1   Which are unimportant and can be ignored for this particular service?
2   What others will need to be added to make a suitable specification for use in this service sector?

Gechuthere Bus Company

The board of Gechuthere Bus Company need a product design specification for their new route to Glasgow. The coach will leave from London's Victoria Coach Station

Monday, Wednesday and Friday, at 9.30am and arrive at Buchanan Street Glasgow at 6.00pm. The return will be Tuesday, Thursday and Saturday, leaving Glasgow at 9.30pm and arriving in London at 6.00am.

Again, all the elements of the specification list (Figure 6.1) will need to be considered, but once again state:

1 Which are unimportant and can be ignored for this particular service?
2 What others will need to be added to make a suitable specification for use in this service sector?

What kind of information do the design team want from top management *before* the design project progresses?

FURTHER READING
BS 7373-3 (2005) *Product Specifications: Guide to Identifying Criteria for Specifying a Service*. London: British Standards Institution.

7
CREATIVITY AND INNOVATION

The reasonable man adapts himself to the space; the unreasonable one persists in trying to adapt the space to himself. Therefore, all progress depends on the unreasonable man.

George Bernard Shaw

New concept generation will be covered in this chapter. In the development of new services it is necessary to be creative. Here will be shown that it is possible to learn how to be creative. Various techniques will be described, including the very latest thinking on creativity. More time needs to be spent in seeking new concepts than most people realize.

LEARNING OUTCOMES

When you have completed this chapter you should be able to:

- Know when to improve existing or innovate new services.
- Know how to identify new concepts.
- Identify the 'best' concepts.
- Compile Concept Assessment matrices.

In most companies strategic plans are an extension or extrapolation on what has gone before, although companies may not admit this. Creative thinking can be the fillip needed to discover new concepts and to break out of this problem. Our lives are changing and despite all the labour saving devices we seem to have less time to do things that we want to do. All this means that there is a potential out there for new ways and new products and services to excite us. Innovation is fundamental to corporate survival. Cooper (1993) has stated: 'The annals of business history are replete with examples of companies who simply disappeared because they failed to innovate, failed to keep their product portfolio current and competitive, and were surpassed by more innovative competitors.'

Terminology

Designers typically use the term 'concept' as the word that initiates the design process. A better word is 'idea'. The concept stage is a part of the process that comes later. There is one main idea but several different concepts that can fulfil that aim. The best idea is the one that best meets the specification and falls within the initial parameters as defined for and by the organization.

THE PAPERCLIP

In Norway there is a 9 foot statue of a paperclip to celebrate its invention by Johan Vala in 1899. Unfortunately for proud Norwegians, the paperclip was, in fact, patented by the engineer, psychologist and philosopher Harold Spencer in the UK nearly thirty years earlier. Harold Spencer was also the first to coin the expression 'survival of the fittest' (not Darwin).

In military circles, paperclips are known as 'court-martial clips' owing to the number of unintended papers that attach themselves to the others and get circulated.

The paperclip is a truly remarkable invention as it can be used for so many more things than merely holding bits of paper together. It has been estimated that of all the eleven billion paperclips purchased every year only about one in five are used to hold paper. Perhaps what is even more remarkable is that somebody has spent their time working this out.

If you think we are going rather over-the-top about paperclips, this is because it is the finest example of a creative exercise to start a brainstorming session. Thinking of lots of possible uses for one (or several) paperclips helps those involved to 'get their blinkers off' and think 'outside the box' before getting on with the more serious part of the brainstorming exercise.

That's a good idea – let's do it

Too often people in companies have a 'bright' idea and then embark on a frantic process to get a prototype on the table and a product out the door. This is not surprising as many 'august' bodies seem to promote this 'artistic' approach to design. Also, many TV programmes, that profess to show people how products should be designed, implement the same action of jumping at the first idea that pops into the designer's head and then pushing the eventual product onto an unwilling, disinterested market. They then blame the lack of customers and product success on everybody else – including the customers, for not fully appreciating their genius. These 'designers' are arrogant and what they do is a fundamental and costly error that contributes to the high failure rate for new products and services, and often companies as well.

In some ways it is understandable that companies act as they do. A budget has been allocated for the development of new services. The top managers want to see that they are getting something for their money and put pressure on those responsible for design to produce something they can see and play with or show around at meetings. Furthermore, non-technical people tend not to understand drawings and do not believe that a pile of paper is really the correct way to manage the early stages of the process.

Management consider achievement is by results. The more visual those results are and the earlier they see them the further they perceive the development has progressed. Designers, too, must share some of the blame. The industrial designers' skill generally lies in the provision of aesthetically appealing opportunities. It is what they are trained and qualified to do and it is what many like to do best. They cannot wait to start rendering on their 3D CAD workstations. Designers enjoy the challenge of solving problems and developing answers to problems through rigorous solutions. They enjoy playing with a prototype as soon as possible. The moral is that although it is important to reduce the time to market for new products and services, this should not be done at the expense of thorough design.

The design manager who is worth his or her salt is one who can get the various parties involved to hold back until enough information is known or has been compiled so that the *right* service is developed. The right service must contain all the features that make it appealing to the customer, be better than the competition and, at the same time, make money for the organization.

> It is one of the unique attributes of a good designer to be able to put themselves in someone else's shoes and experience their daily lives; to literally see the world through their eyes.
>
> Michael Wolff, Principal Michael Wolff Associates

Does a company need a new product or service?

Another cry often heard is to encourage companies to design more. Certainly companies that do not develop new products and services will decline and eventually cease to be, but there are several times when it can be advisable not to do a specific design but to wait until a better idea comes along. Often new ideas emanate from the sales force. They know the existing market but tend not to consider broader markets that may be preferable. As a result, the sales force tend to subdivide existing markets with no overall increase in demand. Those responsible for seeking substantial new services must think to new parameters that can fulfil market need while, at the same time, enhancing rather than damaging the existing range.

It is important to consider the long-term problems of having an ever-burgeoning product range. Back in the early 1980s when the Japanese first demonstrated their leadership in developing new cars, their companies astounded the world with a proliferation of new models. Initially this seemed impressive, but they had overlooked two problems. The first was that before potential customers could become familiar with a product it was withdrawn and replaced by another, and those who had bought the product soon found that they had an old design that had been superseded, with the result that the resale value of their relatively new car was low.

The second problem was a problem for the companies that developed such a vast short-lived product range. They created a nightmare in the provision of spare parts throughout the world. A small change in the design of a product can result in a reduction in economies of scale and a significant increase in the cost of spares supply. Customers want to be sure that they can keep their cars on the road for a good period of time – the total life of a car is typically up to 20 years, through several changes of ownership. Imagine the hassle car companies had supplying, say, a headlamp for a multitude of models for twenty years, enabling these to be delivered to any of their customers world-wide in 24 hours – which is the type of service that customers now expect. They hadn't designed the service end of the design process.

One company that learned from this was the re-born Triumph Motor Cycle Company in the UK. When the original designs were drawn up it was a deliberate policy to maximize interchangeability of parts between models. For example, this even involved using the same twin cylinder block that was cut in half for smaller engines, so the same piston sizes could be used across the range. The service provision of spare parts was subsequently much easier.

This is just one of the potential problems that can be foreseen and planned around if design managers consider the whole life aspect of any new product and service, as far as to its eventual disposal. This thinking needs to be the practice at every stage of the process and the original views held about any new part may alter the further the organization goes through the process. This is Total Design in action and this involves people with a far wider range of disciplines than was thought necessary in the past.

Another area that needs to be considered near the start of the process is the whole-life costs of ownership and opportunities for additional company earnings. The emphasis here may be on the service side and may involve aspects of vertical integration, especially at the later stages, to benefit from the, often, more profitable service stages. As one looks through the whole life of a product the later service stages become more apparent. These service stages will allow more potential for innovation around the product and more potential for profit. They can even indicate new niches where the market may be grown.

It is also important to ensure that new ideas fit inside those guidelines in which a company is prepared to operate. Generally, these include maximum time to market, maximum total cost for the development, potential return on investment, available skills, effect on the existing company products and services and the company's long-term strategy.

Stifling creativity

With all these guidelines, boundaries, limitations and parameters imposed at the start of the process, the accusation could be made that this is restricting or stifling creativity, which is the lifeblood of any designer worth their salt. Well, the days of the 'sulky' designer, who didn't want to 'prostitute their genius to the vagaries of the market', are over. Sure there are a handful of people who manage to make a very nice living from design icons (such as Philipe Starke), but these are a handful. Designers who want an entirely free rein on what they design should work for themselves and not within the confines of an organization that must make profits and satisfy shareholders. And they should consider themselves as 'artists' or 'craftspeople' rather than 'designers'.

Most designers live in the real world and are well able to face up to the necessary restrictions that are imposed on their designs. The better designers work well in new product teams and use the various parameters that are imposed to sharpen their talents to produce effective and innovative designs that still give the company (and the market and shareholders) what they want.

Everything written in this chapter does *not* stifle creativity or innovation. It just gives it a focus and a direction and the overall effect is more success and more potential failures eliminated right at the start before much money has been poorly invested. Furthermore, these improvements in working quickly become apparent after a flurry of extra work at the start. Design ideas that are not 'right' for the company get ditched early on. Suddenly, an overworked and under-performing department becomes more efficient and those working in that department will suddenly find that they have more time to cope with their workload.

As the plan will stretch out into the future for several years, the work plans will become obvious and logical and the boundaries and parameters will be refined to be more workable and accurate.

The only people who believe that it is not possible to plan their new products and service introductions for several years into the future are those who haven't tried to. Chapter 14 on the future shows just what is possible. One of the clear messages that came from the research was that with experience of your own services there is very little that cannot be planned well into the future, several generations ahead.

There are fast-moving areas that are difficult to keep up with unless you are actually working in those areas. These areas change over time but, at the moment, they are electronics, communication, pharmaceuticals, bio-technology and some materials. Most other areas are changing slowly and, therefore, predictably.

Even radical inventions can be identified through patent applications and these usually take up to ten years to become widely available – plenty of time to plan to use them, or plan round them. Legislation takes ten years from proposal to law. Again, plenty of time to plan. An example of this was the law ending duty-free sales in the EU. Those benefiting from the existing rules did nothing for eight years, then they moaned for the next year and finally they clicked that the change was inevitable and they had better learn to live with it, or better still, profit from it. The alternative was to disappear from the scene. It would have been far better if they had spent ten years planning to benefit from the inevitable.

> Innovation starts with people, not with enabling technologies … if you forget this you risk delivering feature-rich rubbish into already over-crowded lives.
>
> Richard Seymour, Principal SeymourPowell Design Studio

What is innovation?

So what is innovation? In the Standard on design terminology published in 1995 'innovation' is defined as:' The transformation of an idea into a novel saleable product or operational process in industry and commerce or into a new service' (BS 7000-10).

Our preferred definition is **'an invention in its first marketable form'**. This means it has to be **new**, and not just an improvement on what has gone before. It requires a new concept. It also means that it must have been put on sale. Designs must certainly be improvements, but not often is a new concept needed.

So where is design management going? The 'infatuation' of those involved in design with innovation continues. But innovation is a double-edged sword. There is increasing evidence that many companies supplying certain types of product should not be innovating but concentrating on product improvement (Hollins and Pugh 1990). Only innovate if customers are prepared to accept the radical change. Many designs have become user standards and, therefore, difficult to change (the 13 amp plug, CD format). Improvement is always welcome but not always radical change. If innovation is being considered it is important that those involved can clearly identify the benefits and the downside for the customer before progressing too far into the process.

Do not just drift into innovating. Many do because it is fun, but only innovate if it is required. In the longer term organizations will need to innovate to survive, and this is discussed more in Chapter 14.

An innovation takes longer so needs a greater amount of time for this part in the design than those parts where people are more familiar with the concept. Innovation thus costs more than an improvement and is more risky as it is more difficult to do market research (more difficult but far from impossible – focus on the fact that people buy benefits, so tell people what they are). On the other hand, if the innovation is successful it can be very successful as there is no exact competition. Therefore an innovation should only be embarked upon when the market actually wants it and the company is able to provide it.

It is important to appreciate when an innovation is required as the way the process is managed and the activities that should be included in the process vary, depending on whether a change is 'static' (incremental or evolutionary improvements) or 'dynamic' (innovation). For example, if a concept is static, aesthetics (décor) and ergonomics are more important, automation is more likely to be viable and necessary, larger companies are more likely to benefit and CAD will be more usable in the design process. The reverse will be the case if the design is to be dynamic. There are many such activities that are related to the status of a service.

> It is very easy to be different, but very difficult to be better.
>
> Jonathan Ive, Head of Design, Apple Computer Inc.

Of course, it is rare that a new product or service is completely an innovation and it is possible for the product to be broken down into its various sub-components, some of which will be innovative and some will require incremental change. It is possible to identify if parts of a new product/market require static or dynamic design and also whether an organization is best able to achieve it.

As most customers and hence most new products do not require a new concept, the existing concept is good enough. If it is *known* that the product is entirely static then the concept stage and the search for new concepts may not be a necessary part of the process. As long as the specification, and hence the market research, is thorough and complete then, for some products, it may be possible to omit the entire concept stage.

There is also innovation in marketing and this is probably one of the more successful areas that can be investigated. How many people would have continued to spend quite a lot of money on pizza (after all it is only glorified cheese on toast) if somebody hadn't thought of home delivery and then included a guaranteed half-hour delivery service? Home banking is another 'obvious' success (only obvious when someone else has thought of it), which works because people do not want the bother of going out perhaps in inclement weather, between fairly narrow opening hours, to have to find a parking space in a town centre and then to join a queue.

> Innovation is more easily accepted in the service sector – there is less of an existing infrastructure to shift.
>
> Bill Hollins (1999)

Seeking new concepts

So, having decided that you need a new concept, how do you find one? Even with a static product in a static market you may need a concept stage to confirm that the existing concept is good enough.

> Perhaps the obvious is the first idea to be rejected. Creative teams are often inhibited by the obvious, by the opprobrium they imagine it brings. They will avoid the direct route from problem to solution, preferring to involve the viewer in an intellectual game, or worse, show off.
>
> David Bernstein, Kelland Communication Management

In spite of what David Bernstein says, when seeking new products and services the first idea is usually not the best. Brainstorming sessions increase the number of new concepts, and the more ideas generated the better.

Brainstorming sessions should have a leader, a maximum of nine participants and last sufficiently long to exhaust all the possible ideas – typically two days if the service warrants this expense. They should be held in comfortable surroundings with no phones and away from normal work, such as in a hotel.

The leader should prevent anybody 'hogging' the conversation or pushing their own idea. When an idea is presented it should then be considered the group idea and not that of an individual. The best ideas do not necessarily come from the most senior people. The leader should co-ordinate the process and write down all the ideas.

BRAINSTORMING SESSIONS

These work just as well for identifying new ideas in many situations as they do in the more familiar use in new product development. The rules for all are the same and although many have heard the term 'brainstorming' not many understand how such sessions should be organized. The 'rules' are:

- *All participants should be given the specification at least one week before the meeting and near the start any queries regarding this specification should be addressed.*
- *No criticism, judgement or evaluation of any kind. Always delay judgement of ideas to a later stage; this reduces inhibitions and eliminates a defeatist attitude: 'All my ideas are useless, it's not worth putting any forward.' Negative statements are not allowed, e.g. 'too silly', 'too stupid', 'not right', you will lose interesting, useful ideas as members of the group evaluate before giving their ideas publicly. There is nothing better than criticism to stifle and restrict creativity.*
- *No dominating role of leader. Everyone has equal status in the group, ensuring that everyone's ideas have equal value.*
- *The group is encouraged to think 'wildly'. It's easier to refine ideas later than to think them up in the first place. If everyone is throwing in wild ideas individuals will be less likely to internally judge their ideas before putting them forward. Often, once thought about and modified, the wild idea may be the ideal solution.*
- *Quantity before quality. Lots of wide-ranging ideas is what is required. Their quality can be judged later.*
- *Members of the group are encouraged to use each other's ideas to build on or modify, 'combinations or modifications of previously suggested ideas often lead to new ideas that are superior to those that sparked them'. (Osborne 1953).*

(Continued)

(Continued)

Running a brainstorming session

This should be coordinated by the product champion.

- *Organize the session in comfortable surroundings at a time when those involved will not be interrupted by other activities that will divert their attention. (A room without a telephone.)*
- *Appoint a recorder for the group, to write up all the ideas as they come in. Using wall space or flip charts so that all the members can clearly see the comments that are being made (if using a flip chart do not 'flip' over so that pages cannot be seen).*
- *Get every member in the group to restate the problem as they see it. You will find that there are several different ways of seeing one problem. There are always other aspects or angles that you did not appreciate. You should then have a number of different restatements of the problem on display.*
- *Have a 'warm up' session. This helps to get the right atmosphere and the members of the group feeling comfortable. For example, ask them to think of uses for a pencil. It should start as being a writing implement and develop into being a piece of wood and a lump of graphite. Allow the group to get 'silly', encourage noise and laughter. The group members will then feel relaxed and comfortable with each other.*
- *Go through each restated problem getting ideas for each. The different ways of looking at the problem will 'cross-fertilise' in the production of ideas and help the group members to look at aspects they would not otherwise have considered.*
- *Persevere when ideas seem to be drying up and when the first 'flush' of ideas is over. Give the group members time to think. This is the time when this method is most effective. When thinking becomes difficult is when the ideas produced are of most value.*
- *Do not evaluate the ideas immediately, wait for a couple of days while the ideas or answers sort themselves out in your mind before evaluating and making your judgement.*

Make it fun!

There also need to be plenty of 'rest' periods as this increases individual performance. These are often called 'periods of gestation' or 'soaking periods'. Here, ideas tend to be 'mulled over' and the thought processes continue in the subconscious. You may have experienced this: you struggle for some time at work trying to solve a problem and then when you are home and doing something else, the solution suddenly pops into your head. This is the effect of this 'soaking' and is a necessary part of the brainstorming activity. The process is summarized in Figure 7.1.

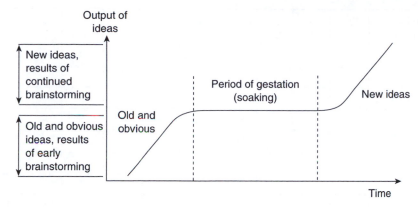

FIGURE 7.1   BRAINSTORMING ACTIVITY

Finding the 'best' concept

Having generated many potential new concepts, how do you then decide which is the 'best'? How do you know it is the best? Trying to identify the 'best' concept is always a hit-and-miss affair and, like generating concepts, one can never be certain and can never prove that the final concept that is taken into production or implementation could not have been bettered.

There are several ways of judging new concepts and the first is against the specification. Eliminate those that do not meet the specification. There are exceptions to this where a concept is discovered that is so good it is worth changing the specification, but this is unusual. Having eliminated those concepts that do not meet the specification you should still have some left. These can be judged through some of the matrix methods as described in the literature. You can never be certain that the 'best' concept has been selected (they may all be failures) but by this stage you will probably have determined the one that is most likely to succeed and also provide the most benefits to the particular organization developing the product or service.

The concept selection system described here is the Concept Assessment Matrix (see Figure 7.2). The first was developed by Stuart Pugh in 1991. Pugh used to go into companies and compile these matrices on a large wall using many concepts and criteria against which the concepts would be judged. He would take about a day over the exercise.

This is how to do it

On the horizontal axis, on the top of the matrix, are a series of concepts that should meet the specification as generated through the brainstorming sessions. On the vertical axis are listed the most important elements of the specification but, of course,

Criteria Concept	1	2	3	4	5	6	7	8	9	10
A	+	–	S	–	+	D	+	S	–	+
B	–	–	+	–	–	A	+	+	–	–
C	+	–	+	–	+	T	+	S	–	+
D	+	–	–	S	+	U	–	S	–	–
E	+	+	–	S	–	M	–	+	–	+
F	S	+	–	+	–	–	–	–	+	–
Sum +	4	2	2	1	3	–	3	2	1	3
Sum –	1	4	3	3	3	–	3	1	5	3
Sum same	1	0	1	2	0	–	0	3	0	S

FIGURE 7.2 CONCEPT ASSESSMENT MATRIX. IN THIS EXAMPLE 4 AND 8 APPEAR MOST LIKELY TO BE THE BEST IDEAS. (AFTER PUGH 1991)

the most important element for any particular service may vary. In practice and with experience one probably knows which are the most important elements in any particular situation.

From the various concepts, which are on the horizontal axis, there will probably be one that already exists and others that are quite familiar. There may be several concepts that are absolutely new, but there may also be one included that is already on the market. Choose this as the datum. The operation of this matrix is to compare all the other concepts, which are on the horizontal axis, with the one chosen as the datum.

For each concept, in turn, compare the specification element with that on the datum. In each case it will either be better, in which case give it a '+', or worse than the concept shown on the datum, in which case give it a '–' and, if it is about the same for this particular specification element, indicate this with 'S'. This activity should be done as a group, as often there is some discussion as to whether one concept is better or worse than the one shown on the datum. For example, does a horse require more maintenance than a motorbike? The activity described in the previous paragraph is undertaken for each concept and each element of the specifications listed on the vertical axis. There should then be a complete matrix consisting of + signs, – signs or S signs. There will, of course, be an empty column, which is the datum.

The next stage is to add up the signs, and enter the total at the bottom of each column. At this stage it should be apparent that some of the concepts have more – signs than + signs. This means that this particular concept is not as good as the datum and can be eliminated. Some concepts will have more + signs than – signs, this means that they are better than the datum and these should be retained.

A word of warning. Do not sum up the + signs and the – signs. Three + signs and one – sign do not make an overall total of 2+s. This is because the elements specified in the vertical axis are not of equal importance.

Another common error is to try to weight, for importance, the elements used in the vertical axis. The problem with trying to do this is that it cannot be done accurately. For example, precisely how much more important is safety than price? Three times? It cannot be done accurately, so do not try. Keep the information in it's broad form and use your knowledge or common sense to assess which is most important. Those who weight the elements end up with a sum and the one that is the highest number wins. This is, in practice, unsound and generally causes the individuals who do this to lose sight of the reality of what they are doing.

The next stage is to alter the datum. With the first datum, there may be several concepts that appear to be as good as each other. By moving the datum about, one can alter the overall best concept slightly. With a few alterations of datum, the overall best concept will emerge. It is also possible to combine concepts or aspects of these concepts to make an overall better concept. It is also possible to modify concepts to improve them. With some manipulation and quite a bit of time (in practice, it should take no more than a day), one should be able to identify a best concept. Grabbing at the first concept, without going through such procedures, can end up with what Stuart Pugh called 'concept vulnerability'. When this occurs the organization develops a product that is not as good as it ought to be and this will be placed on the market, only to be beaten on that market by a better product, with a better concept, from a competitor who has spent more time in identifying which is the best concept.

Blueprinting enhanced: a new design method for improving service

Blueprinting can also be used in an 'enhanced' form to identify how any service can be improved. Blueprinting shows how the customer uses a service. This process can be extended much further to improve services during the early stages of service design. Initially, compile the blueprint as before. Then, in parallel to what has gone before, look at the 'sensory' side of the customer experience and write these in the parallel boxes. What does the customer see, hear, taste, smell and feel at each stage? Then, related to each sense, propose how the service can be improved through the normal concept generation methods. This will allow potential service improvements to be focused more precisely in areas where they are most needed. What the customer feels about each stage and some ideas on how it could be improved should be collected reactively, for example by customer complaints, or better, proactively from customers using the service by interview or other form of market research.

Activity at each stage of the blueprint can be summarized thus:

WHAT DOES THE CUSTOMER:	TASTE?	(T)	HOW CAN EACH BE IMPROVED?
	SEE?	(V)	
	HEAR?	(H)	
	SMELL?	(S)	
	FEEL?	(F)	

For example, consider the customer experience as they would use a new fast food outlet. Initially, the customer approaches the outlet: is the area around the shop clean and free from litter? (V). Does the decor look inviting? (V). The customer walks into the shop: is he or she met by an inviting smell? (S). What is the sound in the shop: would Mozart be the right sound to hear or would there be a better choice of music or even silence? (H). How is the customer welcomed? (H). How long are they expected to wait? Do they feel they are waiting too long? (F). And, of course, how does the food taste? (T).

It can be seen that, having enhanced the blueprint by linking it to the senses of the customers it is possible to make further quality improvements. These improvements can be proposed through a series of brainstorming sessions involving all interested parties. From the supplier's side it would be more of a view from the kitchen or counter and throughout the process, again, quality improvements could be identified. Much of this blueprint would be operating in parallel to the customer experience blueprint.

For an indication of potential new ideas look also to stretching the process – extend it by adding to the stages and, more usually, on the service side. Take the example described above, supposing the addition of home delivery was to be considered. The process blueprint would take a different form as the customer would not enter the shop and their only contact would be through the telephone and when the food was delivered. The kitchen blueprint might be little changed. In this situation time is important so the aspects of time reduction through JIT as described above would become paramount.

Backcasting

The process of speculating back from a desired future to the present is called back-casting. If a future has been identified for a particular product or service it may be possible to speculate back. This can also be done by undertaking a blueprint back to the present indicating the stages or milestones over time. Quality aspects can then be identified and problems confronted very early on so that the service, when eventually designed and delivered, immediately performs at its best.

For the longer-term future planning it is even possible to identify where improvements might occur if a particular technology were available and then either wait for or seek the technology that can make this improvement possible. It may even be possible to enter an alliance to develop the new technology or to do it yourself. In such situations the blueprint can include a series of 'black boxes' to indicate what the technology should deliver and where it should occur in the process.

A failure, but emotion makes it a success

There has been some interesting work done by the consultant Jim Dixon in trying to measure the emotional response to potential designs and trying to see if it can be predicted. This could be a very powerful, if confusing, area of design. How is it certain designs are wonderfully successful in spite of being such apparent failures?

Take the Sydney Opera House. It came in at 14 times over budget, was almost impossible to build and full of design flaws yet you rarely see a picture of Sydney without its being featured. It has inspired the identity of the whole city. So in spite of being a design disaster, it certainly is a design success through the intangible effects of emotion. John Redmond, Dean of Design at Monash University in Melbourne, may well snigger to see how we now openly admit that he was right all along in calling it a design success. (Although we bet he is still glad that he wasn't paying for it.)

There are many similar products. Consider Concorde, up until the time of the tragic accident in Paris. Too expensive to develop, costing more than 20 times the original budget and resulting in less than one-fourteenth of the anticipated number (planned to be 200) produced, yet it inspired admiration and excitement and was one of the mainstays of BA promotion for almost a quarter of a century. Can this 'excitement' be predicted and then designed into a service at the outset – and can it be combined with other positive features that can ensure it is a success?

At the other extreme there are teapots. The traditional brown teapot design is both inefficient and pretty ugly but attempts to radically change the design have, so far, ended in failure. We have affectionate feelings towards the old design. Such irrational emotions can turn a success into a failure and a failure into a success. Can this be anticipated and controlled?

As another example take a look at the 'revamped' VW Beetle car. Volkswagen have designed a success which should be a failure. They have taken the very well-designed Golf floor pan and engine, redesigned the car to make it cramped inside (look at the waste of space between the windscreen and the steering wheel) and only suitable for children and Quasimodo in the back seat. They have made it bulbous and retro in its styling and with a higher price. Then they achieve a success by appealing to those who loved their old Beetle cars 30 years ago with a product which has design clues from, but is actually quite a bit different from, the original. There are quite a few evident on the roads in Britain and certainly a lot have been sold in the United States. The car has been on display at the Design Museum so somebody there seems to think it is an example of exemplary design. Some designers in Germany got that gamble right, but was that by luck, intuition, or some rationality? The BMW Mini has also achieved success with 'identity clues' from the original design, as it was designed in the same factory.

Of course we shouldn't get carried away by this idea that a likely failure can be turned into a stunning success by appealing to the emotions of potential customers. It is too much of a 'let out clause' for some flowery-shirted scoundrel to be able to push through their ill-thought-out feeble efforts by claiming an appreciation of the hidden feelings of the mass market. Certainly the emotion side is important but it really only becomes useful and usable if it can be measurable and more important, be predictable.

Imagination is more important than knowledge. Knowledge is limited. Imagination encircles the world.

Albert Einstein

Lifestyle: A new view on creativity

It would appear that the world is full of 'lifestyles'. These are dictated to us by gurus who set themselves up in business to advise us how to dress, look and where to be seen, all, of course, for a fat fee. You cannot blame these style gurus for having the nerve to get away with it and one should, perhaps, feel sorry for those who haven't the wit or nous to organize their own lives. On the other hand, 'lifestyle' could give a good indication as to what are the new services and products that people may want and, in turn, include what companies should develop and market.

- First we designed products – production led.
- Then we designed things people wanted – market led.
- Now we should design things based on the way people want to live – lifestyle led.

This goes beyond giving the customers what they want. It involves developing services and products that might improve the way people live, without them obviously being aware of exactly what it is that they might be needing. This is most effective when undertaken in conjunction with a blueprint.

This is the type of thing that would emerge through a slightly different view of market research. Rather than asking people whether they want a particular product or service, it starts by asking what people want to improve their lives – they want to look and feel good, be stress-free, have more time to do what they want, keep going and live a long time. So far so good, and trying to satisfy these aspects of their lifestyle can drive the clothing industry, health club/fitness industry, cosmetic industry and, probably even, the cosmetic surgery industry.

Now let's try to take this further. What are the sub-sections of these? People like to alter 'time frames'. Video recording is an example of this. They want to see at one time some programme that was shown at another. They also want to have more time – hence all the labour/time-saving devices that have been promoted for more than a century, from vacuum cleaners to microwave ovens. They also want a good time, hence leisure pursuits and the holiday industry.

So what is the next stage? A possible good extension of looking at lifestyles is to consider different scenarios of people's lives and then see if there are profitable services that can be introduced and supplied by a company. For example, consider a person's typical day and see how it unfolds – what goes wrong? What don't they like? One can learn far more about potential new services through looking at what people do not have rather than what they do. People do not like cleaning their cars (could dust be removed by an electrostatic charge being applied to the car?) People do not like travelling to work (beam me up, Scotty?). How can your company develop a service to improve people's lives at a price that they are prepared to pay for these services.

How can existing products and services be adapted or extended into new profitable areas?

It is not really a 'what if?' analysis. It's more of a 'people do this so how can we make their life in this context easier or better (at a profit)'. Most of the ideas that come up from such an analysis will usually involve the linking of existing products and services to make new ones. It might, though, indicate a need for radical advances to fulfil the envisaged (but unproven) need.

All scenarios should constantly be questioned. For example, if a study of a waiting room in a GP's surgery indicated the need for more comfortable seats the question that ought to be posed is 'Why are these people having to wait in the first place?'.

Invariably, such a scenario analysis will involve blueprinting what people are currently doing and then identifying the areas for potential improvement through new products and services and then applying the proposed potential improvement and then redoing the blueprint to see how the service has been improved. Changes in one aspect of a blueprint may cause problems (or further opportunities) in another part of the blueprint.

The focus all through has to be on more profit for your organization, through services that a company can supply, coupled with real benefit to the customers over and above that which the competition is supplying. If they are outside of a company's abilities, available or obtainable skills, financial reach or strategy then forget the whole thing and look elsewhere.

There are lots of things that can be used to improve the process to increase customer satisfaction. Having identified the scenario and taken the idea as far as its potential, it is still important (vital) that market research is undertaken to see if people actually want it. For example, people watch TV a lot and they are on the move a lot. One would think there would be a demand for a small, hand-held TV. Yet as many have found, including Sir Clive Sinclair, portable TVs are just not big sellers, so will they work if supplied on mobile phones?

One can cast the net wide when considering such lifestyle embellishments but not far into the project the points where the company concerned takes pennies out of the system must be identified. Gardening is popular with retired people but aspects of it can be hard work. First identify the hard bits and then identify the product/ services to make it easier (it could even be a gardening service). One has to be careful that this process does not end up in a series of second-rate 'gimmicks' the like of which appear in those magazines that get pushed through our doors. Such items tend not to do the company image any good.

On the other hand, a clearly demonstrated advantage can be exploited and promoted. Such was the case with the Dyson vacuum cleaner, which really did work better for longer than those with a bag. With his next major design, the washing machine, the stated advantage – a bigger load and your clothes cleaner – was not seen by many to be such an advantage so as to command the very high price, which was significantly more than the competition. The question that should have been asked was 'Do you feel that the washing that comes out of your washing machine ought to be cleaner?' Most people would probably think their washed clothes were clean enough and they didn't need to pay more to get them almost undetectably cleaner. As for the greater wash load in the Dyson, probably most do not do such a large load of washing. Those that do – maybe families with a large number of children – may not be wealthy enough to purchase such a high cost machine. This is moving away from lifestyles to just advantages but it should demonstrate that the lifestyle advantages identified really must be advantages that the consumer wants and wants enough to pay for.

Where this would be used in the design process

A brainstorming session is the ideal forum in which to consider and expand lifestyle ideas. Those involved should be asked to consider problems, what generally irks them or activities that they undertake that might be suitable areas for improvement. These could make the agenda for the meeting. Initially each could present their main ideas (but not solutions). If several people mention or empathize more with certain ideas or problem areas these ought to be considered first. It is best to consider one area thoroughly rather than flit between themes without getting to the root of any. Decide on one important area then undertake a brainstorming session around this. All normal rules of brainstorming must still apply with suitable leadership, rest periods and adequate time to solve the problem.

Of course, all this will mean that (only in these cases) service design will start with a concept stage prior to both the market and specification stage of the Total Design process. This will be followed by a further concept stage. The existing methods can be used but the overall 'frame of reference' will be shifted to apply this thinking in a new way. And unlike most design, no market research has been done prior to the brainstorming session and the urge to just get on and develop the potential new service must be avoided. All this is at the low–cost end of design, but will involve people's time and the lost opportunity of them not doing something else. Furthermore, to explore fully just the 'best' idea will take more time than the brainstorming sessions that occur with the more normal concept stage of the design process.

The first assessment of the ideas will be against the main management guidelines. Normally new concepts would be judged against the specification, but there is no specification with these yet. With each lifestyle improvement concept the customer benefits will need to be listed and where the organization can make their money. Also associated with this evaluation should be an indication of how easy it would be for the company to do and if any radical changes or additions would be needed to the organization's working to be able to take on these concepts. Obviously, the least disruptive concepts are likely to be the most suitable. Now do the market research and write the specification. Having said one doesn't start with a concept, this is an exception. As an indication, customers want services that are easier to use than those already available.

SOME BRIGHT IDEAS

Simon Majaro has questioned why car alarms rely on noise. He has proposed an alarm that send out a strong smell to scare away thieves – an example of analogy, perhaps taking the idea from the skunk.

One aircraft tyre manufacturer sold their product to airlines based on a type of lease and the customer only paid for each landing that the plane made. Rather difficult to administer but the idea proved popular with customers, who only paid when they were actually earning.

(Continued)

The problem is not how to get new thoughts into your mind, but it is how to get the old ones out.

Nancy Austin

So don't get locked into that which has gone before. Be prepared to break out and seek the new to get an important marketing edge.

SUMMARY OF KEY POINTS

- Well-run brainstorming sessions can release untapped talents of creativity but the very group situation and time limitations can stifle these.
- The failure rate resulting from random inspirational sparks vastly outnumber the successes. The 'flashes of genius' from individuals are of little use unless they are funnelled towards organizational needs, strategies and a planned product range.
- Understanding that a service can be changing incrementally or innovatively can direct your emphasis in design management.
- It must be remembered that in most products and services there are parts that are dynamic and parts that are static. It is necessary to split down any such system into its broad component areas and find the product status of each of these.
- New concepts are first assessed against the specification and those that remain can be assessed against these matrices to identify the overall best.

STUDENT ACTIVITY 7.1

Chinese proverb: Involve me and I will understand activities
First, here is an activity to get your blinkers off.

Over a period of 2 minutes, write down all the things you can do with a safety pin or safety pins. (For example, you can hold pieces of paper together with it.)

Having compiled that list, now count how many uses you have written. If you have less than seven you are not (yet) a creative person, but do not worry, as said, creativity can be taught. The test you have done is still used in recruitment to identify a person who is creative. Creativity is not required in every job: for example, air traffic controller. Creative accountancy has got people into trouble (and prison) and you certainly wouldn't want to meet a creative dentist.

Look again at your list. Generally people tend to think in a way that 'spirals out'. For example:

- Initially, you probably thought of single examples, such as a coat hook.
- Then you think in terms of multiples, such as making a chain.
- Then you change the size, such as, a weapon.

- Then you tend to change or use the properties, such as a magnet or a compass.
- Then you change the material and, finally, there is nothing to stop you melting it down and making something completely different. There was no specification and almost anything goes.

You know you are being creative when you have difficulty in thinking of something you *can't* use a safety pin for. (Try it.)

STUDENT ACTIVITY 7.2

We now have a problem with a slightly larger specification, but the brief is still pretty open. There are almost no wrong answers, but some will be better than others. (It is a real problem and the solution that was actually used is given at the end of this chapter.)

Moving heavy machine tools about in a confined space is never easy, especially when they incorporate cast iron beds that are liable to break if dropped. However, they do sometimes have to be moved and the problem becomes even more difficult if, at the end of their journey, they have to be accurately bedded down in a hole in the ground.

Find the best way of coping with one such job, in a situation where the hole is only very slightly wider than the machine. A crane cannot be used because of lack of roof clearance and there are no suitable jacking points on the upper parts. There are quite a few practicable solutions that are worthy of consideration.

The problem: moving the machine

Suggest ways of gently lowering a ten tonne guillotine into a large hole in the factory floor, 4 feet by 8 feet in cross-section and 2 feet deep, without using cranes or jacks. The cavity only offers one inch clearance around the machinery base.

STUDENT ACTIVITY 7.3

1 List three services or products that (parts of) are changing in an innovative manner and state why you consider them to be dynamic.
2 Now list three (parts of) products or services where the change is incremental and state why you think that they are static.
3 Find the status of the following at this time:

- car
- camera
- computer

(**Guidance Note**: You will need to break these products down into their broad characteristics. For example, with the computer, think of the keyboard, the screen, the memory, the software etc. With a car, think in terms of steering, suspension, drive, safety etc.)

You will need to think of possible change but also consider that change has to be a benefit to the customer, at a price they are prepared to pay, and is technically possible.

STUDENT ACTIVITY 7.4

You are to start a small business to deliver parcels (and make money from it, so posting them isn't allowed). The parcels all weigh one kilogram and are to be delivered to various places over a radius of 8 kilometres. It is a 'next day' delivery service but the parcels don't need to get there any quicker. Of course, if the delivery is undertaken in only a little time then you will be able to deliver more and hence, make more money.

(**Guidance Note:** The first stage is to think of all the possible concepts that can achieve the very broad brief. You should have been 'deblinkered' by now and so this shouldn't take too long. The concept generation part is not the main purpose of this exercise.)

Now whittle these concepts down to the eight 'best'.

Now select the most important elements by which you can judge the concepts. From experience, in this example, 'reliability' can cause confusion. 'Accuracy' is a better one for these. Choose eight important elements.

Now to construct the matrix. Put the chosen concepts on the top of the horizontal axis and the important elements chosen (the criteria) on the horizontal axis. You now have a series of boxes that require to be filled.

Now select a 'datum'. This is one of the vertical lines that includes a familiar or existing concept. For example, in this exercise you have probably chosen 'motorbike' as one of the concepts. This is because you are familiar with the fact that many parcels are delivered around town by motorbike. This would make a good datum as concepts that are better than things that already exist have a greater chance of being a success.

Now the important part. For each concept and for each criterion compare it with the datum. If it is better than the datum indicate this with a '+'. If it is worse then give it a '−'. And if it is about the same, then give it an 'S'.

When all the boxes in the matrix have been filled add the +s the −s and the S's and show the number of each at the bottom of each of the vertical columns. An overall 'best' concept begins to appear.

Now try repeating the matrix but change the datum product. The poorer concepts can now be eliminated. It may be possible to combine various concepts to make an overall 'best'.

SELF-ASSESSED QUESTION 7.1

In what areas of business can the design manager encourage creativity?

Write 500 words.

What are the advantages and disadvantages of being a creative organization?

Write 500 words on the advantages of an organization being creative and 500 words on the disadvantages of an organization being creative.

Consider a service that you have used recently. Draw a blueprint of the activity and enhance it by completing the additional 'sensorial' parts below:

Taste?
See?
Hear?
Smell?
Feel?

What did you note and how could the service be improved?

FURTHER READING

De Bono E. (1993) *Handbook for Positive Revolution.* New York: Harper Business.

Ettlie J.E. (2006) *Managing Innovation: New Technology, New Products and New Services in a Global Economy.* Oxford: Elsevier.

Janis I. (1972) *Victims of Groupthink: A Psychological Study of Foreign-Policy Decisions and Fiascoes.* New York: Houghton Mifflin.

Osborne A. (1993) *Applied Imagination,* 2nd edn. New York: Scribner.

Pugh S. (1991) *Total Design.* Reading, MA: Addison Wesley.

Thackaray J. (1997) *Winners. How Today's Successful Companies Innovate by Design.* Aldershot: Gower.

Note

There are many possible solutions to the problem posed in Activity 7.2, but the 'solution' that was used was that they filled the hole with dry ice. They could then slide the machine to the required position and as the ice melted the machine was lowered into the hole.

8 LEARNING FROM PRODUCT AND SERVICE FAILURES

Mistakes are part of the dues one pays for a full life.

Sophia Loren

To achieve success, early identification of potential failure is a natural part of the process. Elimination of failures early on can be considered a success, as this saves resources that would otherwise be wasted and allows the company to 'live to fight another day'.

LEARNING OUTCOMES

When you have completed this chapter you should be able to:

- Identify services that are more likely to fail.
- Thus, avoid the most obvious causes of failure, or eliminate potential failures, during the design process.
- Know the best measure of service success.

We cannot identify failure without first defining success. **The best measure of success is financial** – did the product make any money? People often disagree with this view, with platitudes such as 'it gave us good publicity', 'it was a flagship product', 'it completed the range', 'it created excitement', 'it was a celebration' etc. Put it this way. You can have all that, but what pays next week's pay cheque?

A PREDICTION OF A FUTURE FAILURE

*The **2012 London Olympics** will cost far more than was stated when the bid was won and London taxpayers will have to pay much more than was originally anticipated. How do we know? Because the whole thing has not been design managed! Things will run late and vast sums of money will be thrown at the project to turn it round. Another*

(Continued)

(Continued)

prediction. The Games will no longer be stated to be of financial benefit to Londoners, as originally promised. Success for the event will be claimed because it is 'good publicity', 'a spectacular event', 'a celebration' or 'a great regeneration'. These are the usual claims made when something is a financial disaster.

A new product is introduced every 3½ minutes but most new products fail, and they fail because they do not make a profit. That profit must be greater than just the cost of developing the product, it must also include the lost interest of not leaving the development money in the bank, the waste of exhibition, catalogue and promotion costs, the waste of money and time in setting up the service side and the waste of time for the sales people trying to sell the product when they could be selling something else. Any manufacturing time is wasted, and also the stores and service space taken up with what is, effectively, scrap.

Even failures for one can result in remarkable successes for others. Take, for example, the **Tay Bridge** *disaster of 1879, when a train from Edinburgh to Dundee was swept away with 13 spans of the bridge and resulted in the death of 75 people. The bridge may have collapsed and those in the train may have perished, but the resulting poem by William McGonnagal has endured as a gem of English (or was it Scottish?) literature.*

In most companies success nowadays is determined by the return on investment on their products and services. The greater the profit, over a specified period of time, in relation to that initially invested the more the design can be considered to be successful.

It must also be remembered that even a well-organized new product department will have almost as many product failures as successes. Financial planning must take into account the fact of life that the cost of at least half of the development budget will be wasted on new product failures; failure is a natural part of success and any good organization and manager must accept a certain amount of failure whenever people are trying something new. This does not mean that they should tolerate the stupidity that has been demonstrated in many of the examples given later in this chapter.

You can learn a lot by looking at the product failures of others. By understanding what causes failure and success in others it is possible for an organization to eliminate the potential failures and concentrate on the potential successes. This allows the managers to focus their efforts in the right direction.

To highlight failures, some light-hearted, some serious, some recent and not-so-recent examples of failures and the reasons why these products failed are given in this chapter. As can be seen, in most cases the root cause of the failure was right at the start, and was predictable if only top management had done their work properly near the beginning of the development process. Avoiding most product failures is not rocket science. It is common sense, and a matter of doing the up-front work necessary to identify and correct the potential source of error, or abandoning the project and starting again.

> The trouble with common sense is that it isn't very common.
>
> George Bernard Shaw

As failures are so common (unfortunately, much more common that successes), there will be other well-known cases mentioned in other chapters. Knowing that others make blunders is usually quite gratifying and the big failures mentioned in this chapter will certainly make any blunders of your own seem quite insignificant.

Over-the-wall design

Throughout most of the world, design tends to be carried out in the same way. The market researcher has an idea and throws it over the wall to the 'designer'. This person sits in a window-less box and spends all day twiddling with the CAD equipment. The designer then throws some drawings over the wall to the 'production' or 'implementation' people. They develop it and throw it over the wall to the sales people: 'Here it is, get out and sell it.' If there is any likelihood of any communication taking place then the bureaucracy just builds the walls higher.

Not surprisingly this is called '**Over-the-wall design**' (Figure 8.1). In this book we try to knock these walls down. When we talk about development we are talking about everything that is needed and every one who is needed to create a successful product or service. This means that New Product and Service Development is *big* and involves not only sales, marketing and production (or implementation) but also customers, suppliers, financial departments and, in fact, all who can make a contribution to the success of the product or service.

Reasons for product and service failure

As is said in the chapter on specifications (Chapter 6), there are really very few reasons for product and service failure. Essentially there are three:

- Technical failures
- Market failures
- Financial failures.

Which means:

- It doesn't work (technical failure)
- Not enough people want it (market failure)
- The development costs are too high to be viable to the organization (financial failure).

FIGURE 8.1   OVER-THE-WALL DESIGN (DRAWN BY JANE MINARDI)

Figure 8.2 shows typically where failure occurs in the design process. Assume a company starts with 100 service ideas. After each stage of the process there is a reduction in potential product ideas left for the start of the next stage. In the early stages there is likely to be a large reduction but this is good design management because these are being eliminated at the low cost end of the design process. The problems occur when the potential failures are identified at the high cost end of the design process when significant amounts of money have been spent on them. The most serious failures are those that occur when most of the investment has been made and the service has been put on the market only to find that it doesn't sell.

Producing failures also causes low morale as well as being a shocking waste of time, money and resources.

> For which of you, intending to build a tower, does not first sit down and estimate the cost, to see whether he has enough to complete it?
> Otherwise, when he has laid the foundation and is not able to finish, all who see it will begin to ridicule him saying 'This fellow began to build and was not able to finish'.
>
> Luke 14: 28–29

Right at the beginning it is often difficult to judge a technical failure as these can occur almost anywhere in the process through an inadequate specification, using the wrong concept, faults in the detail or in poor implementation. The other main reasons

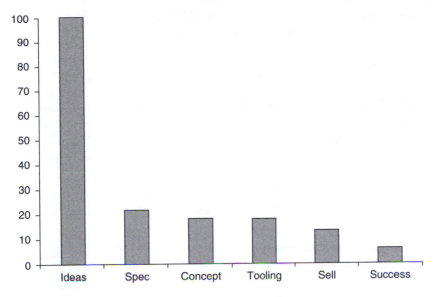

FIGURE 8.2   WHERE FAILURES OCCUR IN THE DESIGN PROCESS

can usually be identified early on. Market failure is the most common reason for a product or service to fail and it is mainly due to 'not understanding the customer requirements' (Cooper 1983). In short, the market research was either not done or was inadequate. Financial failure occurs when the costs of design and implementation of the service have not been sufficiently thought out in the specification stage.

Other products and services are superseded

These need not be commercial failures. If a company enters a market near the start and makes sufficient money during the mature phase of the product life cycle and then leaves the market as it goes into decline, then this is good product management. The problem occurs if a company enters a market late and leaves it without having made a suitable return for the financial outlay. This is when it becomes a failure. For example, if a company spends six months in preparation for a 'trend' product that has a fashion of only three weeks then they could well have a failure on their hands. But generally, as time passes, products and services are replaced by newer ones. This should not, in itself, be regarded as a failure.

If you perceive that any of the 'failures' mentioned are a success, try applying the criterion for product success: **Would you have liked your money invested in them?**

Not unexpectedly, there is a high failure rate at the start of the process, which reduces the further one proceeds through the design process. The fact that most products fail at the start of design is not usually a problem. An organization will consider many ideas and abandon most of these early in the process. It is important that an organization should appraise a large number of potential new products and options and a healthy sign that most are abandoned at this stage.

Spin-offs

Another delusion is that an organization can make a big profit from all the spin-offs that come from a new product failure. As a spin-off from a dish of mould, Penicillin was certainly a huge profit-maker (albeit for the wrong people), but there are cheaper ways of developing the space blanket and non-stick frying pans than going to the moon. David Farrar, formerly of Cranfield University, investigated spin-offs from various products and found that pound for pound the spin-offs from Concorde and the space race were actually less profitable than with most other products.

Communication failures

In some examples the failure was due to a combination of reasons. One may also lay the blame for some as being down to inadequate communication, but the actual cause of the failure blamed on poor communication manifests itself in one of the root causes given above.

Great blunders of our times

We now start looking at some actual examples of product and service failure. Anybody who has spent any decent length of time in managing new products and services has seen the collapse of 'great' ideas at various stages of the design process. Also they can probably tell us why they failed and what should have been done to avoid the disaster – such as not starting in the first place. So let us discuss some of the great blunders of recent times and how they could have been avoided if only somebody had applied just a few simple techniques, a little expertise and a little common sense.

COMMENTS FROM A DESIGNER IN NEW PRODUCT DEVELOPMENT, AS DESCRIBED TO ONE OF THE AUTHORS

In my many years working on new products I have had more than my share of Concordes, Edsels and Sinclair C5s. Fortunately, due to the scale and exposure I have managed to keep these fairly quiet. Amongst these were all-singing, all-dancing products that nobody could afford and few wanted. This was fortunate, because they couldn't be made either.

New products in this particular organization usually started the same way. As soon as one of our salesmen would appear in the office, describing a new product wanted by one of the existing customers, I would grab a pencil and let my creative talents

(Continued)

flow. Innovations are ten a penny (unfortunately, innovations cost a good deal more than that). Invariably, only that one customer wanted the device … or something similar. Like Chinese whispers, the salesman had not heard it right, had mistold me, who, probably, misheard him. The result was something nobody wanted.

Never mind, the following week another salesman would appear and I would have a new project. I was busy, very busy, with a large number of new products getting into the market. The draughtsmen were working flat out to keep up with the demand for detail drawings and production was constantly disrupted with short runs of product variations. The tool room was clogged with prototypes. We had a really lively new products programme … we had an expensive disaster on our hands.

There had to be a better way of organizing and managing new products but finding time to reorganize things, with the mountain of projects on my programme, made this impossible. This was my first mistake. Organizing the management of new products reduces work and also reduces time and cost of new product successes.

My second mistake was to view the new product department as something on its own and not as part of a total process. Everybody who needs to be involved must have the opportunity to make a contribution. This causes communication problems that need to be confronted and overcome. Many companies seem to work this way. Once the project is over the wall the department can, hopefully, forget about it. Communication between departments is kept to an absolute minimum and management of each department is kept quite separate.

We have seen many new product departments and some of what has just been described is apparent in most of them. It was Peter Drucker who said that he saw 'a lot of people trying to do better what they shouldn't be doing at all'.

Let us start this series of failures with a reminder of some 'biggies'. One of the biggest design failures of all time is reputed to be the **Premier 'Safe' cigarette**, which cost RJR Nabisco $500 million and seven years' work before being abandoned. The loss partly resulted in the break-up of part of the company. The idea was to have an inner cardboard tube with holes along its length. This held the tobacco. At the end of this was some charcoal and when this was lit the tobacco was heated (but not burned) and this released the nicotine. This nicotine passed through the holes in the tube into an outer tube and into the mouth and lungs of the smoker. No smoke and no tar and therefore safe?

After years of development the first test marketing showed that the device was difficult to light. It also tasted horrible. But these were not the given reasons that the device failed. The Premier Safe cigarette was withdrawn for two reasons. First, if the product was sold as a safe cigarette what would be the market perception of the rest of the company's products? Second, if the product was sold as a safe cigarette and just one person became ill with a smoking-related disease what would be the legal implications?

The point that needs to be asked is, why weren't the company lawyers and marketing people contacted *before* all the years of product development? A quick question at that time would have saved a fortune and some of the company. Clearly, a serious omission in the product specification.

This pales into insignificance, however, next to our own **Poll Tax**, a design failure that cost the British government £18 billion before it was eventually abandoned. Widespread protest following its introduction resulted in millions of pounds owed in unpaid tax (especially in Scotland) and those charged with collecting the outstanding debts decided to simplify the whole collection system by computerizing it. Everyone in Scotland who had yet to pay (which was a very significant percentage of everyone who was supposed to pay) was sent a form to fill in which was then to be read through a bar code system. People filled in these forms and sent them back, *but*, with the aid of a black ink ball-point pen, also added one extra 'bar' to the bar code. All the returned forms were fed into the computer which, with a cough, kicked them out again. It is believed that this was 'the straw that broke the camel's back' and the authorities officially abandoned trying to collect the back-tax owed. The lesson to be learned here is twofold. First, it was a market failure as many people considered that the tax was unfair. Second, it was a technical failure because it didn't work. A tax must be easy to collect, for example PAYE is collected at source and it is difficult to avoid VAT when buying goods and services. If people decided that they would not pay the Poll Tax it became difficult to collect it.

A more recent government blunder is the **Internet University** (UkeU), launched in September 2003 and abandoned after only 900 of the expected 5,600 students enrolled for courses at a cost of £44,000 per head. Less than 1% of money from the private sector was obtained to fund the scheme. Estimated losses were £50 million (anticipated profits were £110 million). The Commons Education Committee review in March 2005 condemned it as being 'a disaster' and stated 'there was no formal market research undertaken to assess either the level of demand or the nature of the demand or the type of e-learning required. There was no systematic evaluation of the markets … and no understanding of consumer demand'. The committee chairman Barry Sherman said 'the UkeU was a terrible waste of money.' This demonstrates the need for doing market research at the start of the service design process, where costs are low.

ALL WITH THE BENEFIT OF HINDSIGHT?

Below is part of an article written by Bill Hollins in Engineering Designer *in 1998:*

The Millennium Dome
There is just about time to stop it all without throwing away much more money. Now with the Millennium Dome the figures, which show that the project will be a failure, are so blatant that it is hard to see any reason why it should be kept going. The only reason that it is being continued is that politicians want it. Quite often politicians seem to be devoid of some of the more basic attributes of life, such as brain cells.

Look at the figures: the anticipated cost of the Millennium Dome is £750 million. Add to this the cost of putting something inside that we will actually want to

(Continued)

see. That should bump the costs up to the round £1 billion. Currently, although they are not certain as to what they are going to put inside the Dome (I propose a large stuffed white elephant), they still anticipate that there will be 12 million visitors (one-fifth of the country's population) and these will be happy to pay £20 each (family ticket £65). This means they are actually planning for an income of £240 million but an actual expenditure of about £1 billion. In other words, they plan a deficit of £760 million.

Of course, they may have underestimated the number of visitors. If everybody in Britain visits the Dome they would actually make £200 million profit, but that hardly seems likely and I, for one, don't intend to go as there is nowhere to park, and alternative transport to the Dome hasn't been described yet [Note: The Jubilee Line extension was finished on time but at a very large overspend] and no doubt this will also add to an already expensive entrance ticket. We do have something to compare it with. The Festival of Britain in 1951, with an existing infra-structure of public transport, managed 8 million visitors.

But what price do you put on a celebration? Incidentally, in April 1998 it was announced that eleven new hospitals would be built in Britain. Total cost? One billion pounds. I know which decision I prefer to celebrate.

No design disaster in your organization can match these and the company still survive to pay your salary on a regular basis.

Postscript: *There were 6.5 million visitors to the Dome, of which 1 million went in free and 2.3 million were given a discount (Janet Anderson, Tourism Minister, Metro 8.2.2001).*

As can be seen from the above, by applying the simple techniques proposed in this book it is possible to predict, and therefore avoid, many failures.

Eventually it was admitted. On 21 July 2001, Dome boss David James pinpointed the failures when he said that the pressure to complete on time and the confused reporting structure – including government departments, the Millennium Commission and the company board – meant proper management and financial controls were not put in place.

Amongst our list of big failures there are other **millennium muddles.** It seems that anything with 'millennium' in the title is a problem. Millennium Dome (enough said), Millennium Wheel (a triumph for things made abroad and a snub to British manufacturing, but even this was a couple of months late due to faults in the bearings; it started to operate better after the 'millennium' bit was removed and it was renamed 'The London Eye'). Then we had the Millennium Bridge (the one in London' that is; the one on Tyneside is a big success).

It is, after all, only a footbridge and doesn't have a great deal of weight to carry, so what was all the fuss about? (For detailed comment on this design disaster see the Box.) Some of the bridges we are using for cars were built long before the horseless carriage was invented and they seem to be holding up pretty well. They were probably over-engineered, but the Victorians (and those before them) were designing using a fair degree of the 'factor of ignorance'. Isambard Kingdom Brunel had a footbridge built across the Thames at Hungerford Dock in London in 1835. It apparently worked without a wobble.

A BRIDGE TOO FAR?

Comment by Bill Hollins in Engineering Designer, *vol. 26 no. 4 (Sept/Oct 2000) 21.*

I started writing this on the first day that this new £80 million footbridge across the Thames was opened. By the time you read this it will be apparent if my initial fears have come to anything. It is a nice-looking footbridge, 'like a shaft of light across the Thames' we have been told. It ought to be nice-looking because it has been designed by an architect (Norman Foster) and a sculptor (whose name I can't remember). No mention of engineering designers, which was my first cause of concern but as soon as things started to go wrong suddenly it was the engineers who were the 'fall guys'.

You may have seen pictures of the Tacoma Narrows Bridge (Galloping Gertie) that eventually swayed itself to pieces because the designers did not take into account the effect of cross winds. I think a model tested with a hand-held hairdrier may have predicted this problem – and they did have hand-held hairdriers back in 1929. I think we can assume it was an example of bad design.

Nowadays we are far more enlightened. We have computers with which to design things, programs that allow you to simulate performance and check the calculations long before 'metal is cut', and wind tunnels in which to test models of any proposed structure. It could be said that design today should be fool-proof, providing all the correct tools are used.

The day the Millennium Bridge was opened to the public we saw pictures of people swaying as the bridge pitched in the cross winds. It looked to be worse than the old Galata bridge in Istanbul and that did a fair bit of swaying. A 'spokesman' for the bridge said the cause of the problem was that too many people were crossing it (so what is it there for?). The bridge was designed with a planned usage of 4 million people crossing it each year, that is about 11,000 per day. It was also said that the winds on the Thames were too strong that afternoon.

Now I live not far from that bridge. We could hear the fireworks display that heralded its opening. I spent the afternoon in question at a local park on a bright and sunny day. I did not notice this 'strong wind' … It wasn't the sort that would blow an umbrella inside-out and not as bad as could be expected at many times of a typical year.

*I accept that a bridge must sway, as must any building, but sway that much in a pretty light breeze? Perhaps we should worry about the future of this nation if we can't even design a pretty rigid footbridge. Incidentally, real designers can cross the Thames, or any other river for that matter, without the aid of a bridge. Just be confident in the knowledge that **Designers walk on water**.*

Comment: *This was a technical failure and the lesson to be learned here is to use the existing available knowledge when designing. There are several books published by the Institution of Civil Engineers that give details on rigidity and stiffness including how to minimize the bad effects of a large number of people crossing bridges. Much of the information dates to Victorian times.*

Let's focus next on the **New Wembley Stadium.** At the time of writing it has been declared that the cost of the new 80,000 capacity national football stadium has gone up from the original estimate of £400 million through the next estimate of £660 million to £800 million. The first question to ask is why the sudden jump in price in these times of low inflation? The next question is why did the very successful Olympic stadium at Homebush, Sydney, which holds 110,000 people, cost only £200 million? Wembley works out at over five times the cost per person for each seat. It is also significantly more than the cost per seat of every recently built football stadium. Will each person be in a heated armchair with a toe-warming foot rest?

Then consider the number of events at Wembley per year, let's say two per month with an average attendance of 50,000 (it's not all major cup finals, think of the Conference play-off final). Now consider an average ticket price of £40, which is far more than many would want to pay.

Total annual income: 50,000 × 40 × 24 = £48 million.

At first glance this looks quite healthy until one considers that the initial cost of building has to be borrowed and then paid back with interest – say 10% interest. Total interest payable each year is £80 million. Of course, you have other income besides just the gate money but that is a huge shortfall to make up with hamburgers etc. and they haven't even started to pay off the initial loan yet.

It is the same situation as exists with the **Humber Bridge**. This bridge is an example of one of the few political promises that were kept. Barbara Castle was the Environment Minister at the time and promised that if a by-election went the Labour Party's way then the bridge would be sanctioned. It cost about £64 million to build back in the 1960s to take the 74 or so people who want to travel from Lincolnshire to Hull (or back) every day. Whenever the toll is increased just to meet the cost of interest accruing, many of the few customers choose to drive the extra 23 miles round the outside to avoid paying the high toll. A lovely bridge, but a financial disaster. The lesson here is to plan the project cost in line with the likely income as identified through market research.

The next area that should send chills up any observer's spine is the infrastructure around the proposed new stadium. Wembley is a residential area. This is the age of the car, and if you have one then why not use it? Supporters need somewhere to park. No parking? Then cut down on the original estimate of the size of the gate. Did you ever try to visit the old Wembley Stadium by public transport?

This is the era of Total Design. One doesn't just design a stadium. One also has to design the whole infrastructure including adequate parking, adequate roads to the stadium from motorways and a complete system of public transport. This has not been well thought through. The misery that one had in getting to the old stadium is to be carried over to the new stadium. Perhaps the only sensible site for the new national stadium would have been around the National Exhibition Centre in Birmingham. This has a good road network, good parking, rail links and an airport and is in the centre of England nearer to the heartland of football support.

As another example let's take the **Media Centre at Lord's Cricket Club**. A good-looking building that performs well and it won architecture awards. But it cost £7 million pounds, which was twice as much as the original estimate. It perhaps demonstrates the apathy of the architectural profession that they can present awards when the project was clearly out of control and shows again that skills in any aspect of design cannot be taken in isolation of the needs of business – which is survival first (Drucker 1955) and then profit. The lesson here is to design a project within the finance available or do not start it.

Yet another incredibly badly planned project was the new **British Library**. Not only did it come in at more than three times over budget and many years late, but the final building was insufficient to undertake the role that it was initially projected to do. In short, it cannot hold all the books it needs to.

The architect, St John Wilson, was pleased with the project, which is not surprising as he had been working on it for over thirty years (we would all like a job for life!). He was also quoted as saying, 'I bet the Pyramids and the Sistine Chapel overran their budget'. Maybe, maybe not. One thing is certain, a pyramid couldn't overrun its completion date, because there was a mummified stiff that needed to be put in it. And can one really compare the British Library to the Sistine Chapel?

This is another example of inadequate planning at the start of the project that led to an over run of budget and timeframe resulting in a financial failure. The lesson to be learned is plan the project at the outset.

Now for something less heavy – a nice little failure this. Some years ago a bright designer thought it would be a good idea to develop a **cat-flap** that would allow only the owner's cat in. This would exclude neighbours' cats, who let themselves in, eat your cat's food then wait behind the door to mug your unsuspecting moggie when it returns home. A noble and worthwhile concept, but it was its execution that let it down.

The design was put on the market and, initially, it sold well. The cat-flap door was opened by a magnetic collar worn by the cat. A simple, effective but flawed idea. Owners soon found that their cats were going missing, although they were usually quite easily located – often stuck to a parked car! It was a great idea to use a magnetic collar, but the magnet, it seems, was just a little too strong.

The product in its faulty form remained on the market for quite some time before the original model was removed and replaced by a less 'exciting' version in which the collar activated a relay that unlocked the cat-flap.

This is an example of a technical failure. The original design concept was flawed and this should have become obvious when the prototype was tested. The lesson to be learnt is that all new products and services need to be tested before they are put on sale and preferably in situations where they are likely to be used.

Don't understand? Your fault or theirs?

A seminar some time back involved a discussion on 'the critical role of design in overcoming technophobia'. Technophobia is clearly a recently made up word, which presumably means a fear of technology. Whenever people want to impress (or is it confuse?), they create a new word for something so that they can then make money out of it. Perhaps the prize for this goes to the word 'cellulite', which has no meaning in medicine but by identifying it cosmetic companies have been able to make a fortune out of selling women products to get rid of it.

'Technophobia' is in the same category. First, a second-rate company produces something that is too difficult to understand how it is to be used. Rather than go back to the drawing board (or workstation) to correct the poor design, they make excuses that the consumer is to blame. They can then accuse the consumer of being 'technophobic' and try to make more money by taking the consumers' collective hands and leading them through the mystery of this confusing new technology, until, that is, a better company comes up with a simpler way of achieving the same ends.

As consumers we should make it clearer to such companies that it is not a fear of technology that we have with their products and services, it is positive action in avoiding something in which insignificant thought has been given to the ergonomics. Technophobia should not exist. Products should be easy to use. If you have difficulty in using something then once again, it is not your fault, it is the fault of the company who produced it.

Not enough failures?

It was said earlier that the failure rate of new products and services is much too high and needs to be reduced. We will now suggest that, perhaps, it is not high enough. What *is* too high is the cost of these failures.

Reducing the investment in failures can be a major step forward in the management of services. Consider the cost of the various stages of the process. Initially these are relatively low as there are not many people involved, no investment in capital equipment or materials and most of the work (market research etc.) is still only on paper. As the design progresses the costs increase dramatically, especially during the implementation stage. The early stages or 'front end' is the low cost end. A product failing at the market research end of the process is much less expensive and therefore far less dangerous to the company than one failing after it has been put on the market.

It used to be so much easier. The people who used to cast the cannons in the Middle Ages were also taken to the battle to fire them. A fault in the design and/or manufacture of the cannon usually resulted in a nasty 'accident' that left the bits of those responsible scattered around the battlefield. And the same recipe was identified by Igor Sikorsky, who wrote: 'In the early days of aviation the aircraft designers were also the test pilots. This had the automatic effect of weeding out the bad designers.'

This policy hasn't altogether been superseded. In China those responsible for sorting out any 'millennium bug' (another con trick) problems in Chinese planes were ordered to be 'air-borne' as the century turned. As far as is known, they had a Happy New Year and many happy landings.

So emphasize your effort at the front end to identify and eliminate potential new product failures before they become a heavy investment and before they become financial disasters. Furthermore, because the cost of the front end is relatively small, it is possible to double the effort and the cost of these early stages, without seriously increasing the overall cost of the entire process.

Coping with failure

The research that Alan Topalian and Bill Hollins did for the standard BS 7000-1 *Guide to Managing Innovation* (which is more fully described in Chapter 14) gave an insight into how those people who were dealing with planning products for the longer term coped with design failures. The thread that ran through these findings was that those people learn from failures and learn how to avoid making the same mistakes the next time.

Several organizations had a formal evaluation process that was used whenever a project was abandoned to see what lessons could be learned from the failure. These did not take the form of apportioning blame but were used to improve the existing processes. Encouraging experimentation and accepting failure was a feature of the most successful innovative organizations. One director said: 'The trouble here is that we do not have enough failures … with every failure we learn so much.' Another said: 'We do learn a great deal from technical failures. We … consult the problem and then come out with products that are even better.'

Certainly, however, some of those interviewed in the research considered a failure to be 'a waste of time and money' and felt that resources were 'too thin on the ground' to risk failures. You can't win them all!

> This thing we call 'failure' is not falling down, but staying down.
>
> Mary Pickford

SUMMARY OF KEY POINTS

- Aim to eliminate potential failures early in the process so that more time is spent on those services more likely to be successful.
- There are three main reasons for failure – market, financial and technical.
- Two of these reasons for failure are right at the start of the process.
- The main measure for a service being a success is financial.
- With a front end focus, poor ideas can be easily eliminated and better ideas more fully thought out whilst still 'on paper'. This avoids changes later in the process – at the high cost end of design. This will result in a more efficient use of the resources available within tight constraints.
- Failure can be a learning process to improve the next service to be developed.

STUDENT ACTIVITY 8.1

1   Write down some more great design failures of the past ten years. Take your time and make your list long.

   When they think of failure, most people in Britain start with the Sinclair C5. It certainly was a spectacular flop, losing most of the £8 million spent on its development, but there are many more important failures than this – Chernobyl, for example. Think widely, and don't forget to include services.
2   Now write down next to each example the causes of the failure.
3   What could have been done to avoid these failures?

STUDENT ACTIVITY 8.2

Write a list of any successful products and services you can think of. Write down why these were a success.

So what is a product success? In most cases the answer is financial. It is nice to have other measures as well, but all of these are secondary.

STUDENT ACTIVITY 8.3

Investigate the failure of one new product or service from a company in which you have worked and, preferably, one in which you have been personally involved.

1   Briefly describe the product or service and why it is considered to be a failure.
2   Comment on the financial, market, technical and any political implications of this failure.
3   Discuss the costs and actions necessary to correct the problem.

STUDENT ACTIVITY 8.4

It is often said that top managers must learn to tolerate design failure. What kind of failure should they tolerate? What kind of failure should not be tolerated?

FURTHER READING
It is best just to look at newspapers to identify potential failures. Look at the fragile excuses given for these failures. Identify the high cost of these failures and see who or what was to blame. Soon you will become proficient at spotting failures before they are even admitted.

PART 3

Management of Service Operations

9 Service Quality Management

The most important aspect of any product or service is reliability – something performing to specification. This is achieved through quality. Quality can be achieved through inspection, quality assurance, or Total Quality Management (TQM). The merits of all of these will be discussed. Tools will be introduced that can be used to improve the quality of services: philosophies and tools; problem diagnosis; customer care programmes. The chapter considers qualitative measurement of customer expectations and satisfaction, including the use of the SERVQUAL instrument.

10 Global Supply Chain Management

In this chapter we recognize the different operating systems and the circumstances that determine their appropriateness. This allows an optimization of scheduling and allocation of resources focusing on the need of differing service types.

This chapter also explores the impact of e-commerce and the use of information technologies on supply chain management. It will look at outsourcing, the service side of controlling inventory management, Just-in-Time MRP (Materials Requirements Planning) MRP II (Manufacturing Resource Planning) and its spin-off ERP (Enterprise Resource Planning) – a theory developed for manufacturing but found to work better in the service sector.

11 Services Location and Distribution

Deciding on the location of a service facility is one of the most expensive decisions any organization can make. A wide range of factors have to be assessed in deciding a location strategy. Different weighting is applied whether a service facility or a manufacturing facility is under consideration. Tools to use to aid decision-making are discussed. There is consideration of service layout designs.

12   Managing Capacity and Variations in Demand

Customers do not make their purchases at a constant rate throughout the year. There are variations in demand whether the product is a Christmas decoration or a summer holiday. Here we investigate some of these variations and describe how companies can forecast and plan their capacity or alter customer demand to cope and to optimize their performance. Topics include: methods for optimizing the balance between varying levels of demand and supply; scheduling and planning; queuing strategies for service industries; marketing implications; how to manage queues; how to eliminate or reduce them.

13   Evaluation and Performance Measurement

In this chapter measuring performance, growth and experiences will be considered. This will include planning and control using techniques such as the Balanced scorecard. The role of benchmarking in performance measurement will be discussed.

14   Thinking about and Managing for 'the Future'

Is change happening faster than ever before and as a result, is it too fast to manage? Here we will look at research into this difficult area. The findings of our research into how organizations plan their products over a much longer time scale are presented. This shows that it is possible to plan far further ahead than most managers believe and manage new services up to ten years into the future.

9 SERVICE QUALITY MANAGEMENT

All instances where customers come into contact with our organization constitute 'moments of truth' – unique, never-to-be-repeated opportunities for us to distinguish ourselves memorably from competitors.

Jan Carlzon, then President of Scandinavian Airlines, 1980; quoted in Peters and Austin, *Passion for Excellence*, 1985

Quality is not related to the price of products. A well-made suit may cost more but there is no reason why the cheapest pen or T-shirt should not be a quality product. People buy products that they think will give them good service and which represent value for money. Increasingly they are prepared to pay more for, what they perceive to be, good quality. On the other hand, if customers buy a product or use a service that they believe was not good quality, they will go elsewhere and may avoid particular products or companies in the future.

LEARNING OUTCOMES

When you have completed this chapter you should be able to:

- Define quality.
- Identify the milestones in the evolution of quality management.
- Describe the more successful management quality initiatives such as Total Quality Management (TQM) and Six Sigma.
- Identify the quality tools used by businesses to improve their services.

Your most unhappy customers are your greatest source of learning.

Bill Gates, Microsoft Corporation

Quality can be defined as 'fitness for purpose'. This is easy to measure with manufactured products against technical drawings. This is far more difficult when measuring services, where the quality of a service is often embodied in the person giving it.

Companies in Europe and the United States consider that improving quality is one of their main objectives. Quality is important for you as consumers, because you want the things you buy to work and continue working. If you expect the products that you buy to be of the highest quality, it is also of prime importance to producers.

History of quality

During the nineteenth century, and exhibited at the Great Exhibition of 1851 at the Crystal Palace, was first shown the concept of 'interchangeable parts'. In this case, rifles were shown, where one part of one rifle would fit onto another rifle in the batch. While there was little interest at the time, the implications for future manufacturing and assembly were enormous. It meant that parts could be made in one part of the world and then assembled onto parts made in a different part of the world. For this to work, quality of components had to be ensured.

Prior to this, products were made as individual items and, if any part failed, it had to be replaced by an individually made component often produced by a skilled craftsman. With the introduction of interchangeable parts it was possible to store a selection of these parts and use them to replace parts that had broken. Because of interchangeable parts, mass-production became possible. Large numbers of components could be produced and assembled by unskilled workers.

Early in the twentieth century, demand exceeded supply, but during the latter half of the century this situation reversed. Increasingly in the twenty-first century customers have a choice for practically everything that they purchase, be it electricity supply, telephone services or Internet Service Providers. With so much choice, customers become more focused on obtaining good quality and rejecting poor quality.

Definitions of quality

As we have indicated, there are different approaches to defining quality. Professor David Garvin categorized some of the definitions into what he called 'five approaches' to quality, summarized in Table 9.1.

1 **The transcendent approach**
   Quality is synonymous with innate excellence. Quality can be defined as the absolute best possible in terms of the product's or service's specification. A Rolls Royce car is a quality car, a Barbour coat is a quality coat and a quality flight is offered by Cathay Pacific Airlines.
2 **The manufacturing approach**
   Organizations following this approach focus on error-free production and items that conform exactly to their design specification. A Swatch watch may be cheaper than a Rolex but can also be defined as a quality product provided it has been made to its design specification.

TABLE 9.1   DEFINITIONS OF QUALITY

Transcendent	Innate excellence. Recognized through experience. You know it is quality when you see it, touch it, experience it
Manufacturing-based	How well the product matches the design specification
Product-based	Quality defined by measurable characteristics e.g. 100% cotton or 1000 hours of light for a light bulb
User-based	Fitness for purpose as perceived by customer
Value-based	Achieving a balance between price charged and conformance or performance

3 **The user-based approach**

It is not enough for a product to adhere to its specification for it to be a quality product, the specification must be appropriate for the customer. The product must be fit for its purpose. Reliability is a key factor in delivering fitness for purpose.

4 **The product-based approach**

In this approach quality is a set of precise and measurable characteristics that are required to satisfy the customer. A light bulb may be designed to last for 750–1000 hours (depending on the type of bulb) or a watch to run without the need for servicing for at least five years.

5 **The value-based approach**

This is the term given to defining quality in terms of cost and price. Customers have an understanding of what represents value for money for them. Passengers using easyJet or Ryanair do not do so for the sake of the in-flight refreshments and are prepared to put up with cramped seating in order to take advantage of the competitive prices.

Service quality parameters

It has been determined that **service quality** has five identifiable parameters and these can either be designed into a new service or brought about through training of the personnel (which should also be an element in the design of the service). These dimensions are:

- **Tangibles** – the appearance of physical facilities
- **Reliability** – the ability to perform the promised service dependably and accurately
- **Responsiveness** – the willingness to help customers and to provide prompt service

- **Assurance** – the knowledge and courtesy of employees and their ability to convey trust and confidence
- **Empathy** – the provision of caring, individualized attention to customers (Parasuraman et al. 1985).

History of quality experts

Quality standards and management have been developing since the 1950s. A number of 'quality gurus' have stressed particular aspects of quality.

Armand Feigenbaum

Feigenbaum wrote the first edition of his book *Total Quality Control* in the 1950s. His definition of Total Quality Management (TQM) was:

> an effective system for integrating the quality development, quality maintenance and quality improvement efforts of the various groups in an organization so as to enable production and service at the most economical levels which allow for full customer satisfaction.

Feigenbaum found that his writings were taken up in Japan, where the concept was made to work on a large scale (Feigenbaum 1986).

W. Edwards Deming

Deming was considered to be the father of quality control in Japan. In the 1950s Japanese companies adopted his approach to quality wholesale and it is this which is credited as being behind the success in terms of quality of Japanese products. His basic premise was that quality and productivity increase as process variability decreases. Through his 14 points for quality improvement Deming emphasized that quality is a strategic priority which starts with top management (see Table 9.2).

When Deming first proposed to American industry that, rather than making things and then checking if they are right, why not make them right in the first place, his compatriots thought that this was impossible (Deming 1982, 1986).

J.M. Juran

Juran was one of the first quality gurus who defined product quality as fitness for purpose. According to Juran, this consists of quality of design, quality of conformance, availability, safety and field use. We have touched on the importance of each of these in the chapter on new product development. Juran highlighted the fact that goods could conform to specification but not be fit to use from the customer's point of view (Juran 1989).

TABLE 9.2   DEMING'S 14 POINTS FOR QUALITY IMPROVEMENT

1	Create constancy of purpose
2	Adopt new philosophy
3	Cease dependence on inspection
4	End awarding business on price
5	Improve constantly the system of production and service
6	Institute training on the job
7	Institute leadership
8	Drive out fear
9	Break down barriers between departments
10	Eliminate slogans and exhortations
11	Eliminate quotas or work standards
12	Give people pride in their job
13	Institute education and a self-improvement programme
14	Put everyone to work to accomplish it

Genichi Taguchi

Taguchi was concerned with ensuring that quality was designed into products and combined this with statistical methods of quality control. He pioneered the idea of setting up interactive teams to criticize and develop product design. In Taguchi's definition of quality is the concept of the loss that is imparted by the product or service to society from the time it is created. The quality loss function includes factors such as guarantee/warranty costs, customer complaints and loss of customer goodwill (Taguchi and Clausing 1990).

Phillip Crosby

With Phillip Crosby the focus came on the cost of quality. He had found that many organizations did not know how much they spent on quality, whether in putting it right or getting it wrong. Crosby's book *Quality is Free* highlighted the costs and benefits of implementing quality programmes. He stressed the need for a zero defects programme. Crosby's 1979 text was misunderstood by some, who could not see beyond the title. Crosby was saying that there is an initial investment in improving quality and then after a period of time, sufficient improvement will have been made to the companies' processes to save money from the cost of bad quality. So, in effect, after some years the financial savings that accrue will have more than paid off the initial investment. He should have called the book 'Quality is Free – Eventually'.

Quality control

The first quality standards were produced by the military in the 1950s and 1960s. During this era quality control was still the main way of ensuring quality. This was known as 'end of line' because the problem was made and then checked to see if it was correct. In the manufacturing sector in the 1970s one third of employees were employed checking the work of others. Of course, this is a shocking waste of manpower, especially as the best workers were used to check the work of others and were themselves unproductive.

The main problem with quality control is that it does not work. It is very difficult to achieve 99% quality through inspection. In the service sector often 99.9% quality is unacceptable (one item in 1000 fails). How would one cope with 1/1000 days of poisoned tap water, 1/1000 planes missing the runway, 1/1000 babies dropped in a maternity ward? For example, what percentage of badly performed operations should we tolerate? Often services require a higher level of quality – 100% perfect – and this means error-free. Yet, in the service sector we still tend to check quality through inspection when it is a thing of the past in manufacturing.

At first glance this would appear to be an impossible dream but an absolute necessity. For example, the National Health Service is now paying out literally tens of millions of pounds each year due to (quality) mistakes. We will now discuss how this can be approached and continuously improved (*kaizen*).

A serious error that still appears in some operations management books is to show a graph of cost of inspection against cost of correction and where the two curves cross is stated to be the optimum quality level. In practice this means that there is an acceptable level of quality that might be less than 100%. Of course this is unacceptable. Actually, quality control is not quite dead, but instead of checking the product for faults the control should be on the process to ensure that faults cannot be produced. In manufacturing this is often called *poka yoke* and the best author on this is Shigeo Shingo.

Shingo was concerned that statistical quality control methods could not prevent defects so there should therefore be controls within the process to try to prevent defects. Defects occur when people make errors. According to Shingo, defects can be prevented if there is feedback immediately after the errors are made which leads to corrective action. This requires inspection on all the items being produced, by successive check, self-check or source inspection. Successive check inspection is undertaken by the next person in the process or by an objective evaluator such as a team leader. The result can be instant feedback for the worker who produced the item, who can then make the repair. With self-check, as the name implies, workers check their own work. The individual worker is also required to undertake source inspection but this time for errors that will cause defects. The aim is to prevent the defects ever occurring. All three types of inspection rely on control consisting of fail-safe procedures or devices called *poka yoke* (Shingo 1986).

Probably the first example of quality control was instigated by the great civil engineer (later Sir) Joseph Basalgette when building the London sewer tunnels in the 1860s. Portland cement had recently been introduced but it was untried. Tests by

(Continued)

Basalgette (this was in the days when managers actually did the work themselves) showed that it was stronger than any other cement available at that time and became hard in wet conditions. But it had the drawback that if the mixture was wrong, then the cement lost a great deal of its potential strength. Both Brunel and Stevenson, the greatest engineers of their day, warned Basalgette against using Portland Cement because of the problems of maintaining consistency in the mix. Basalgette ignored their advice and went ahead with it but instigated a rigorous quality control exercise in which each batch of mixed cement was tested before use. This proved to be successful and almost all of the 308 million bricks are still in position held by the cement nearly a century and a half later.

Quality assurance

In much of the world, manufacturing companies have moved away from inspection and quality control to quality assurance. Quality inspectors have been retrained in quality assurance.

In the mid-1970s the Japanese started importing cars into Europe. They were ugly, they tended to rust, but people bought them because they worked. In the late 1970s Lord Stokes of BMC contacted Geoffrey Fielden, then Chairman of the British Standards Institution, asking if there was anything that could be done to increase the quality of British cars to enable them to compete with the influx of Japanese. Based on military standards BSI produced a standard for quality assurance, BS 5750. Quality assurance is the 'beginning of line'; procedures are put in place to which people work, and by doing so good quality is ensured. This proved to be very successful and has been developed into what is, now known as ISO 9000. It is the world's biggest-selling standard.

ISO 9000

The International Standards Organization undertakes major reviews of its standards roughly every five years. The ISO 9000 standard was reviewed in 1994 and more recently in 2000 to take better account of the needs of services companies.

Quality assurance has some drawbacks. The latest version of the standard, BS EN ISO 9001 (2000), is more flexible than the one it replaces. There were two problems with implementing the original standard: first, people tended to over-complicate the amount of documentation that went with the processes within an organization. Once this documentation had been approved then companies had to work to it and often this involved a vast 'paper-chase' within the organization. What quality assurance did achieve was consistency that things would always be produced the same way every time. But it is possible to be consistently bad as well as consistently good. It was found that certain companies that had been approved and certified were consistently producing things badly. Early in the 1990s a cavity wall insulating company, one of the few that had been approved at that time, was found to be consistently producing the worst results in the sector.

Another problem with specifying a consistent method of doing things is that it can result in unresponsiveness to change. If the procedures are so firmly established that altering them becomes difficult, the effect can be to stifle innovation or improvement.

Companies insisted that their suppliers had achieved ISO 9000 before they would deal with them, as it was one of the few ways of ensuring that their suppliers delivered good quality products to them. Initially, companies in the United States refused to adopt ISO 9000 but more recently, as they found they were losing market share, they have become enthusiastic adopters.

The European Union has recently required that quality systems of many suppliers of products related to health, safety and the environment be formally registered, by a third party, according to the ISO 9000 Series standard. This action has made adoption of the ISO standards a prerequisite for doing business in Europe. Countries in Asia, Africa and South America are more and more considering adoption of these standards as a means to increased trade among themselves and with the United States.

Under BS EN ISO 9001(2000) there are now four core standards comprising the series:

- ISO 9000: Concepts and Terminology
- ISO 9001: Requirements for Quality Assurance, 'To provide confidence as a result of demonstration in product/service conformance to established requirements.'
- ISO 9004: Guidelines for Quality Management of Organizations. 'To achieve benefits for all stakeholders through sustained customer satisfaction.'
- ISO 10011: Guidelines for Auditing Quality Management.

The accreditation of complying with ISO 9001 (2000) is awarded after an accredited, independent third party conducts an audit of the company's operations against the requirements of the ISO 9000 standards. Upon successful completion of this audit, the company will receive a registration certificate that identifies its quality system as being in compliance with ISO 9000 standards.

The move from the 1994 standard was not intended to require organizations to substantially revise their existing quality systems. The aim is for the standards to provide a process-orientated structure, showing the five main clause headings of ISO 9001 and ISO 9004:

1 Quality management system
2 Management responsibility
3 Resource management
4 Product realization
5 Measurement, analysis and improvement.

TABLE 9.3   BENEFITS OF EXTERNAL QUALITY STANDARDS

Internal benefits

Defines responsibilities

Written procedures form a point of reference for all staff

Reduces costs of failure

Improves morale and motivation

External benefits

Enhances marketability (as some customers only buy from registered suppliers)

Enhances customer confidence

Enhances image and reputation

The revised ISO 9001(2000) quality standards are based on the following eight principles:

Principle 1 Customer focus

Principle 2 Leadership

Principle 3 Involvement of people

Principle 4 Process approach

Principle 5 System approach to management

Principle 6 Continual improvement

Principle 7 Factual approach to decision-making

Principle 8 Mutually beneficial supplier relationships

Table 9.3 sets out the number of perceived benefits accruing to the use of external quality standards.

Although ISO 9000 was widespread in manufacturing it was adopted much later in the service sector. There was an initial scepticism that it could be applied away from the context of machinery and where people are more involved. It was not until the mid-1990s that companies in Europe started to apply ISO 9000 to the service sector, but now its adoption is widespread. It should be noted that the majority of loss through poor quality is at the service end of the product.

Increasingly, there are companies that are 'empty organizations', those that import items that are made elsewhere and put their own labels on them. These companies that put on the labels are the service companies whose reputation increases, declines or can be destroyed if the quality of items for which they are not actually responsible for their manufacture is deficient.

Total Quality Management

The introduction of Total Quality Management (TQM) has further improved the quality of products so that companies can now compete on world markets. As mentioned earlier, W. Edwards Deming at first proposed to American industry that rather than making things and checking if they are right they should make things right in the first place. American industry thought his views were impossible to implement, so he went to Japan, where his views were instantly adopted as common sense. This was the start of TQM and was the reason why Japanese cars were so much better than European cars in the 1970s. TQM is a step beyond Quality Assurance.

Deming was of the view that 85% of quality problems could be attributed to management and 15% of quality issues are decided on the shop floor. But on the shop floor is where quality should first be noticed. Workers need to let management know of quality problems so they can correct them at source. There also needs to be a formal method for recording and reporting quality problems. The ISO standard makes clear what is needed in terms of quality management systems.

Empowering the workforce to make decisions that affect quality is one of the keystones that make TQM possible. Workers must then be empowered to make decisions. There should be mechanisms for employee involvement and good communication. A crucial part of Total Quality Management was the acknowledgement of internal customers. The end customer is often obvious: it is the person parting with their money. Internal customers are those one deals with inside the organization. Employees can examine what they can do to make their work colleagues' job easier. This is often undertaken in group meetings called 'Quality Circles'. Groups of employees are brought together to discuss how they can improve the product, process or their working environment. As staff enjoy greater empowerment, managers have more time to manage the strategy of the organization and they spend less time fire fighting. Furthermore, there is a change of role for service employees, as they now become representatives of the company. Efforts can be made to help them feel proud of their company, e.g. a smart uniform. This approach has been taken up in the financial services sector in the UK.

Under a total quality management programme it is recognized that every person contributes to quality. They are expected to improve the way they undertake their jobs. Within any organization the employees are the prime source of knowledge and ideas for improvement. Since TQM is about embedding an attitudinal change to quality within the organization, staff development and training is an important element.

Total Quality Management is a long-term strategy. The aim is continually to improve the product or service, and this is known as *kaizen*. It is said that TQM is a journey not a destination, as improvement is always possible and what customers would accept yesterday is no longer considered good enough today. Deming said that TQM involves 'delighting the customer', therefore effort and care must be put into identifying who the customers are and what their needs are.

Quality is expensive and this expense will continue for quite some years. So companies should not embark on a TQM programme unless they have the foresight and the finance to keep it going. It does take time, typically five to seven years, to achieve worthwhile successes. TQM is not a quick fix. This can cause problems in maintaining the initiative to go forward but it is worth persevering.

Good quality starts with design and must be designed in from the beginning. It is inefficient to try to design it in at the end. The cost of poor quality goes up by a factor of ten at each stage of the process (Oakland 1993).

For TQM you need to ensure quality at each stage of the customer or product 'chain'. The process that the work passes through must be broken down into its component parts, then you can start to identify where quality problems, wastage and bottlenecks occur.

The prerequisites for success in the introduction of TQM are generally accepted as being:

1   Commitment by senior management.
2   A strong emphasis on communication to and by the workforce.
3   A determined attempt to improve and structure lateral communication and cooperation between departments.
4   Sound mechanisms for employee involvement.

As Deming said about TQM, 'You don't have to do this – survival is not compulsory.'

More recently, the shadow of Total Quality Management has reached to the service sector. Some service companies do not have the ethos of quality and little experience to call upon. Their customers demand a higher level of service and continuous improvement. In an ever-increasingly competitive world companies are striving to improve quality just to ensure their survival.

Pleasing customers is the name of the game

In management education there is an increasing focus on customer satisfaction. Deming went beyond merely proposing that we satisfy customers when, in 1955, he introduced the idea of 'delighting the customer' through Total Quality Management in his book *Out of the Crisis* (Deming 1986). In design, Robert J. Cooper (1988) has long been saying that the main cause of failure is 'not understanding the customer requirements'. More recently, relationship marketing has had an important emphasis. As said by Ziethaml and Bitner (1996): 'There has been a shift from transaction to relationship focus in marketing. Customers become partners and the firm must make long-term commitments to maintaining those relationships with quality, service and innovation' (p. 171). So in this we are encouraged to build and sustain long-term customer relationships through customer satisfaction, this being more cost-effective than constantly seeking new customers. All of these come together to provide a focus on customer satisfaction right at the start of an effective design process.

Getting close to customers and understanding their requirements and complaints involves the organization having a mechanism for collecting, assessing and *discussing* corrective action on aspects of its work or customer complaints.

Finding out what customers want

The new service design idea will delight the customer by being reliable, good quality, easy to use and better value than the competition.

Once you have identified the various customers you need to find out what they want and, where possible, give this to them. This is often easier in the service sector because of the close interaction between customer and supplier. One of the keys is to ensure that a good cross-section of all customers are questioned with a well-structured and well-formulated questionnaire. A faulty questionnaire can only result in faulty data.

In the service sector measures of quality tend to be more qualitative than quantitative. In manufacturing there are drawings with tolerances and anything outside of the tolerance is wrong and anything inside the tolerance is right. In services it is often not possible to give quantitative measures: you cannot measure the smile on somebody's face. Unfortunately, because quantitative measures are easier, companies still focus on these – how quickly the customer gets their hamburger rather than whether the hamburger tastes nice.

Customer complaints

When companies in the service sector are asked how they determine customer satisfaction or the quality of the service they provide, quite often they say that they rely on customer complaints. This is a good starting point but a company should quickly move away from this measure from being reactive to being proactive. It has been said that customers who complain are the best customers, because they have taken the time and made an effort to let the organization know that they are dissatisfied with the service. Most people just walk away. The aim should be to reduce and then eliminate complaints.

Attempts have been made to determine the percentage of people who do complain related to those who are dissatisfied with the service but do not complain. These results are bound to be inaccurate. In simple terms, if customers do not complain how can one know they are dissatisfied? There have also been estimates on how many people a dissatisfied customer will tell, but again the accuracy of these results must be drawn into doubt.

Furthermore, complaining is a cultural thing. In the United States customers complain more. In the UK they tend not to complain but quietly accept the poor service then go away and look for an alternative supplier. In Sri Lanka they have a culture of not complaining at all. One of the authors delivered a complete talk there using an inoperative microphone because the audience was too 'polite' to shout out that the microphone was not working.

What can be said is that not every dissatisfied customer will complain to the organization but they will probably tell others. Curing complaints is a good starting point and noting the reduction in the number of complaints as part of a Total Quality Management programme is a good measure. But move on, actually seek out what is wrong and cure it before the complaints start.

Mystery shoppers

'Delighting the customer' means exceeding the customer's expectations. Parasuraman, Zeithaml and Berry (1988), in their work on SERVQUAL, endeavoured to show that certain gaps exist between what the customer expects and what the service is set up to supply. This work has been expanded by others such as Fahmia Huda (1997), who have identified additional gaps that may exist in different types of service provision. The aim is to eliminate these gaps so the service provided meets that anticipated by the customer. Of course, this relies on knowing what the customer anticipates – easier said than done.

Service providers must aim to go just a little further in their attempts to satisfy customers. There may be a point at any one time and place (accepting that service is cultural) that there is a level of service beyond which the customer is not delighted but made slightly 'nauseous'. For example, how ingratiating can service be in a restaurant before it becomes embarrassing and then intolerable.

Part of being proactive and overcoming the problem of identifying what determines a quality service can be solved through the use of 'mystery shoppers', which are also sometimes known as 'secret customers'. Generally, an organization will employ an outside consultancy to undertake this, but there is no reason why the organization should not do it themselves. The 'mystery shoppers' are often senior citizens or students. They are given a booklet that has a series of questions in it and also facts of the organization's performance that they should observe and comment on.

For these the starting point is, again, to have a blueprint of the service. This will show better the areas about which questions can be formulated for the mystery shoppers. For example, if it was decided that the quality performance of the London Underground was to be determined, these 'mystery shoppers' would be given their booklet and it would include questions such as, 'How long did the customer have to wait to buy a ticket?', 'Is the station clean? Mark out of 5 if the station is clean, a low score being that the station is covered with litter and a high score being that the station is free of litter.' The first of these two questions requires a quantitative answer, a time in seconds. The second of these is a qualitative question and requires the observer to make some kind of judgement. To be able to answer the qualitative questions, with any degree of consistency, the 'mystery shoppers' need to be trained using some standards for, in this case, unseemliness, so that the 'mystery shoppers' can then make a repeatable judgement.

Some questions will have two answers: for example, if the ticket seller is asked the question 'What is the last train to the folk museum?' there are two answers – one is the accuracy of the time given, which is a quantitative measure, and the second is the manner in which the answer was given by the clerk, which is a qualitative measure of the clerk's politeness. It is important that the answer to the first questions is right and that the measure of the second question is high.

From the use of 'mystery shoppers' it can be seen that the quality of an entire service can be measured and the parts that require improvement can be identified. It should be realized that in breaking down the process into a series of events, not all are of equal value. For example, in the case given above, a customer is more concerned about the time taken to get a ticket than they are about the time on the platform waiting for a train. In a study on the Swedish railway system it was determined that the reason is that if a customer is waiting for a ticket they may miss the train, but if waiting on the platform they will not.

Quality gap model

From their research into service quality dimensions, Zeithaml, Parasuraman and Berry went on to develop a model of service quality, commonly known as the 'gaps' model. This model examines service quality on the basis of differences between customers' expectations regarding the five dimensions and their perceptions of what was actually delivered. Where there are differences they are called gaps. (See Figure 9.1 for a graphical representation of the gaps.) To measure these gaps, they developed a 22-item questionnaire called SERVQUAL, which is a useful quality assessment tool. That is not to say that it is not without problems. The model does not allow the possibility that customers might actually have low quality expectations. If a customer got better service than expected from a service organization, the service could not then be classified as a quality service if the customer expected poor quality. When considering complex services in the legal or medical fields, customers do not always know what to expect and may not know how good the service was even after the service has been delivered. The gaps model works well for large service organizations but is less applicable for small firms.

- **Gap 1 Not knowing what customers expect.** The first gap occurs because of the difference between what customers expect and what managers perceive they expect. This may be because of insufficient marketing research or inadequate use of research findings. Too much distance between management and customers, whether because of too many layers of management between front line staff and top management or poor upward communication, can result in a lack of interaction contributing to this gap.
- **Gap 2 Concept–specification gap.** If there is a mismatch between the product or service concept (see Chapter 6) and the actual specifications established for service delivery, poor quality can be perceived. This gap could be due to lack of perception of feasibility, inadequate commitment to service quality, inadequate task standardization and lack of goal-setting.
- **Gap 3 Service performance gap.** This gap is created where there is a discrepancy between service specifications and the actual service delivered. This might be because employees are unable or unwilling to perform at the desired level. See Chapter 3 for further discussion of role conflict, role ambiguity, poor employee–job fit, poor technology–job fit, inappropriate supervisory control systems, lack of perceived control and lack of teamwork.
- **Gap 4 When promises do not match delivery.** A discrepancy between what a firm promises about a service and what it actually delivers. Has the marketing department over-promised, and set unrealistic expectations in the minds of customers or is it the operations department failing to provide the level of quality expected by customers?
- **Gap 5 Expected service–perceived service gap.** The first four gaps contribute to Gap 5 emerging, which is the difference between what a customer expected to receive and what they believe they actually did receive. These

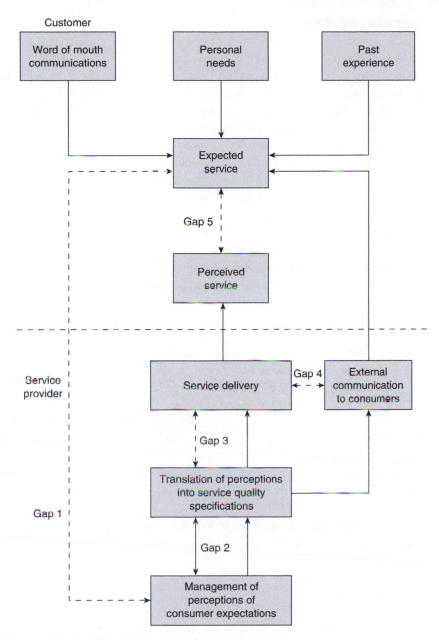

FIGURE 9.1 THE GAP MODEL (AFTER PARASURAMAN ET AL. 1985)

perceptions are influenced by word of mouth communications, communications from the service organization, personal needs and their past experiences. Where the perceived service falls short of the customer's expectations they are disappointed and dissatisfied. But when the perceived service exceeds the customer's expectations, the result is delight. So perhaps the route to delighting the customer as advocated by Deming is to under-promise and over-deliver.

Service recovery

Research has shown that customers who have had a service failure resolved quickly and properly are *more loyal* to a company than are customers who have never had a service failure, significantly more loyal. A key part of an organization's approach to quality therefore has to be to develop a service recovery programme. The goal of service recovery is to address customers' issues to their satisfaction. Customer relationship management includes service recovery or customer complaint handling processes. Service recovery is more than complaint handling. It is about recovering a customer's positive feelings about a company after a bad experience and taking action to resolve the root cause of the problem. Organizations that just concentrate on complaint handling are only addressing the negative. Service recovery means turning the issue into a positive – both for the customer and for the company through the learning opportunity. The focus for successful service recovery is to recover quickly, recover effectively and improve the situation. Effective recovery comes with the recognition of the key role of employees.

British Airways' customer relations department is reported to have developed a four-step process that it incorporated into all its technical and human systems:

1   Apologize and take up the problem. Customers do not care whose fault the problem was; they want an apology and they want someone to champion their cause.
2   Do it quickly. Aim to reply to the customer the same day, and if that is not possible, certainly within 72 hours. British Airways research showed that 40–50% of customers who contacted it with complaints defected if it took company staff longer than five days to respond. A speedy reply demonstrates a sense of urgency; it shows that the company really cares about the customer's feelings and situation.
3   Assure the customer that the problem is being fixed. Customers can be retained if they are confident that the operational problem they encountered will truly be addressed.
4   Do it by phone. British Airways found that customers with problems were delighted to have a customer relations person call them.

This may be the theory but it is not easy to maintain consistently, as one of the author's experienced in 2005 when she complained to BA about a service failure.

For some organizations part of service recovery is to offer an effective service guarantee. For such to be effective it has to be unconditional, easy to understand, meaningful, easy and painless to invoke, easy and quick to collect on, builds customer loyalty by making expectations explicit and sets clear standards. Examples are FedEx and Domino's Pizza.

Six Sigma

Following the TQM imperative of forever seeking improvements, organizations such as General Electric, Motorola and Honeywell have been following a TQM

TABLE 9.4 KEY CONCEPTS OF SIX SIGMA

Critical to quality	Attributes most important to the customer
Defect	Failing to deliver what the customer wants
Process capability	What your process can deliver
Variation	What the customer sees and feels
Stable operations	Ensuring consistent, predictable processes to improve what the customer sees and feels
Design for Six Sigma	Designing to meet customer needs and process capability

programme with a high process capability (99.9997% accuracy) called Six Sigma. This is the equivalent of only 72 passengers through Heathrow Airport having misplaced baggage out of some 20,000,000 passengers a year. General Electric have spent some half a billion dollars training their professional workforce in the concepts. There are some 10,000 black belts in General Electric trained to roam the plants full time to set up quality improvement projects.

Six Sigma is a statistical term that measures how far a given process deviates from perfection. The central idea behind Six Sigma is that if you can measure how many 'defects' you have in a process, you can systematically figure out how to eliminate them and get as close to 'zero defects' as possible. To achieve Six Sigma quality, a process must produce no more than 3.4 defects per million opportunities. An 'opportunity' is defined as a chance for non-conformance, or not meeting the required specifications. This means we need to be nearly flawless in executing our key processes. At its core, Six Sigma revolves around a few key concepts (see Table 9.4).

For some years manufacturing has been incorporating the theories of Six Sigma, that is, one failure in 1 million. Certainly, if the service incorporates and 'rides on the back of' manufactured products then those parts of the service should be virtually error-free. The aim then is to make the less predictable service part more predictable and repeatable. One way is to automate parts of the service (e.g. automated telling machines) to remove the human element of the process. This should improve reliability (something performing to specification for a specified period of time). But, at the possible expense of the human contact that many customers like.

The next step is to break down the stages of the process into its components, which will then allow each of these to be analysed. This is called blueprinting and was discussed in detail in Chapter 4.

Now, at this stage it is necessary to define what is 'good quality' in each stage. It may well be multifaceted, with both quantitative and qualitative elements in each stage. The quantitative element tends to be easier to control, as it will include 'numbers'. For example, staff must answer the phone within four rings or a customer must be served in 30 seconds; easy to 'impose' and easy to measure if it has been achieved. The qualitative parts are much harder to measure, specify or control: for example, how does the person at the end of the phone 'behave' or what is the human interaction like when the customer is eventually served? Those operating the service tend to concentrate on the easy-to-measure, quantitative quality measures.

In the blueprint specify all the aspects that are good/bad quality and if the blueprint is outlined in small enough steps it should be possible to state what could go wrong with each element of the service (and if it can go wrong it will).

Many services incorporate elements that run in parallel, such as the blueprint for passenger check-in, luggage handling, cleaning and refuelling, that all occur together in the build-up to an airplane flight. Each must be analysed and, in such cases, a 'critical path' should be identified. The critical path is the journey through the process in which a delay in any of the elements on the path will result in a delay in the whole process. Some delay in elements of the process not on the critical path need not effect the overall length of the service and, hence, all those stages of the critical path contain what is called 'float'. Start by trying to make improvements to the activities on the critical path – if reduction in delay/speed is important to the service.

So, by this stage, one should have identified all the potential problem areas and whether they are on the critical path or not on the complete blueprint. Also, whether the problem areas are likely to be quantitative or qualitative in nature. It may be possible to apply Six Sigma techniques to the qualitative problems. The quantitative areas are far more difficult. 'Acceptable' services need to be identified and then these could be written up as 'codes of practice' and incorporated into staff training programmes and their effectiveness 'confirmed' by customer questionnaires etc. (as long as such measures are proactive and not relying on customer complaints).

Quality awards

A number of studies have identified 'quality droop' over time. This occurs when after successful implementation of TQM programmes the impetus for long-term improvement starts to wane. As a counter to this droop, various bodies have sought to stimulate quality improvements through quality awards. Organizations are increasingly using these external awards as a way of reinvigorating the company's approach to quality and revitalizing the company's efforts.

The Deming Prize

The Deming Prize was instituted in 1951 by the Union of Japanese Scientists and Engineers and is awarded to those companies who have successfully applied 'company-wide quality control' based upon statistical quality control. Originally it was only open to Japanese organizations but has more recently been opened up to overseas companies. Applicant companies have to submit a detailed description of quality practices, reporting against the following assessment categories: policy and objectives, organization and its operation, education and its extension, assembling and disseminating of information, analysis, standardization, control, quality assurance, effects and future plans. This form of self-evaluation is valuable in itself.

The Malcolm Baldridge National Quality Award

The early 1980s saw the American Productivity and Quality Centre recognizing the need for an annual prize for quality, similar to the Deming Prize, which would be available to American companies. The aim of the award was to encourage American companies to improve quality and productivity, to recognize achievements, to establish quality criteria and to provide guidance on quality improvement. The process consists of a detailed application and site visit. Assessment examines internal leadership, information and analysis, strategic quality planning, human resource utilization, quality assurance of products and services, quality results and customer satisfaction.

The EFQM Excellence Model

The European Foundation for Quality Management (EFQM) was formed by 14 leading Western European companies in 1988. Five years later there were more than 300 members from most business sectors and most Western European countries. The European Quality Award was launched in 1992 to reward companies that demonstrate excellence in the management of quality. Interestingly, to win, companies had to demonstrate that quality management has led to the company meeting the expectations of customers, employees and other stakeholders in the company. The model was subsequently modified in 1999 and renamed the EFQM Excellence Model. The modifications reflected developments in management thinking which emphasized customer and market focus and innovation and partnerships.

Quality tools

The **Plan → Do → Check → Act cycle** – credited to Walter Shewhart – was first mentioned in *Economic Control of Quality of Manufactured Product* (1931). This text provides the basis for the philosophy of Total Quality Management and was the foundation of modern statistical process control (SPC). Under SPC each individual part produced was no longer inspected for quality, instead the process was monitored through sampling. Adjustments are then made to the process to ensure quality production dependent on the results from the sample.

The Shewhart cycle reinforces the notion of a never-ending approach toward process improvement. W. Edwards Deming, who had worked as Shewhart's assistant, further developed this radical approach to improving quality. In Japan the Plan→ Do→Check→Act approach is known as the Deming cycle.

Statistical process control

This involves the use of methods such as control charts that signal shifts in a process that could lead to services/products not meeting customer requirements.

Benchmarking

To know what is acceptable today one can embark on a benchmarking programme. Benchmarking, as the name suggests, is comparing the operations of your organization with the 'best in class'. This may be other competitors, but it is more usual to learn from organizations operating in different spheres of business. For example, car companies looked at next day delivery companies to improve their methods of distribution. It is better not to benchmark against competitors for two reasons. Copying the best of a competitor can only make you as good as that competitor and an organization needs to go beyond that. Secondly, if you choose a non-competitor organization you can, perhaps, elicit their help in your benchmarking programme, in exchange for you helping them in a different aspect of their benchmarking programme. Thus, benchmarking clubs have grown up to mutually improve each other's performance.

Xerox was one of the pioneers in the use of benchmarking in Europe. Its use has now been extended to services such as hospitals and banks.

There are essentially four types of benchmarking (see Liebfried and McNair 1992):

- Internal benchmarking compares different operations or parts of operations within the same organization. In the retail sector the performance of different stores is compared.
- External benchmarking compares an operation with an operation belonging to an external organization.
- Non-competitive benchmarking is the benchmarking of performance against other external organizations that do not compete directly in the same markets.
- Competitive benchmarking is a direct comparison between competitors in the same or similar markets.

Benchmarking is discussed further in Chapter 13 on performance measurement. The five key stages to implementing benchmarking are shown in Figure 9.2.

Input–output analysis

This analysis establishes the context in which an operation is set by identifying inputs and outputs from the process, identifying the source of the inputs and the destination of the outputs and then examining the requirements of internal customers served by the outputs from the process and the requirements of the suppliers of the process inputs.

Flow charts

A flow chart is a natural, more developed technique from the input–output analysis. Flow charts can highlight problem areas where there is no existing procedure to cope with a particular set of circumstances.

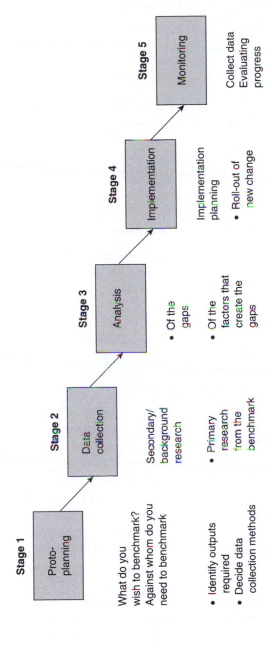

FIGURE 9.2 BENCHMARKING'S FIVE KEY STAGES IN IMPLEMENTATION
(DIAGRAM DESIGNED BY TANER OZSUMER AND OSEAR SANTACRUZ. REPRODUCED WITH PERMISSION)

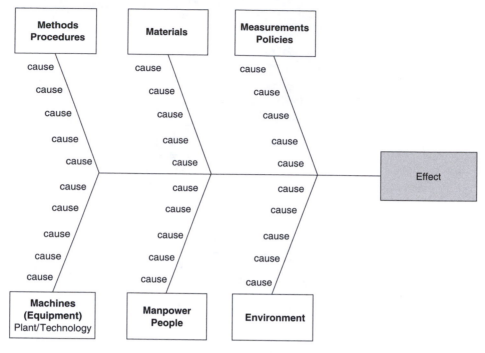

FIGURE 9.3 CAUSE AND EFFECT DIAGRAM

Scatter diagrams

Through a scatter diagram it is possible to identify whether there is a connection between two sets of data. While useful in establishing whether a relationship exists, it does not establish the existence of a cause–effect relationship.

Cause–effect diagrams

This technique is also known as the fish-bone analysis or Ishikawa diagram. It is meant to explore the root causes of problems by asking the what, where, when, how and why questions and adding some possible answers. The focus is on examining the people, systems, materials, methods, manpower, machines, place, procedures, policies, surroundings, suppliers and skills issues which all have an impact on service or product quality to a greater or lesser extent. (See Figure 9.3 for an example of the cause and effect diagram.)

Categories used in the service sector tend to be policies, procedures, people and plant/technology while manufacturing companies focus on machines, methods, materials, measurements and manpower. The advantage of this technique is that categories can be adapted to fit particular circumstances, such as the process steps for example. Figure 9.4 shows possible causes of customer complaints in a particular service encounter.

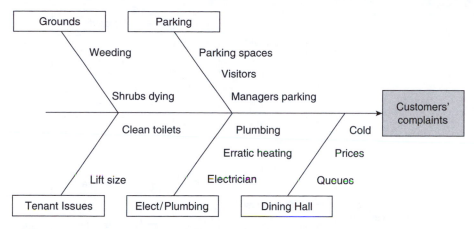

FIGURE 9.4 CAUSE AND EFFECT DIAGRAM SHOWING POSSIBLE CAUSES OF CUSTOMER COMPLAINTS. (DIAGRAM DESIGNED BY TANER OZSUMER AND OSCAR SANTACRUZ. REPRODUCED WITH PERMISSION)

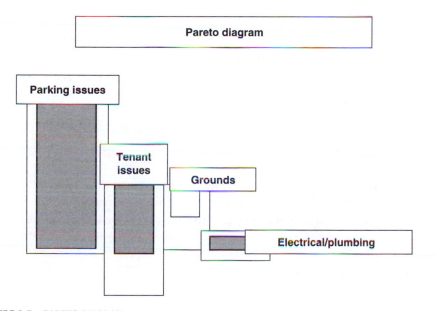

FIGURE 9.5 PARETO DIAGRAM

Pareto diagrams

Applying the Pareto analysis enables companies to distinguish between those factors which are crucially important, usually few in number, and those which could be classified as the 'trivial many'. The technique involves organizing information on the types of problem or causes of problems into their order of importance. The areas that actually need some decision-making can then be highlighted (see Figure 9.5).

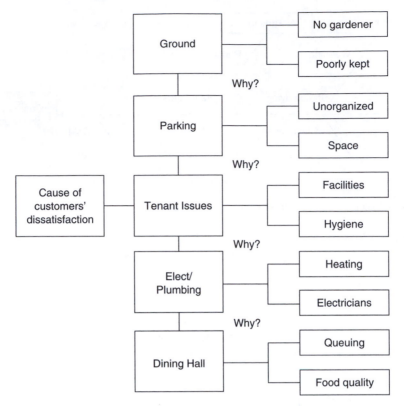

FIGURE 9.6 WHY–WHY ANALYSIS. (DIAGRAM DESIGNED BY TANER OZSUMER AND OSCAR SANTACRUZ)

Why–Why analysis

This is a structured problem-solving technique which states the problem and asks why it has occurred and then follows up each of the major reasons for the problem in turn and poses the question as to why these have happened. The procedure continues until no more answers to the question Why? can be generated (Figure 9.6).

SERVQUAL instrument

In measuring service quality a standard approach is to look whether there is a gap between what customers expected and their perceptions of the service provided. The size of the gap will highlight the areas that need to be improved. The SERVQUAL questionnaire consists of 22 expectation and matching perception questions relating to the five dimensions of service quality (Parasuraman et al. 1988).

Blueprinting

Blueprinting involves: looking at the process; looking at the customer chain; breaking the process into components and identify quality and other bottlenecks; designing problems out of the process; understanding how customers relate to the process.

The similarity between the current usage of the word 'blueprint' and its original meaning is that in both the whole arrangement is shown. A Blueprint is defined as a 'process broken down chronologically into sequential constituent stages' (BS 7000–1: 1999). In other disciplines it is sometimes called a Project schedule, Project or Process Plan, or a Process Map.

The aim of blueprinting a service is to identify accurately the stages of the process and match the length of time of one process with the next. A quality service is deemed to have been delivered when a customer goes straight from one stage to the next with no queuing. This engenders a feeling of satisfaction among participants and customers.

Case Study

A few years ago Bill jointly headed up a 'Teaching Company Initiative' aimed at introducing Total Quality Management into an organization. Here is the reality, with the company name omitted. The particular branch of this organization was closed a couple of years later. Having said that, there were quite a lot of good things achieved, from which others could learn.

TQM: Learning from mistakes and getting it right second time

It has been estimated that up to 80% of Total Quality initiatives have failed during implementation in industry (Brown 1993; Fisher 1994). This company, based in southern England, had already made one false start. The original attempt did not follow a structured approach. It was championed by a person who was already over-worked and he could not spend sufficient time on the venture. It also used a glorified redundancy scheme which meant that far from gaining the workers' acceptance, they did everything to stop it. It was bound to fail.

In spite of the loss of morale from that first attempt, the company could still see the advantage of Total Quality. Trying to restart a TQM programme after previously failing brings with it its own set of difficulties. Those previously involved feel that they have already wasted their time once and are naturally very sceptical the second time around.

Poor quality is more expensive than many people realize and the cost of a batch being rejected for poor quality soon adds up to big money. In this particular company almost all rejects ended up as scrap and the time then spent redoing the order was a lost opportunity, time that could be better spent producing other new orders.

The main focus of this particular programme was the reduction of waste. This included damaged or spoilt material and production over runs, and this will eventually include an appraisal of lost value along the lines of 'waste elimination profit' (Japan Management Association 1987).

For example, management commitment is vital but what exactly does this involve? This meant an agreed willingness to change and implement change right from the outset. This required total active involvement from the MD down. Quality needed to have a high priority in the organization and it must be part of the business strategy, but sadly, this was not the case. It also required a large commitment in funds. Far from being free, quality is very expensive at the start and if there is an insufficient budget to implement change, then do not bother to start. It must be one of the greatest causes of loss of morale in any programme if genuine improvements are identified then shelved through lack of money to implement them.

It is also important to get away from the piecework mentality that still prevails in many organizations. Any bonus payments must depend on quality performance rather than only on quantity of output. Payment by output is now certainly less prevalent in manufacturing but is still widely used in the service sector. If you pay people to produce more then they will, but quality will take a back seat.

Near the start of the programme, the total plan, process chain or 'blueprint' (Shostack 1984; Randall 1993, Hollins and Hollins 1999) of the information and material flow between departments and other various processes leading to customer satisfaction was drawn up. Any change in one area will affect some other area, so the total picture of any proposed improvement needs to be seen and should show up on a blueprint. Most people must have experienced the situation where some changes have resulted in a small improvement in one area or department but caused a snarl up in several others. The blueprint should identify such potential problems before they occur.

It has been written, 'what you cannot measure, you cannot manage' (Nesbit 1992). This is certainly the philosophy the McKinsey Consultancy firm advocates. Having an accurate measure of the current situation in problem areas at the start of the programme was vital in order that the extent of any subsequent improvements could be shown. Two teams investigated scheduling and customer complaints/credit notes. These key failure areas having been identified, Pareto analysis (the 80:20 rule) was then used to identify the most frequent causes of problems. This gives focus and priority. Put against the cost of correction, it is possible to identify those areas that are of greatest urgency and, therefore, are of top priority.

We started with an investigation into the reasons why credit notes were issued. This identified that most of the problems were not so much associated with the actual products being manufactured but more with the administration system associated with orders. It proved easy to put in better administrative systems that would, subsequently, avoid these problems. This incorporated a 'closing of the loop' feedback system so that corrective and preventive action could be taken to ensure that problems and errors of this type did not occur in the future. This and other measures of continuous improvement have been very successful and issued credit notes were reduced by a factor of 200%.

When people were operating in the teams they said that they felt things were being achieved. Change was being accepted and long-held barriers were being broken down. Awareness Sessions were held for all the employees but, stupidly, they were held (unpaid) outside of works time, as the MD did not want to disrupt production. As a result, few attended these meetings. This is an example of where management commitment was needed and the finance was required to cope with either the loss in production or the cost of overtime payments.

Ishikawa fishbone diagrams were used at the Quality Improvement Team meetings and one of the problems identified early on was the need for greater empowerment. It would appear that in this organization greater autonomy was welcomed. It was an encouraging finding that employees were keen to take on more responsibility.

Many employees would like the interest and involvement that a greater degree of decision-making would give them.

We recommended that there was a full-time facilitator overseeing the programme, as the coordination that is involved cannot be left entirely to improvement teams. The 'champion' must also be a special kind of person. This person must be well qualified in understanding how the organization works and must also be an expert in the theory of total quality. This may involve quite extensive (and expensive) training of the leader *before* starting the programme.

Also, the leader must be a good communicator who can make him- or herself understood and be accepted by top management as well as those on the shop floor – the latter group is the more difficult. Communication certainly improved when the champion was sited at the 'coalface', on hand to offer advice and information.

Near the start of the exercise the programme was discussed with the managing director. He opened the discussion with the statement: 'My view is that a manager's job is to deal with problems as they occur.' In effect, this meant that he reacted to crises as they occurred rather than actually planning the future to avoid most of these crises. It sounded as if he spent his life fire fighting. Unless he could be persuaded to start planning, then the TQM initiative was doomed right at the start. So although we employed someone to head up the quality team, the person put in charge of the programme was taken off it to 'fire fight' whenever a crisis occurred in production, which was often.

We found that implementing Total Quality was easier where there had been an effective use of quality control and certainly we found that it was important to have process control before trying to introduce Total Quality. It is often said that Total Quality and BS EN ISO 9001 do not necessarily sit well together, but this was not what we found. There was a culture in the organization that was against taking measurements and their subsequent analysis but this was changed. Another change of culture taken on board was that reports on progress or measurement must not be used to chastise various groups of employees, but the focus must be on using the information discovered to take the continuous improvement a stage further.

Total Quality needs to be done and needs to be seen to be being done and it requires careful planning, execution and perhaps above all, patience. We conclude that more resources were needed to implement the ambitious quality plans. It is, perhaps, understandable that the company were unable to allocate a greater share of their budget to Total Quality, with all the other calls for finance in a struggling company. There was far too little in the budget to do what was needed. As a result, once again their TQM initiative faltered and was abandoned after 18 months of the two-year programme. There were certainly some improvements achieved. Two years was far too short to complete the programme anyway. TQM must be on-going. It may be a cliché, but a true one, that 'TQM is a journey not a destination'.

SUMMARY OF KEY POINTS

- Quality should be defined in terms that are meaningful to your customer.
- A wide variety of assessment tools are available to help identify current problems and point the way to possible quality improvements.

- Total Quality Management programmes require time and resources and a commitment to change management to achieve successful implementation. Without these the following can go wrong:

  1 Expecting quick results, insufficient patience
  2 No real management commitment – only 'lip service'
  3 Insufficient finance
  4 Lack of measurement
  5 Linking TQM with redundancy and cost-cutting
  6 Too much paperwork
  7 Focus on quantitative measures only
  8 Not involving everybody and not seeking their approval
  9 Not seeing that the initiatives are working
  10 Not aiming for continual improvement (a journey not a destination)
  11 Nobody in overall control

STUDENT ACTIVITY

1 Name three leaders in quality thinking and outline their contributions.
2 Who is responsible for quality?
3 Discuss the difficulties in implementing TQM and suggest ways of overcoming them.
4 Explain how the costs of quality concept could apply in a fast food restaurant.

FURTHER READING

Brysland A. and Curry A. (2001) 'Service improvements in public services using SERVQUAL', *Managing Service Quality*, 11(6): 389–401.

Kandampully J. and Butler L. (2001) 'Service guarantees: a strategic mechanism to minimize customers' perceived risk in service organisations', *Managing Service Quality*,11(2): 112–20.

Liebfried K.H.J. and McNair C.J. (1992) *Benchmarking: A Tool for Continuous Improvement*. New York: HarperCollins.

Longbottom D. (2000) 'Benchmarking in the UK: an empirical study of practitioners and academics', *Benchmarking: An International Journal*, 7(2): 98–117.

Luk Sh. T.K. and Layton R. (2002) 'Perception gaps in customer expectations: managers versus service providers and customers', *The Service Industries Journal*, 22(2): 109–28.

Parasuraman A., Zeithaml V.A. and Berry L.L. (1994) 'Reassessment of expectations as a comparison standard on measuring service quality: implications for further research', *Journal of Marketing*, 58: 111–24.

Sohal A. (2002) *Total Quality Management Text with Cases*. Oxford: Butterworth Heinemann.

10 GLOBAL SUPPLY CHAIN MANAGEMENT

'An Asda spokesman said after the integration with WalMart: "We can track stock more effectively at depot, shelf and warehouse levels. This means we are beter at availability, and the cost savings from the operational efficiencies means we can invest in price competitiveness and pass that on to our customers."'

Computing, October 2004

As companies buy in a greater proportion of their materials, goods and services than they did some ten years ago, they are becoming more dependent on their suppliers. This has led to a refocus on the relationship with suppliers and how managing the supply chain can reduce organizational costs.

LEARNING OUTCOMES

When you have completed this chapter you should be able to:

- Define supply chain management.
- Explain e-procurement.
- Define Just-in-Time.
- Explain supply chain strategies.

Definitions

Supply chain management is the management of activities that procure raw materials, transform them into intermediate goods and final products, and deliver these products to customers through a distribution system (Lee and Billington 1992). It encompasses purchasing, logistics and transport.

As such, it encompasses the management of the flow of materials and information through the supply chain. Technology has enabled a shift in focus from engineering – efficient manufacturing processes to the coordination of activities in the supply chain through knowledge management. The supply chain now consists of transporters, warehouses, retailers and customers as well as manufacturers and suppliers.

There has been a growth in the number of organizations such as TNT Logistics, for example, offering end-to-end supply chain management through logistics design, IT, transportation, warehousing design and management, order fulfilment and merchandising (www.**tntlogistics**.com).

A key component for successful coordination is information. Programmes such as continuous replenishment programmes (CRP), Just-in-Time (JIT) and quick response programmes all rely on the dissemination of scheduling, shipment or manufacturing information to the parties involved. In CRP, for instance, the retailer's warehouse inventory movement is the key information that the manufacturer requires in order to determine the product replenishment quantity and frequency (Tan and Shaw 1998).

Value chain

The importance given to supply chain management has grown as organizations have become more adept at analysing and understanding the value chain in their organizations. The value chain describes different value-adding activities that connect a company's supply side with its demand side. Value is added by reducing cost and adding value to customers.

Porter (1985) defined the value chain as 'a model that describes a sequence of value-adding activities of a single organization, connecting an organization's supply side with its demand side and includes supporting activities'.

There is an internal value chain within an organization as well as an external value chain where activities are performed by partners. Value can be added for the customer by reducing cost and adding value to customers within each element of the value chain and at the interface between elements of the value chain.

Porter's Value Chain Analysis (see figure 10.1) examines those areas of the business that can be designated **primary activities** – inbound logistics, operations, outbound logistics, marketing and sales, service – and how they interface with his designated **support activities** – firm infrastructure, human resource management, technology development, procurement. Analysing where costs are occurring throughout this value chain provides an opportunity to identify waste and a suitable case for treatment.

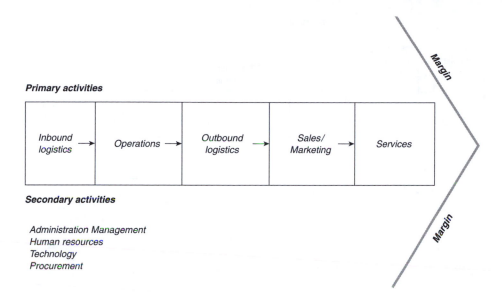

Primary activities

| Inbound logistics | Operations | Outbound logistics | Sales/ Marketing | Services |

Secondary activities

Administration Management
Human resources
Technology
Procurement

FIGURE 10.1   THE VALUE CHAIN

Importance of the supply chain

The supply chain is seen as a source of competitive advantage as firms increase their competitiveness, product customization, high quality, cost reduction and speed to market. The goal of good supply chain management is about reducing waste and maximizing value. It is based on the view that the only customer with real money is the end customer, so everyone in the supply chain should focus on satisfying the end customer.

It has been estimated that total supply chain costs represent half, or in some cases three-quarters of total operating expenses for many organizations. (Quinn 1997). In the year 2000, American companies spent $1 trillion on supply chain related activities (Simchi-Levi et al. 2003). Inefficiencies in some supply chains due to redundant stocks, inefficient transportation strategies and other wasteful strategies mean that unnecessary costs build up in these supply chains despite the scale of the investment.

The objective of supply chain management is to integrate the entire process of satisfying customers' needs all along the supply chain. As production costs are reduced and quality functionality and speed of delivery are improved, costs and delays in distributing goods and services are taking a greater fraction of total cost and time. If each segment of the supply chain tries to maximize its own position there can be unnecessary costs; if an integrated view is taken then there can be opportunities for savings. Hence the drive for supply chain management.

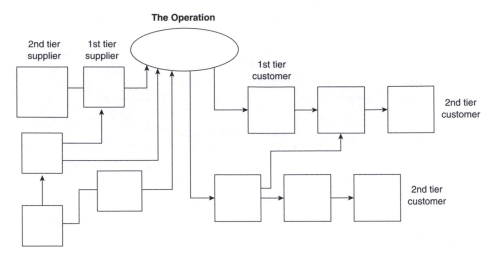

FIGURE 10.2   THE SUPPLY CHAIN WHICH INCLUDES INTERACTIONS BETWEEN SUPPLIERS, MANUFACTURERS, DISTRIBUTORS AND CUSTOMERS

Supply networks

Supply chain management is about managing the operations that form an organization's supply side and those that form the demand side (see Figure 10.2). So, on the supply side, **purchasing and supply management** is the recognized term for the operation's interface with its supply markets. **Physical distribution management** is the activity of supplying immediate markets. **Logistics** is the management of materials and information flow from a business down through a distribution channel to end customers.

Of course the reality for organizations like Wal-Mart and Tesco is far more complex than the simplified diagram in Figure 10.2 shows. Such organizations, rather than having a single supply chain, are at the centre of a supply network or supply web.

Chaffey (2002) described procurement and inbound logistics as being upstream supply chain activities and talked of this as being buy side e-commerce. For him the downstream supply chain activities of sales, outbound logistics and fulfilment were sell side e-commerce.

There has been a move from a push-oriented supply chain that emphasizes distribution to a pull-oriented system that uses the supply chain to deliver value to customers who are actively involved in product and service specification (see Figure 10.3).

E-business has led to a change in supply chain thinking in a move from push models to pull models. A distribution channel is then created to push the product to the market. Pull models start with analysis of customer's requirements through market research and cooperation with suppliers and customers in new product development. Technology like electronic data interchange (EDI) helps develop closer links between elements of the supply chain.

The key is balancing the production stream with ever-changing customer demand.

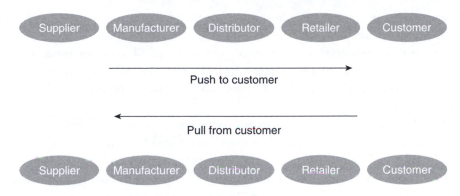

FIGURE 10.3 PUSH AND PULL MODELS OF THE SUPPLY CHAIN

Procurement

Purchasing

This is the most costly activity in many firms. Purchasing is critical whether it is sourcing components for the automobile manufacturing sector or operating in the restaurant and hotel sector. Procurement encompasses all the activities involved with obtaining items from a supplier: that is purchasing and in-bound logistics such as transportation, goods in and warehousing.

One of the first decisions to be made is whether to purchase items that an organization's operations then transform into finished goods and services or to buy in a complete service from a third party. In the manufacturing sector this has been traditionally known as the make or buy decision.

The purchasing department need to evaluate alternative suppliers and provide current, accurate and complete data.

Types of purchasing

There are two types of purchasing: direct and indirect.

Direct materials are those whose use is planned and scheduled for. Usually they are not shelf items; they are usually purchased in large volumes and after negotiation and contracting. They have a direct part to play in the creation of products.

Indirect items are usually used in maintenance, repairs and operations activities and are known as MROs. These could be anything from the light bulbs in the office, to catering services, to paper for the organization's printers.

Indirect items include those that relate to the manufacturing of products, and items related to operating procurement that support the operations of the whole business, such as office supplies, furniture, information systems, catering, travel and professional services and MRO goods.

Procurement management refers to coordination of all activities pertaining to purchasing goods and services necessary to accomplish the mission of an enterprise: 80% of an organization's purchased items, mostly MROs, constitute 20% of total purchase value.

A traditional paper-based procurement system involves the end user of an item selecting an item by conducting a search and then filling in a paper requisition form that is sent to a buyer in the purchasing department. A buyer fills out an order that is then dispatched to a supplier. After an item is delivered, the item and a delivery note are reconciled with the order form and invoice and then payment occurs. E-procurement systems offer the opportunity to transmit this information electronically rather than by fax.

All manual processes of requisition creation, requests for quotation, invitation to tender, purchase order issuance, receiving goods, and payment can be streamlined and automated. To implement such automation a company needs internal workflow, groupware and internal marketplace and collaboration with suppliers' websites. Some organizations develop an intranet for their internal marketplace and an extranet for bid sites.

The question can be 'How to move people away from paper to online?' The UK Benefits Agency worked out it cost something like £76 to process a paper-based order and that this could be reduced to one-tenth that if done online. The UK government recognized the potential of e-procurement to drive considerable savings from public sector procurement. To facilitate this it established the Office of Government Commerce (OGC) on 1 April 2000 with the aim of achieving substantial value for money improvements in the government's annual procurement budget of over £13 billion. (For more detail and latest news on OGC visit www.ogc.gov.uk)

The OGC merged the procurement services previously provided by The Buying Agency (TBA), the Central Computer and Telecommunications Agency (CCTA), Property Advisers to the Civil Estate (PACE) and procurement units from the Treasury to create OGC Buying Solutions on 1 April 2001.

Public sector organizations use OGC Buying Solutions because they trust it to get the best deals for them and to ensure compliance with European Commission procurement directives. Known national suppliers are used, which reassures buyers about the quality of what it is on offer.

Turban et al. (2004) quotes the following transaction costs: $2 by telephone; $1.20 by EDI; 20 cents by Internet. Chaffey (2002) spoke of e-procurement reducing transaction costs from £60 to £10 per order. While the actual numbers vary according to the different pieces of research, the scale of reduction in costs if there is a move to electronic procurement is clear.

Many items are rebuys, either straight or modified. E-procurement can make these easier. Direct cost reductions come about through improving efficiency. Less staff time is spent in searching and ordering products and reconciling deliveries with invoices. Automated validation of pre-approved spending budgets for individuals or departments leads to fewer people processing each order and in less time.

There are indirect benefits, such as reducing the cycle time between order and use of suppliers. Greater flexibility in ordering goods from different suppliers may be enhanced. E-procurement enables buyers to spend more time on value adding activities rather than placing orders and reconciling deliveries and invoices. Traditionally correcting errors has been a major part of buyers' role.

The goals of e-procurement are increasing purchasing agent productivity; authorizing requisitioners to perform purchases from desktops, bypassing the procurement department; lowering purchase prices through product standardiza-tion and consolidation of buys; improving information flow and management; minimizing purchases made from non-contract vendors; improving the payment process; streamlining the purchasing process making it simple and fast; reducing administrative processing cost per order by as much as 90%; finding new suppliers and vendors who can provide goods and services faster and/or cheaper; integrating the procurement process with budgetary control in an efficient and effective way; minimizing human errors in the buying or shipping process.

Cost savings are quoted as a reason for embarking on e-procurement yet many organizations have not got figures for the costs of procurement under their current systems. Chaffey (2002) calculates that savings equals number of requisitions times (original cost minus new cost). Such savings can of course have a big impact on profitability. The largest savings and biggest impact on profitability come in the manufacturing sector where procurement is a major cost element and there are many requisitions for relatively low value items. Service industries have a lower potential for savings.

Many e-procurement programmes fail to achieve their objectives. This is due to a failure to use project management methodology to aid the implementation and a failure to grapple with the process and people side of a business transformation process. Successful procurement programmes require using business transformation methodology. This involves a focus on the benefits to be gained. Breaking down large programmes of work into smaller projects enables more effective project management. Successful procurement implementation comes from working in this way from day 1 as well as selecting the right piece of software. Never underestimate people's capacity to be wary of change.

Purchasing strategies

A fundamental question is, What purchasing strategies might be pursued?

Many suppliers
This is also called competitive bidding or market transactions. The pros of this strategy are that this technique can result in prices being driven down through competitive tendering; the organization is able to switch sources in case of a supply

failure. It may also increase the circle of knowledge and expertise that an organization can tap into.

The disadvantages are that suppliers are unlikely to feel commitment to the organization if they know they are being judged on price alone. Poor service quality can result.

Few suppliers This is also called the partnership approach. Those organizations which are proponents of single sourcing claim that it results in better quality, better communication, strong durable relationship, greater dependency, higher confidentiality. Given that it is possible to award longer-term contracts for greater volumes improved scale economies can result, which can then lead to better discounts.

The downside to single sourcing is that the organization can find itself vulnerable to disruption, a particular problem for those who have adopted a Just-In-Time approach to resource management. There is also the view that this strategy results in upward pressure on prices. The dangers of single sourcing were played out in the summer of 2005 when British Airways faced massive disruption as a result of an industrial dispute at its single supplier of airline meals, Gate Gourmet.

To achieve the best from customer–supplier partnerships, a basic understanding of human psychology and motivational theory would lead to stressing the need for a win–win approach.

With this in mind perhaps it is not surprising that BCG research on the auto supply sector in 2004 found that alongside an annual reduction in costs of 3% over the past 10 years, suppliers' profits have halved over this period and there has been an increased number of product recalls. BCG found that there was a correlation between customers' satisfaction with product quality and suppliers' sense of satisfaction.

Businesses tend to buy either by systematic sourcing – negotiated contracts with regular suppliers, typically in long-term relationships; or by spot sourcing – the fulfilment of immediate needs, usually for commoditized items for which it is less important to know the credibility of the supplier. These items usually have a very tightly defined specification.

The earliest and biggest trend in e-procurement is the use of tools to automate processes related to the purchasing of indirect goods such as those offered by Oracle, Ariba and Clarus. For direct sourcing, tight integration with suppliers along the supply chain is essential.

All commentators in this area currently identify procurement visibility as a big issue. It seems obvious that managers cannot control what they cannot measure yet many organizations still have inadequate information on their current spending. The 2004 LBS research published as the EU Spend Management Study found that 70% of UK firms found service contracts more difficult to measure and control than non-services. Procurement evaluation starts with spend analysis which provides a baseline that all future activity can be measured against. It also appears that there is less visibility associated with the purchase of services than with the purchase of other goods.

Too much emphasis on buying the right bits of technical kit and not enough on how to get buy-in from staff to the change process leads to failure.

An issue that organizations have to decide about is whether to use an exchange to buy or sell their goods and services. If an exchange is being considered the next question is whether to use a private or public exchange.

Trust and integrity are important issues when it comes to B2B (business to business) marketplaces. What has been established as a result of the failures that there have been are:

- The need for very clear security statements.
- The need for very clear statements of what the site will do for the users.
- Reinforcement of the proposition of ease of use.

Cooperation is fine in theory but the reality is different. Competitive rivalry is too strong. Technology companies themselves are reticent about the idea of technology exchanges. Oracle and Sun Microsystems regard their approved vendor list as top secret and not something to be laid open in a marketplace. Volkswagen was reluctant to become involved in Covisint, the exchange established and owned by a number of automobile manufacturers and their suppliers.

> *Covisint, formed by DaimlerChrysler, Ford, General Motors, Renault and Nissan in 2000, has faced challenging times creating a virtual marketplace and auction house for suppliers and manufacturers in the automotive industry. Creating the technology to operate such a marketplace turned out to be more difficult than expected, while suppliers remained hesitant to compete for business online. In February 2004, Compuware acquired the products and technology of Covisint. At that time, Covisint had more than 135,000 users in more than 96 countries.*

Sell side – many catalogue-based B2B suppliers – has the advantage to the buyer of searching, with the onus of maintaining data on the supplier; the disadvantage to the buyer is a different interface on each site, a restricted choice, poor integration with ERP (Enterprise Resource Planning)/procurement systems, and limited purchase control.

Buy side has the advantage to the buyer of simplicity, a single interface, wider choice than sell side, integration with ERP/procurement systems and good purchase control; the disadvantages to the buyer are of software licence costs, retraining and the onus of maintaining data.

Large buyers open their own market place, called a buy side market place, and invite potential suppliers to bid on the items the buyer needs. This model is a reverse auction or bidding model. Searching e-stores or e-malls to find and compare suppliers and products can be very slow and costly, so this way works better.

Two early examples of market places were www.vertical.net and www.chemdex. com, which started out in the early days of the dot.com boom. They offered simplicity, a single interface, potentially widest choice of suppliers, products and prices, often unified terms and conditions and order forms. Disadvantages to the buyer were that it was difficult to know which market place to choose, poor purchase controls, uncertainty of service levels from unfamiliar suppliers, difficulties interfacing with the market place data format and relatively poor integration with ERP.

Other approaches to procurement include aggregating suppliers' catalogues – centralizing procurement by placing suppliers catalogues on a central server – and aiming to reduce maverick buying and control the purchasing budget.

Group purchasing   Orders from several buyers are aggregated so that better prices can be obtained. Small and medium-sized enterprises (SMEs) join together through a third party to gain quantity discounts. Some sites developed which aggregate demand and then negotiate with suppliers. Group purchasing started with commodity items such as MROs and consumer electronic devices.

Implementation of e-procurement

Successful adoption of e-procurement systems can be affected by what Chaffey (2002) termed organizational risks, that is to say, that the threat of redundancy or redeployment can lead to resistance surrounding the introduction of the system. Change management techniques are necessary. All the consultants working in this area agree that if the introduction of e-procurement is seen as simply the introduction of a new IT system then it is likely that the initiative will fail. Changing the way the organization thinks and overhauling its processes are also necessary.

There could be a risk of maverick or off-contract purchasing as people are empowered to directly purchase their own items. Maverick purchasing is buying items that are unnecessary or too expensive.

Of vital importance to any organization is consideration of how the new systems should integrate with the existing financial systems. Software vendors can argue the case for starting from scratch with a clean piece of paper or acquiring an interface between the old and new systems that does not hinder functionality. What is important is that any organization builds flexibility into any new system.

Implementing e-procurement   What an organization is looking for when implementing is recognition that different types of information systems cover different parts of the procurement cycle. There is a need for a stock control system – which highlights that re-ordering is required when the number in stock falls below reorder thresholds – and for the introduction of a CD/web-based catalogue, e-mail or database-based workflow systems and order entry on website capabilities. These systems need to integrate with the organization's accounting systems. The capability of integrated e-procurement and ERP systems is also necessary.

The earliest trend in e-procurement adoption is the use of tools to automate processes relating to purchasing of indirect goods. The decision has to be made to try to link different systems or purchase a single new system that integrates facilities of previous systems.

Inventory management

Inventory is rightly identified as a source of cost when analysing the value chain yet organizations cannot function without some level of inventory. Effective management of the supply chain will only come once the approach to the management of inventory within the organization has been agreed.

Consider the real cost of inventory. Not only has it been purchased but it also takes up space, which has to be paid for in some form. The parts have to be kept dry and protected from theft or damage. People are used to putting the parts into stock and to taking them out again. Records must be kept of where everything is and all the parts counted periodically (stocktaking). And, of course, the stock itself depreciates. While parts rust and eventually go out of date, food depreciates at a much faster rate. The reduced-to-clear shelf in supermarkets is a familiar site as store managers try to minimize the volume of items they are left with which are past their sell by date. In the retail sector there has been a move to reduce store stockrooms and expand the sales floor. Such moves are dependent on timely and reliable deliveries from a distribution centre.

In theory, nearly all stocks of parts should be unnecessary; in practice, even in the most efficient plants it is very difficult to achieve this with all stock items. As said earlier, small parts such as printer cartridges, computer disks etc. can be bought in batches and stored. It is the high value items that should be delivered when required.

The stock cannot be eliminated overnight. The aim is to have a faster throughput in the stores. This requires a better level of communication with suppliers, as well as an accurate knowledge of what is required and how often it will be used – keeping records, planning and scheduling again.

If supplies are to be delivered only when required, it will often be necessary to source products that can be delivered fairly easily, which means local sourcing. When purchasing from abroad this can often be impossible. Therefore, the purchasing department must compare the price of parts that can be delivered at short notice to the *real cost* of buying components from further away. The item which has the lowest price may not be the best buy.

There is a dilemma between, on the one side, the accountants who want to do away with all stock and release all the capital tied up with it and on the other side the materials engineer who can have an easier life if there is always the part held in stock for whatever eventuality arises – an infinite stockholding. So who has got it right? The correct answer lies somewhere between the two, but generally British industry holds too much stock and a lot could be run down to provide a 'windfall profit'.

Just-in-Time

Initially JIT meant that parts were delivered to an organization as they were required and fed straight onto the production line. In theory, this makes the storing of the component unnecessary. Inventory costs are low and the effect on the balance sheet can be quite significant. Furthermore, not holding stock saves a lot of space that can be better utilized, for example, converting storage space to sales floor.

Of course, this will not work if one is in retailing or running a pub. Holding stock is the very nature of such businesses. It would not be much fun to go into your local pub and order a pint just to be told that you would get it next day! Approaches to inventory vary depending on whether you are Tesco or AsdaWal-Mart or the independent local corner shop. It is affected by the store throughput. How many customers visit your store each day, each week? What is the pattern of their purchases? This influences the decisions that have to be made about how frequently replenishment needs to take place. Replenishment is about ensuring the capability of meeting the required service levels.

JIT requires that:

1 Components are delivered when they are required, which might be daily.
2 Components that come in go straight onto production without inspection and, therefore, must be Quality Assured. Suppliers must either be registered for ISO 9000 or operate Total Quality Management themselves.

This can go much further. JIT, in effect, is a lead time reduction system. In manufacturing a poorly operating production line has a lot of 'work in progress'. This takes the form of stocks waiting to be used and also stocks, part way through the process, having come off one machine and waiting to be put on the next. If a particular component is traced through the process, it can be seen that it may take several weeks, from the time that it comes into the factory, to go out of the factory on the finished item. Even worse, a large amount of finished stocks, where all the value has been added, can be hanging around for a long period of time until the item is sold. By reducing this work in progress the lead times can be reduced and, therefore, there is a shorter time between components being purchased and the item being sold. Blueprinting (as discussed in Chapter 4) can be used to map out the process and to identify where the worst bottlenecks occur. These can then be eliminated. Each time a bottleneck is cured another will appear, which in turn must be cured. This, in effect, is a process of continuous improvement of production through producing only what is needed when it is needed and thus eliminating waste.

Suppose each stage of the operation is considered to be the customer of the stage before it and parts are delivered only when they are needed. This means that work in progress (WIP) is effectively eliminated and work should move in an uninterrupted manner through the plant, but only if each stage of the process is producing items with zero defects.

The eventual aim is to eliminate all of these buffer stocks and, in some cases, even reach the situation where a customer order is made one day and produced and delivered the next. This system in itself can only work effectively if there is Total Quality because any breakdown in quality will stop production.

This also means that parts are converted into saleable items and sent out to the customer more quickly. This avoids tying up capital and a vast amount of factory space.

A problem occurs if one activity in the chain does not produce total quality (zero defects). As no WIP is held, any failure in quality stops the whole process. The same will happen if a machine breaks down. It has been found that simple machines are more successful for the implementation of JIT rather than multi-function machines. Also an important aspect is the speed of changeover from one job to another which often requires fast changeover tooling for these machines. With JIT, bottlenecks become immediately obvious and, therefore, must be cured immediately.

Site layout is planned to optimize the fast throughput and a U-shaped layout seems to work with greatest effect. This is so parts can come off the delivery lorry, go through the process and then end up again where the trucks are for reloading and dispatch. In a service this would be customers entering and leaving from the same part of the facility.

JIT forces the production process to be extremely efficient and immediately shows up where something is going wrong. It also requires good communication and multi-skilling of staff. Materials supply systems are vital for JIT, as they must ensure the supply of the right parts at the right time.

Generally, fewer suppliers are used and long-term agreements are made with them. Schedules agreed for delivery only when required means more forward planning. The principle of not holding inventory is not applied to small low value items, such as nuts, bolts and washers, but would be applied to any high value item such as electric motors.

What can go wrong with JIT?

First, will suppliers deliver the quantity you want, when you want it, with the quality you require?

Secondly, how do you deal with variation in demand? (One reason for multi-skilling.) You may end up with a pile of high value added finished stock or stock-outs.

Successful JIT requires good relationships with your suppliers. Both sides need to come to a common understanding of the standard of quality, dependability, flexibility and speed that is required.

Good communication is the key to making JIT work, and one way of achieving this is through Quality Circles (Ishikawa 1961).

When Toyota drove down the production cycle time by making cars efficiently in a few hours, they then found it was taking 12 weeks to distribute and sell them. JIT can be applied throughout the marketing and distribution process.

One aspect of JIT is that it is a 'pull through' technique. With most production there is a schedule for a batch to be made. With JIT the demand should come from an actual order, and the detail of this order is written on a card called a '*kanban*'. Some companies have already introduced aspects of this with order 'menus' which give the customer a (limited) choice in the product features that can be purchased. These order details are fed down computer lines to the factory where the details are fed into the production schedule. A true 'pull' system. Of course, restaurants have worked this way for years.

The theory of JIT sounds fine, but in practice very few companies (if any) have introduced the theoretical model as it leaves them too vulnerable. But elements of the system are now essential for efficient manufacturing. JIT forces a company to be very efficient.

JIT in the service sector

It will now be shown that Just in Time (JIT) can be applied more easily, with greater effect and better results, in the service sector than in manufacturing. Much as WIP slows the lead time in manufacturing, the application of JIT in a service situation can make the passage of customers through the system more efficient. In manufacturing WIP takes up space, increases transport distances within the operation and ties up capital. All of this also applies to customers in the service sector – only more so. Waiting customers before or between stages of the process (e.g. at a hairdresser's shop) have to be housed in comfortable (expensive) surroundings and are likely to complain if kept waiting. Lumps of metal do not! Furthermore, the one real failing with JIT in manufacturing is the potential build-up of finished stock if the capacity planning is inaccurate. This is the worst type of stock as all the value has been added and the items then have to be stored – slowly depreciating (finished cars in a field waiting to be sold). In a similar service situation, customers have finished they pay and go – there is no finished stock.

In JIT, bottlenecks in the production process can be identified and eliminated and whenever this occurs, the process becomes more efficient. This efficiency often appears as a reduction in lead time. In the service situation, this is shown as a faster thoughput of customers, a reduction of queuing and a more effective utilization of space. The analogy of 'daily deliveries' can be drawn with the use of an appointment system where suitable.

For example, if you consider a hairdresser's shop, without JIT there could be a queue of people outside (that could be considered raw material stock) and people waiting between each stage of the process – hair wash, cut, dry, pay. These people would need space to wait in. This has the effect of making the overall premises larger, with unproductive (and expensive) space in which people can be kept waiting in comfortable surroundings and, perhaps, entertained. But these people are actually cluttering up your premises: and what is more, they don't like it and nor do you. The application of JIT can eliminate queues of people trying to join a service or part way through the process.

Queues would be eliminated by an effective appointment system and, with knowledge of the operations within the salon, the waiting time between the stages of the process would be eliminated. There is one further advantage of JIT applied to the service sector. In manufacturing, if the anticipated demand is incorrect, it is possible to end up with a large amount of finished stock. This is stock of the worst type because all the value has been added. In the service sector the 'finished stock' is people leaving the premises and these need not be of concern to the service provider.

How to introduce JIT

Just-in-Time takes years to implement fully. For example, you cannot achieve JIT without TQM and, as has been said already, the implementation of TQM itself takes years. Implementing JIT must, of necessity, take longer. It probably is not advisable to implement a complete JIT system, as this would be operating too near the edge of a precipice. A buffer stock allows some 'safety' into the system. To our knowledge, although quite a few companies have got near it, nobody has fully implemented a JIT system.

There is a sequence that should be followed when attempting to implement JIT. First introduce planned maintenance. This will reduce unanticipated and unpredicted downtime. It has been found that smaller single process machines are better for JIT. These can be moved more easily out of their line for easier fixing should failure occur. In Japan it is common to operate machines at only 90% full capacity. This has been found to increase their reliability. In this country, machines tend to be run flat out, because accountants like to get their money back quickly. It is advised that the machines are, in fact, run at full capacity, as if machine suppliers sell a machine to operate at a certain capacity then it should be able to operate at that capacity. Nowadays it would be expected that they should operate reliably at the manufacturer's rating.

Then introduce 'quick changeover' for tooling (faster loading for a coffee maker?). If the product is to be changed regularly then more time will be spent in changing tooling. A quick changeover of tooling will reduce this unproductive downtime.

Introduce TQM. Any loss in quality during the production cycle also causes production to stop. At the same time, ensure that suppliers are also operating to TQM. This will be easier for your suppliers and, therefore, beneficial to you if you move towards single sourcing of components and sub-contracted activities and, also, if your favoured suppliers are involved in any design changes you are to introduce. If you ask these chosen suppliers what is easier for them, you will get better quality.

Retrain operators for multi-skilling. As JIT is very much affected in variations in demand, it will be necessary for operators to move to different activities and different products during times when demand for other items is low. It will also be necessary for operators to cover for other operators during periods of absenteeism for illness or holidays etc.

Now introduce the horseshoe process line, perhaps with a cellular layout. There need not be much space between the machines and, therefore, not much transport required between operations. This is because work in progress is kept to a minimum and space between the machines will not be piled up with this WIP.

The final stage to be introduced is that which many people think is JIT. This is the daily deliveries from your suppliers. In practice, only very large companies can expect daily deliveries. It must be remembered that the supplier must feel it worthwhile to deliver the stock and, therefore, they must have, say, at least a van full to make it worthwhile bringing these components from their plant to yours. Rather than just introducing daily deliveries, do this in stages. First, increase stock turnover to five times a year, then ten times a year, then twenty times a year and so on. To do this it is often better to have a few trusted suppliers in the supplier network. Single (trusted) suppliers are better than multi-sourcing. Always avoid playing one supplier off against the others in an attempt to, say, reduce prices, as this may affect their quality and reliability.

It is too simplistic to assume all stock is a bad thing and should be eliminated. Such a policy is often advocated in operations management books and accountancy books.

ABC classification of inventory items

The ABC classification system is derived from the Pareto 80:20 principle and is commonly applied to inventory management to help management identify the appropriate control policies. It classifies inventory items into groups (A–C), typically according to the amount of annual expenditure they incur, calculated by multiplying the estimated number of items used annually by their unit cost (see Figure 10.4). Usually, 60–80% of annual expenditure is accounted for by 10–20% of inventory items. These are then called A items and should be closely controlled so as to reduce overall inventory expenditure. The importance of these items may demand a strategic approach to their purchasing and the development of close buyer–seller relationships which are the cornerstone of the JIT approach to inventory management. Class B items account for the next 20–30% of items and 10% of total expenditure. Class C items comprise the remaining 50–70% of items but by value represent around 10% of total expenditure. Less rigorous inventory control techniques are required for these items because the cost of inventory tracking would outweigh the cost of holding additional stock.

Inventory management models

There are a number of inventory models which organizations can adopt to help them decide how much to order and when to place that order.

In **fixed order quantity inventory systems** the order quantity remains the same each time the order is placed but the period between orders varies according to the rate of use of the inventory item. Under this system, the order

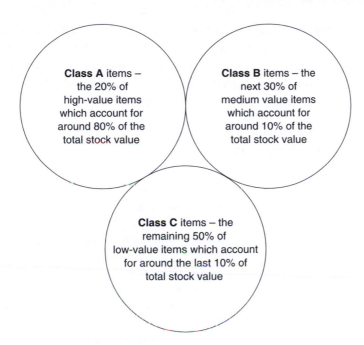

Class A items – the 20% of high-value items which account for around 80% of the total stock value

Class B items – the next 30% of medium value items which account for around 10% of the total stock value

Class C items – the remaining 50% of low-value items which account for around the last 10% of total stock value

FIGURE 10.4   INVENTORY CLASSIFICATIONS

for further inventory is placed when the stock level has reduced to a certain level, named the reorder point (ROP). Depending on their level of sophistication, organizations might use IT systems to calculate the ROP or use the two–bin system. With the latter, inventory is held in two containers, termed 'bins'. When one bin is empty a replenishment order is made and inventory is taken from the second bin until the replacements arrive. This system requires that the inventory record is updated as inventory is used and replenished, hence it is sometimes called a perpetual system.

Less important items as identified through the ABC classification may only have their inventory levels checked at certain levels such as once a week or once a month. Many small and medium–sized enterprises deem that approach appropriate for their needs.

The **reorder point model** calculates the timing of the inventory order on the basis of when the stock level drops to a predetermined amount. This amount is calculated to ensure there is enough stock to cover the delay between an order being placed and delivery being received. This is usually termed safety stock and is to reduce the likelihood of stock outs occurring. Stock outs have a detrimental effect on customers' perceptions of the quality of service. Factors to take into account include variability in delivery lead time, variability in rate of demand, the cost of holding safety stock and the cost due to stock outs (likelihood of lost sales, damage to reputation etc.).

We do not propose to discuss the economic order quantity (EOQ) model because, as Brown, Lamming, Bessant and Jones (2005) identified, the assumption of one delivery per order and the use of that stock over time increases inventory levels and does not fit with the JIT approach. EOQ is no longer relevant given the complexities organizations are faced with in the twenty-first century.

RAPID REPLENISHMENT AT TESCO

Graham Booth, when director of supply chain at Tesco, identified a rapid replenishment system triggered by customer demand as being the source of competitive advantage. His strategic aim was to use the same suppliers, cross-dock facilities and vehicles serving multiple store types. The program could then work across multiple store formats. He recognized that the best way to operationalize this aim was to use blueprinting to map the supply chain of soda from bottler to the shelves of Tesco stores (Womack and Jones 2005).

As Booth and a group of managers walked the supply chain, they spotted a number of problems or weaknesses in the supply chain that needed addressing, from: 'Why are products missing from the shelves?', 'Why are products from roll cages that have just come off the truck from the regional distribution centre (RDC) re-sorted in the stores?' to 'Why is so much stock needed in the back of the grocery store, and at the Tesco RDC, and again at the soda bottler's RDC?' and 'Why are there huge warehouses of cans waiting to be filled near the bottling plants?'

Booth and his team concluded that the supply chain could be transformed if:

- *Store-level point of sale data were connected directly into the order–ship decision-making process. This ensured that it was consumer demand that was driving store deliveries.*
- *The number of deliveries could be increased: Tesco trucks now leave the RDCs multiple times per day to replenish what was sold in the past few hours.*
- *Cola was received from the bottler on cages, which were then rolled directly onto delivery trucks, and then from the store backroom to the retail floor. In this way the cages serve as the retail 'shelf', eliminating many touches along the way.*
- *The former Tesco warehouses were turned into true cross-docking facilities. Fast-moving items generally spend only a few hours there from the time they are received until loaded onto an outbound store truck.*
- *Tesco worked with the bottlers to help them make the transition to becoming virtually make-to-order businesses rather than the old make-to-stock, resulting in greatly reduced inventories at its plants. While some buffer inventory is held, it is very small. This required changes to production processes to enable smaller batch sizes and increased flexibility.*
- *Tesco embraced new processes such as Tesco trucks picking up empty cages from the stores, then delivering them on the return trip to suppliers, where they also then pick up new full cages.*

From Womack and Jones 2005

Supply chain models

A number of configurations of supply chains can be found.

Vertical integration relates to the extent to which supply chain activities are undertaken and controlled within the organization. Under this configuration the majority of manufacture is in-house; there are distant relationships with suppliers. In forward or downstream integration, an organization expands on the demand side. This involves taking the organization closer to customers, allowing more freedom to contact people direct. It has been described as an offensive strategic move.

The extent of vertical integration has to be decided. Vertical integration affects quality in that it impacts on the closeness of the operation to its customers and suppliers. The origins of problems are generally easier to find in an in-house operation than through outside suppliers. On the other hand, there is danger of a lack of competition leading to less incentive to cooperate with quality improvements.

A fundamental business decision that companies have to make is to decide which components to produce internally and which from outside. The vertically integrated corporation, with an ownership relationship with its suppliers and distributors, is fast becoming extinct. Successful outsourcing of non-core activities has encouraged companies to focus on their core competences and look to form strategic partnerships.

In the food sector, Del Monte Foods has a product line of fruit and vegetables ranging from A to Z. It operates 17 production facilities and 18 strategically located distribution centres in North America and state-of-the-art food and pet food research facilities in Walnut Creek and Terminal Island, California. Additionally, Del Monte has operating facilities and distribution centres in American Samoa, Ecuador and Venezuela. In recent years it has been developing innovative packaging.

Nike, Inc., the largest supplier of athletic shoes in the world, outsources 100% of its shoe production. The athletic footwear sector is both technology- and fashion-intensive, thereby requiring flexibility in both production and marketing. Nike creates maximum value by concentrating on research and development and post-production activities such as marketing, distribution and sale. The link between these activities is one of the best marketing information systems in the industry.

Vertical disintegration: this is also known as disaggregation. In this configuration there is a greater move to outsourcing; the organization focuses on managing its network of suppliers. The rationale behind this move is cost reduction and a focus on core capabilities.

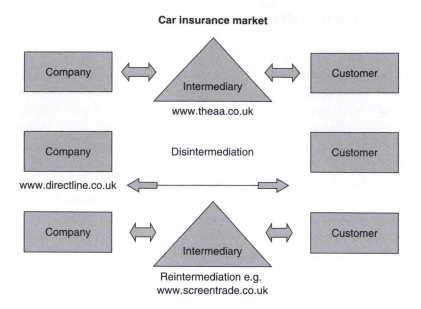

FIGURE 10.5 BUSINESS MODELS IN THE CAR INSURANCE MARKET

Virtual integration: in this pattern the majority of supply chain activities are undertaken and controlled outside the organization by third parties. There is total reliance on linked third parties; a close relationship with suppliers; and rapid market penetration can be achieved.

Virtual organization: the processes transcend the boundaries of a single form and are not controlled by a single organizational hierarchy. Production processes are flexible with different parties involved at different times. Parties involved in the production of single product are often geographically dispersed. So coordination is heavily dependent on telecommunications and data networks.

Supply chains and value chains can be revised by disaggregation or reaggregation. Disaggregation may involve outsourcing core supply chain activities to external parties. It is sometimes called **disintermediation** and involves the removal of intermediaries such as distributors or brokers that formerly linked a company to its customers. As more activities are outsourced, a company moves towards a virtual organization. It is possible to find examples of disaggregation and reaggregation in the same business segment. Reaggregation or **reintermediation** is the creation of new intermediaries between customers and suppliers providing services such as supplier search and product evaluation. The car insurance sector in the UK provides examples of this (see Figure 10.5).

Types of relationships in supply chains

From the point of view of *individual* operations within a supply chain, one of the key issues is how to manage relationships with immediate suppliers and customers. The behaviour of the supply chain as a whole is, after all, made up of relationships which are formed between individual pairs of operations in the chain.

A question to be addressed is whether the relationship is with the final link in the chain, involving the ultimate consumer, or whether it concerns one of the prior links in the supply chain, involving two commercial businesses. So, business to business (B2B) relationships are by far the most common in a supply chain context. Business to consumer (B2C) relationships include both 'bricks and mortar' retailers and online retailers.

Supply chains developed to serve mainly national markets have had to adapt since the Euro was introduced as the main currency within the European Union. Large food retailers operate today on tight margins and overstocking is kept to the minimum with short supply chains and using techniques such as efficient consumer response (ECR) that assume a highly predictable demand.

The other issue to be considered when examining the types of relationship within a supply chain is where the power lies within the supply chain. There is a huge difference in being the equivalent of Wal-Mart in your supply chain or of Jack Scaife, a speciality sausage maker in Yorkshire, UK (see www.walmart.com and www. jackscaife.co.uk).

Types of B2B relationship

A convenient way of categorizing supply chain relationships is to examine the extent to which a company chooses to buy in from suppliers. Two dimensions are particularly important – *what* the company chooses to outsource and *who* it chooses to supply it.

In terms of what is outsourced, key questions are:

* How many activities are outsourced?
* How important are the activities outsourced?
* How many suppliers will be used by the operation?
* How close are the relationships?

Companies that sell to other companies typically operate as both suppliers and buyers. For example, Boise Cascade Office Products currently sell through 400 e-market places and e-procurement solutions. These solutions represent a huge variety of data formats, data requirements, taxonomies, unique pricing, unique product selection and more. Most suppliers have internal IT systems designed for internal use, with acronyms and abbreviations that only make sense to company employees. The Internet creates a demand for this information in a format that is usable to the general public and thereby places a big demand on the organization.

Managing information across the supply network

If supply chain management is all about managing the flows of materials and information through the network, it is greatly aided by close synchronization of schedules which speeds up throughput. Being close also has the advantage of being able to help forecasting, which as we shall shortly see can have a major impact on the profitability of the supply chain.

Improved communications can result in realistic delivery promises, which gives an improvement to the dependability factor. Forward integration gives the potential for products to be developed specifically to customer needs. There is a danger of dissipation of management attention if attention is spread too thinly. Ownership of suppliers can give the potential to dictate volume changes to match downstream fluctuations. There is the potential to share costs.

Sharing information

Being able to share information on forecasting, production and inventory control activity is important for the smooth operation of the supply chain. There are a wide range of software and other technologies now available which facilitate this exchange. Quick response programmes, which link manufacturing, warehousing, sales and retailers, are used by organizations such as Benetton. Under this system a Benetton retailer anywhere in the world can reorder a product through a direct link with Benetton's mainframe computer in Italy. Part of the order could be fulfilled from the Italian warehouse and the rest manufactured. It will take four weeks maximum to reorder, manufacture and transport the product. Quick response programmes combine bar code scanning and electronic data interchange (EDI) to enable a Just-in-time replenishment system. Efficient customer response (ECR) is the term given to the system of bar code scanning and EDI used by some organizations in the United States to bring together distributors, suppliers and grocers.

Dell Computers' plants depend on component suppliers being tightly integrated into the manufacturing process and holding inventory ready for shipment. Accurate forecasting and sharing of information becomes crucial. Network computing facilitates this.

Bull-whip effect

As information becomes distorted from one end of the supply chain to the other it can lead to inefficiencies, resulting in excessive inventory investment, poor customer service, lost revenues, misguided capacity plans, ineffective transportation, and missed production schedules. These distortions in information have come to be called the bull-whip effect or the Forrester effect.

Stockpiling can occur at seven or eight places across the supply chain, which can lead to 100 days of inventory being kept just in case. A 1997 US study projected that streamlining the information sharing process in the grocery sector could result in savings of $30 billion (Lee et al., 1997).

There can be fluctuations in output as each operation reacts to orders placed by immediate suppliers. If information is shared throughout the chain then the wild fluctuations should be minimized. EPOS systems (electronic point of sale) help this – data from checkouts is consolidated and transmitted to warehouses. EDI helps share information with the transportation companies and supplier manufacturing operations that form the supply chain.

Electronic data interchange (EDI)

Electronic data interchange shares information between the various parties in the supply chain. Details of orders placed with suppliers, orders received from customers, payments made to suppliers and payments received from customers, can all be transmitted through information networks. Suppliers, customers and banks then share the information in a digital form, avoiding the need for rekeying.

The advantages of EDI are: quick access to information, better customer service, reduced paperwork, better communications, increased productivity, improved tracing and expediting, cost efficiency, competitive advantage and improved billing.

Traditional EDI systems in the 1970s were implemented through value added networks (VAN), limiting the accessibility for smaller companies. Value added network services were usually run by third parties rather than traders themselves. The biggest user in the UK was Tesco, which was one of the pioneers using EDI. Significant initial investment was needed so relatively few companies took it up. The other drawbacks were that business processes needed to be restructured to fit EDI requirements, a long start up time was needed and the use of private, expensive VANs was necessary. The result was high operating costs and multiple EDI standards so one company might have to use several standards. Overall, it was a complex system and so it was not surprising that there was resistance to taking up the technology, particularly among SMEs.

The Internet has had a big influence on how this exchange of information can be effected. Through standard data formats, it is now possible to bring the advantages of EDI to everyone, not just big companies who can afford it. Electronic communications have helped drive introduction of new models of supply chain management: e-mail, web-based ordering, EDI of invoices and payment, web-based order tracking. The advantage is more efficient processes; lower cost execution of processes; reduced complexity of the supply chain; improved data integration between elements of the supply chain; reduced costs through ease of dynamic outsourcing; enabling innovation and customer responsiveness.

For business partners to communicate online, they need some type of secure interorganizational network like an extranet and a common protocol such as EDI. In the twenty-first century traditional electronic data interchange in which trading information such as orders and invoices is transmitted in an open format across secure, privately managed networks is being replaced by web-based EDI in which secure messages are passed over open networks. This enables smaller companies to join electronic commerce networks, allowing direct communications between suppliers and customers and making it possible to rationalize the supply chain by cutting out distributors. Internet-based EDI can replace traditional EDI or supplement it for SMEs. Accessible and cheap, Internet-based applications can complement many current applications, and have additional functionalities such as workflow, collaboration and search engines not available under traditional EDI, which make them very attractive for SMEs.

Intranets connecting internal business applications such as operational enterprise resource planning systems and decision support oriented data warehouses enable effective management of the supply chain. Such systems increasingly support external links to third parties, such as suppliers.

Substituting the VAN, the platform that EDI originally operated on, with Internet-based EDI can dramatically lower EDI transmission costs and EDI over the Internet can be faster than other VANs (Radosevich 1996).

Applying e-business to the supply chain entails synchronization of supply and demand, more flexible manufacturing processes and the ability to treat the supply chain as a virtual assembly line. It allows real time data exchange and collaboration. Consumer demand for cars ordered via the Internet to their personal specification and delivered quickly will force manufacturers to focus on their logistics. The global car industry has dreamt of the possibility of delivering a customer-specified car to the customer within a working week. Most industry analysts believe that the key to making this dream a reality is the distribution chain. The time-consuming element of car production is not the production line. Once the necessary components are to hand, assembling a car is quite quick. The key is how to best synchronize the flow of materials, getting materials in the right place at the right time. What developers of systems to facilitate these flows have had to come to terms with is the need to think of the supply chain as a whole. For example, Ford has around 19 assembly plants in the United States dealing with several suppliers on any given day. Since 2001 Ford has used the Ford Supplier Portal provided by Covisint Communicate to manage this interaction.

A company can create an extranet that enables trading partners to enter data in a web form whose fields correspond to the fields in an EDI message or document. Procter & Gamble replaced its traditional EDI system with 4,000 business partners to an Internet-based system with tens of thousands of suppliers.

Marks & Spencer invested in technology to enable their main suppliers to link to a single supply chain and integrate this with their customer transaction system to enable streamlined deliveries through shared information. The system was designed to enable the collection of customer transaction details from more than 300 stores in almost real time. This information allowed suppliers to deliver more efficiently to the distribution centres, thereby allowing greater product availability and selection.

The bolstered supply chain replaced a daily batch file transfer solution over EDI between M&S and its suppliers. The BizTalk software allowed the exchange of information in real time, helping overcome problems quicker. (Computer Weekly, March 2000)

Office Depot, a large US office supplies company, is fairly typical of a number of companies in how they have used the Internet to refashion communication in their supply chain. Initially the company focused most of its effort on the consumer side, creating Internet sites and resources to draw in consumers and boost sales. Following on from that success, it turned its attention to electronic links with its vendors. The company developed an extranet to automate several layers of paperwork between the company and its suppliers; now data from Office Depot goes to suppliers on inventory levels and products and vendors transmit back all data involved in providing and moving goods. There are faster and more accurate information flows. Some users find EDI an intimidating technology so there is a special section of the extranet to explain EDI. When the extranet went online, Office Depot concentrated on getting the 250 suppliers who provided up to 85% of its sales online. Under this system suppliers are able under this system to analyse current demand, shape marketing strategies and manage inventories to match demand. Operational costs have been reduced 10–15% by providing suppliers online access to inventory data. Both suppliers and Office Depot have gained under this system.

No discussion of supply chain management is complete without reference to Dell. Michael Dell's original concept of revolutionizing the supply chain for personal computers by taking out the middleman has shown the savings that can be made when intermediaries are removed from the supply chain. Dell customers can configure, price and order computer systems 24 hours a day, 7 days a week. They are able to get current order status and delivery information and have online access to technical reference materials through accessing the company website. (www. dell.com). Dell's supply chain strategy has been to focus on capital efficiency and low inventory. Focusing on the virtual integration of suppliers and customer orders helped inventory drop from 33 days in fiscal year 1994 to 5 days at the end of fiscal year 2001.

Suppliers are located right next to Dell's assembly plants, and they deliver a constant stream of components on a Just-in-Time basis. Monitors are shipped directly from the companies that make them and merged in transit with Dell's own shipments, arriving in matching Dell boxes in a single customer delivery.

Physical distribution and logistics

The management of outbound logistics or inbound and outbound logistics is essential to the efficient management of the supply chain.

The Internet has led to information being more readily available along the distribution chain. Transport companies, warehouses, suppliers and customers in the chain can share a knowledge of where goods are in the chain and where they are going next.

Operations within the chain can coordinate their activities more readily, which gives the opportunity to make cost savings. When a company is contracted to transport goods from A to B, its vehicles may have to return from B to A empty. Back-loading means finding a potential customer who wants their goods transported from B to A in the right time frame. Companies that can fill their vehicles on both outward and return journeys will have significantly lower costs per distance travelled than those whose vehicles are empty for half the total journey. Freight2mail.com is a UK and European return loads freight exchange. This site's primary function is to display and notify members of available return loads and available empty vehicles. In October 2005 Freight2mail was free to join and use for bona-fide transport providers or transport users.

While goods are sold over the Internet they still have to be physically transported to the customer. Early e-tailers ran into problems with this order fulfilment task. Traditional warehouse and distribution operations were not designed for e-commerce fulfilment. Traditional bricks and mortar operations require large vehicles to move relatively large quantities of goods on pallets from warehouses to shops. Distributing to customers who have bought online requires a large number of relatively small individual orders to be delivered, all of which may be different.

LOGISTICS IN ACTION

Hallmark Flowers.com, a US company which guarantees next day delivery if the order is placed online before 7:00 in the evening Central Standard Time. Most orders come in after 4:00pm. Orders are received on their website, then the 'Move Demand Centre software' reserves flowers in the inventory system and generates the orders to put together the bouquets. Accompanying cards produced by electronic printers and documents for FedEx are generated automatically. Hallmark Flowers leases a 106,000 sq ft facility in Southaven, Mississippi, just outside Memphis, Tennessee, where fresh flowers arrive and are shipped out daily. The arrangement centre is just 7 miles from the Memphis airport, allowing for quick transport to FedEx, the company Hallmark uses to guarantee overnight shipment of flowers. There is real time inventory management and complete integration; the order data helps forecast demand; flowers are a highly perishable commodity which cannot be kept for more than 48–72 hours. The company has found that they can restrict business through the website to ensure volume is manageable.

Once upon a time customers specified parts required and a logistics company took the parts from the warehouse to the factory. Now collaboration between those in the supply chain leads to shared operational, strategic and planning data so whole processes can be streamlined, thereby reducing costs and complexity.

Today's logistics companies work with customers to provide a full consultative service, offering help with problem-solving, product development, materials and methods of fixing. When it goes wrong the costs can be huge. In 1998 production at the UK factory of one of the world's largest car makers was brought to a standstill for several days because of the non-availability of a single door latch component, worth no more than a few pence. Costs to a car maker in terms of lost production, plant downtime and wages, not to mention bad publicity and lost orders, can be estimated at thousands if not millions.

Organizations need to ensure that stocks of even the smallest component must be in the right place at the right time. For some years many companies devolved management of the supply for high volume components to specialist companies. Outsourcing responsibility for supply of low cost yet high volume and production critical components presents an opportunity to combine pressure relief for the manufacturer's own resources with the potential for cost savings. As part of this process the logistics specialist might include 'tear down' facilities, where a final product is completely disassembled and its components examined in detail in an attempt to rationalize type variety and number of parts used in order to simplify assembly. Cost savings can ensue.

Companies want their logistics specialists to respond quickly, flexibly and efficiently to their needs. Anglian Home Improvements is one of Europe's largest manufacturers of windows. The fasteners used to be sourced from 14 different suppliers, generating between 400 and 500 separate orders each year. Each order created a different purchase order, delivery note and invoice. Anglian then gave responsibility for fastener supplies to a single logistics company: now 200 different fasteners are supplied on a JIT basis. The first step in outsourcing is to establish the client's exact consumption of parts. Any supplier currently delivering direct now has to deliver to a logistics company which stores, quality checks and collates stocks ready for delivery to the production line, exactly where and when they are needed.

The use of third party logistics providers is becoming more common, first for transportation and warehousing, but next to be outsourced are freight consolidation and distribution. The advantages in international business in particular are the reduction in uncertainty and complexity and the minimizing of risk while maintaining flexibility.

Integrated solutions are crucial to supply chain management. A key to the developments here is the use of real time data. Organizations need to be able to monitor their product throughout the supply chain. Hence the extensive use of bar code-based tracking, mobile computing and laser scanning. Using a number of Internet applications that allow real time access to information across organizations enhances customer service and improves inventory management. If there is a lorry going into a factory four times a day, many other products can be added onto the delivery, creating a more efficient supply chain.

Real time links between the website and the inventory system are needed so that inventory is updated with every order and as soon as an item is out of stock it is removed from the website. So an organization must integrate its e-commerce systems with catalogue sales systems. It is not enough to have an item in stock if it cannot be shipped quickly. Order systems have to communicate with shipping systems that generate packing orders and get shipments out of the door. There is now a wide choice of formats to transfer data between e-commerce platform and back-end systems.

Not all orders are filled from warehouses. Some ship from bricks and mortar stores and some have suppliers drop shipments directly to customers.

Logistics is not just about getting goods out to customers it is also about managing the returns process. The reverse supply chain requires efficient management. This requires product and shipping information to be tracked, stored, referenced and reported. Customer credits need to be processed efficiently. Many organizations will use rules-based decision support programming to control which products are accepted for return and how they are sent back. Organizations can minimize the number of items that need to enter the return flow by ensuring that the quality of product and user-friendliness for the consumer is at the highest attainable level before being sold and shipped, or changing promotional programs that load the trade when there is no realistic chance that the product shipped to the customer will actually be sold.

Of concern can be the cost associated with returning products that should not have been returned or the cost of products that have been returned to the inappropriate destination. Rogers, Lambert, Croxton and Garcia-Dastugue (2002) talk of the need for successful gatekeeping to control and reduce the rate of returns without damaging customer service. The point of entry into the reverse flow is the best point to evade unnecessary cost and management of materials by screening unwarranted returned merchandise. Reverse logistics is big business.

> Of the approximately $96 billion in online retail sales in 2003, over $20 billion were sent back to retailer.
>
> AMR research, *Beyond the Shopping Cart*, 2003

Reverse logistics help organizations plan for the return of defective products, product disposal after end-of-life, product upgrades, product recall, warranty returns, product defect analysis. So reverse logistics costs are affected by innovation rates and by quality problems. At a conference on trends in reverse logistics in 2006 it was reported that 'improperly handled returns erode 30–35% of potential profits.' (Gartner Research) and that 'There are up to 12 times the number of transactions involved in the returns process than in selling the product in the first place' (AMR, Nigel Montgomery).

SUMMARY OF KEY POINTS

Supply chains are dynamic systems involving hundreds of activities and decisions to be made. Effective supply chain management oversees the flows of materials and information between each tier of supplier and customer. Procurement encompasses all the activities involved with obtaining items from a supplier: that is purchasing and in-bound logistics such as transportation, goods-in and warehousing. E-procurement leads to direct cost reductions which come about through improving efficiency. Two fundamental approaches to procurement: buying from many suppliers in a pure market manner or buying from a few key suppliers with whom one develops a long-term, trusting relationship. Inventory is rightly identified as a source of cost when analyzing the value chain, yet organizations cannot function without some level of inventory. Effective management of the supply chain will only come once the approach to the management of inventory within the organization has been agreed.

JIT requires that components are delivered when they are required, which might be daily, and components that come in go straight onto production without inspection and therefore must be Quality Assured.

STUDENT ACTIVITY 10.1

Look at the websites for these two organizations: www.walmart.com and www.jackscaife.co.uk. Can you identify who might be their key suppliers? Who has the most power in the relationship between supplier and purchasing organization? How did you come to that judgement?

STUDENT ACTIVITY 10.2

1   Visit supplyworks.com and examine how they streamline the purchase process. How does it differ from ariba.com?
2   Enter govexec.com. Identify recent e-procurement initiatives and summarize their unique aspects.
3   How far do you think UK government policies are driving e-procurement?

STUDENT ACTIVITY 10.3

On the face of it, it would appear that holding stocks is a 'bad thing'. This is an oversimplification of the situation in most organizations.

List all the cases where it is necessary to hold stocks (don't forget the service sector). You should be able to compile a list of about 20 cases. Having done this, you can use it to appraise any stock-holding situation in the future. If the case is not on your list, it may be a reason for eliminating these stocks thereby freeing up space and capital. (Did you write your answer on a piece of paper taken from a pile of paper? That was a necessary stock – wasn't it?)

Check out what has happened to www.vertical.net and www.chemdex.com and outline the reasons for this.

What do you think could be termed the 'danger of drop shipping'?

How quickly should customers' orders be processed?

FURTHER READING

Chaffey D. (2002) *E-Business and E-Commerce Management.* Englewood Cliffs, NJ: Prentice Hall.

Lee H.L. and Billington C. (1992), 'Managing supply chain inventory: pitfalls and opportunities', *Sloan Management Review*, 33 (3): 65–73.

Lee L. Hau, Padmanabhan V. and Whang Seungjin (1997) 'The bull-whip effect in supply chains', *Sloan Management Review*, Spring, pp. 93–102.

London Business School (2004), *EU Spend Management Study.*

Lyons Review Team (2004) *Well Placed to Deliver? Shaping the Pattern of Government Service*, www.hm-treasury.gov.uk/Consultations_and_Legislation/Lyons/ consult_lyons_index.cfm.

Radosevich L. (1996) 'The once and future of EDI', *CIO Magazine*, 1 (6): 66–77.

Reekers N. and Smithson S. (1994) 'EDI in Germany and the UK: strategic and operational use', *European Journal of Information Systems*, 3(3): 169–178.

Tan Gek Woo and Shaw M. (1998), 'Applying component technology to improve global supply chain network management', ICIS 1998: 296–301.

Turban E., King D., Lee J., Warkentin M. and Chung H.M. (2002), *Electronic Commerce: A Managerial Perspective*, 2nd edition. Upper Saddle River, NJ: Prentice Hall.

Womack J. and Jones D. (2005), *Lean Solutions: How Companies and Customers Can Create Value and Wealth Together.* Free Press.

11 SERVICES LOCATION AND DISTRIBUTION

> There are three important things in retailing: location, location, location.
>
> Lord Sieff, Marks & Spencer
>
> You can be the best retailer in the world, but if you set up your shop in the wrong place, you'll never do much business. If you operate from the wrong properties, you start with your hands tied behind your back.
>
> George Davies, Fashion Brand Designer and Retail
Consultant cited in Clarke and Rowley 1995

LEARNING OUTCOMES

When you have completed this chapter you should be able to:

Identify or define:

- The objective of location strategy.
- The factors affecting location decisions.

Describe or explain three methods of solving the location problem, such as:

- Factor-rating method.
- Locational breakeven analysis.
- Centre-of-gravity method.
- Geographic Information Systems.

This chapter explores the information an enterprise needs to be able to make decisions about the optimum location of its operations. It introduces students to some of the tools commonly used in making location decisions.

The operations function exists within the overall framework of the total organization and its external environment. While the business strategy determines the services offered and the service quality provided it can also limit the resources available to operations. The operations manager is forever charged with balancing the conflicting priorities of efficient use of resources and customer satisfaction. In the short to medium term existing resources constrain overall feasibility and quality and price. The location or premises from which an organization conducts its business is both a major resource and a major constraint. In terms of location decisions an organization is faced with making the most of existing premises and selecting new alternatives.

Location decisions

The objective of location strategy is to maximize the benefit of the location to the firm.

If we consider industrial location decisions, a *Cost* focus is paramount, since in fact revenue varies little between locations. Location is a major cost factor which affects shipping and production costs (e.g. labour). So costs can vary greatly between locations. Management's strategy has to be to adopt the strategies that will minimize these costs.

In contrast, when it comes to locating services the focus has to be on revenue, both actual and potential. Costs actually vary relatively little between different market areas. However, location is a major revenue factor. It impacts on the amount of customer contact achieved and the volume of business that is possible.

Generally location decisions will be long-term decisions and difficult to reverse. They affect fixed and variable costs, such as the transportation cost, and other costs like taxes, wages, rent etc. Heizer and Render (2004) estimate that as much as 25% of product price can be accounted for by transportation costs.

Location can also influence such costs as tax, wages, raw material costs and rents. The pattern of location decisions over the past 30 years has been to site manufacturing plants in low wage economies.

James Dyson, leading innovator and strong advocate of British engineering, found that modern economic realities pulled him in a different direction to his stated beliefs. 'I do not believe that the nation that was home to the Industrial Revolution can remain great if it loses its ability to make things,' he said. From the time he opened his Malmesbury, Wiltshire factory for the production of his bagless vacuum cleaners in 1993, James Dyson became the leading evangelist of British manufacturing, frequently bemoaning government's failure to invest adequately, in his opinion, in research and engineering. Yet in 2002 he moved vacuum cleaner production to Malaysia, where production costs were 30% lower. The following year he switched production of his washing machines from Malmesbury to Malaysia too. China was also considered as a possible location for the washing machine production. Dyson justified the move as follows: 'We need an enormous amount of cash to invest in new technology, to launch into new markets and to launch more products faster. Most of our suppliers are also in the Far East. And our markets are there too. We're the best-selling vacuum cleaner in Australia and New Zealand. We are doing well in Japan and we are about to open in America. It makes more sense for us to produce in the Far East.'

(Continued)

Certainly, given 30% reduction in labour costs and reduced transportation costs between component suppliers and the production facility, it was no wonder that the entrepreneur took the decision to base production in the Far East and to maintain head office and research and development facilities in the UK.

Costs

UK worker: £9 per hour   Malaysian worker: £3 per hour
UK office rent: £114 sq m a year   Malaysia office rent: £38 sq m a year.

Source: Economist Intelligence Unit and BBC

It was also easier to obtain the necessary planning permission to expand the factory as and when required. The workforce were well skilled and able to maintain the product's high quality. Malaysia also formed a good distribution centre for exporting the appliances to Japan and the United States. Sales of the Dyson vacuum cleaner in North America increased 350% between 2003 and 2004. The increase in profits has been re-invested in research and development and more rapid innovation. This is deemed to be necessary as UK sales have slowed down since the first Dyson vacuum cleaners appeared in 1993, indicating a market approaching saturation and a need for new, improved models.

There are broadly three strategic options for an organization: not moving but expanding the existing facility, maintaining current sites but adding another facility elsewhere, closing the existing facility and moving to another location. Expansion may require new planning permission and the site's physical constraints may prevent the desired redevelopment.

In the global market place decisions about where to locate have to be made, first, at the country level, then which region, then the actual site.

Country level

At the country level the factors that have to be weighed up are:

- Political risks, government rules, attitudes, incentives.
- Cultural and economic issues.
- Location of markets.
- Labour availability, attitudes, productivity, costs.
- Availability of supplies, communications, energy.
- Exchange rates and currency risks.

The introduction of the euro in the European Union has removed consideration of exchange rates and currency risk as an issue for many EU-based firms.

The stability of the political leadership is likely to be given greater weight than its record on human rights abuses. Another delicate issue is the concept of incentives or bribes. Incentives that are openly declared and visible to all are very different to bribes. Accepting that the giving or receiving of bribes by UK businesses is illegal, it is still recognized that to do business in some parts of the world, particularly to locate operations there, may require the payment of a 'facilitator fee'.

Disney's decision to locate its European themepark in Paris, France illustrated the weight corporations give to the different location factors. A Disneyland had been successfully opened in Tokyo and it was thought that Europe would be a good location for the next roll out of the format given the success Disney films had had in Europe. Two potential sites were considered: Paris and Costa del Sol, Spain. The weather was better and more predictable in Spain but the transport infrastructure was better in Paris. There were good motorway links, the proposed site was midway between two airports and the suburban railway would link with the Paris metro system. The Channel Tunnel was also expected to make it eaiser for British holiday makers to get to Paris. In addition the French government offered considerably more financial inducements. Due to its transportation availability, Paris offered Euro Disneyland a wealth of potential guests and employees.

Regional level

At a regional level the questions arise around the attractiveness of the region (culture, taxes, climate etc.), labour availability, costs, attitudes towards trade unions, the cost and availability of utilities, local environmental regulations, government incentives, proximity to raw materials and customers and land/construction costs. The clustering of high-tech companies around particular universities reflects availability of skilled and educated labour and the desire to cluster like-minded businesses near each other.

For example, from the 1970s onwards many semi-conductor firms chose to locate in the southern part of the San Francisco Bay area in northern California. They found themselves clustered alongside the computer firms that used such devices and programming and service companies, which served both. Soon the area was re-named Silicon Valley. It had the advantage of plentiful industrial space and relatively cheap housing. The development of the venture capital industry provided the funding to fuel the growth in the area.

The quality of life issues in the community include all levels of education, cost of living, health care, sports, cultural activities, transportation, housing, entertainment and religious facilities. All other things being equal, the decision may well come down to where are the best golf courses.

In 1989 Toyota took the strategic decision to expand its manufacture of vehicles to Europe, where a significant volume of customers were based. The UK was chosen as a suitable location because at that time it had a large domestic automobile market, a well-established component supply base and good transport links with the rest of Europe.

The selection of Barnaston in Derbyshire owed a lot to the availability of skilled workers. The decline in manufacturing at that time meant that skilled workers were looking for jobs. Toyota was also keen to site its plant away from the heavily unionized car manufacturing sector in the West Midlands.

The good road and rail network meant suppliers could get components in to the plant and Toyota could get cars out to its dealers. The site also had to be big enough to be capable of future expansion.

The proximity of the world famous golf complex at The Belfry added to the attractiveness of the Midlands area with Japanese executives.

Site level

When it comes to choosing between different potential sites, the site size and cost become very important, as do the air, rail, highway and waterway systems, any local planning restrictions, proximity of services/supplies needed and environmental impact issues.

Siting a brandy distillery alongside the railway line that will be used to bring in the grape needed the distillery process makes sense in terms of minimizing transportation costs.

When BMW decided to build its first major manufacturing plant outside Germany in Spartanburg, South Carolina, it was attracted by the lower manufacturing labour costs – $17/hour (US) *vs.* $27 (Germany) and higher labour productivity, as measured by comparing 11 holidays (US) *vs.* 31 (Germany) (Heizer and Render, 2004). BMW's assessment was that the move would result in a lower cost per car of $2,000–3,000 as new plant and equipment increased productivity. There were lower wage costs in South Carolina and $135 million in state and local tax breaks were available as well as a free-trade zone from the airport to the plant.

The spatially variable location costs can be distinguished between tangible costs, such as transportation cost of raw materials, and intangible and future costs, such as attitude toward unions. Table 11.1 gives some further examples of such spatially variable costs. Part of the labour costs to be considered is not just the actual hourly rate but an assessment of productivity rates and absenteeism levels.

TABLE 11.1   SPATIALLY VARIABLE LOCATION COSTS

Tangible costs	Intangible costs
Transportation cost of raw materials	Attitudes towards unions
Shipment cost of finished goods	Quality of life
Energy and utility costs	Education expenditures by region/state
Labour costs	Quality of regional and local government
Raw materials	
Taxes	

Service location

Traditionally it has been considered that there are organizations that need to be close to their customers: such as government departments, fast food restaurants, super-markets, bakeries, dry cleaners, newsagents and some services like doctors, solicitors, accountants, barbers/hairdressers and banks. However, this depends on the nature of the service being delivered. Some government services can be delivered remotely and the physical location of the offices is not an issue. There is no real need for departments to be based in the capital close to the politicians. In the UK there has been a policy of moving certain agencies outside London and the South East to other parts of the country where the influx of jobs can aid regeneration. Wage rates are also cheaper in the north-east, for example, than in London so savings can be made on the labour costs. The Lyons' report of 2004 stated that:

> there should be a strongly enforced presumption against London and South East locations for new government bodies and activities; for functions such as back office work and call centres which do not need to be in London; and for bodies and functions whose effectiveness or authority would stand to be enhanced by a loca-tion outside London.

Certain factors will feature on the lists of all organizations choosing between poten-tial sites, others might be there to reflect a particular retailer's trading style. For instance, petrol retailers will be analysing a different checklist of factors to that of fashion retailers.

As stated earlier, the purpose of service location decisions is to identify where rev-enue can be maximized. McGoldrick (2002) reckoned location factors could be examined under four main headings: population, accessibility, competition and costs, and these certainly ensure that the key factors are considered.

Population

It is a truism to say that population is the major determinant of success but the basic building blocks of any analysis of service locations would be data on population size, the age profile, household size, income levels, disposable income per capita, occupation classifications, main employers, economic stability, unemployment levels, seasonal fluctuations, housing density, housing age/type, neighbourhood classification, housing ownership, building/regeneration plans, lifestyle measures, current shopping patterns, cultural/ethnic groupings.

Some of these data are available from the census but this has the drawback of rapidly becoming out of date, particularly for inner city areas where there is greater population mobility. GIS providers such as Experian or CACI are major providers of these data. Information in all these areas is sought because, for example, by itself income level is a poor indication of the spending power, actual and potential, within an area. Hence retailers are interested in information on disposable income and current spending habits which take account of family and mortgage commitments since this is what will determine the purchasing power of potential customers.

Accessibility

The key variables to be considered under this heading are driving times and parking provision. There may well be government planning advice about trying to increase the use of public transport which has to be factored in. Accessibility issues are also influenced by whether a visit to the proposed retail location is likely to be the primary purpose of a customer's journey or forms part of a multipurpose journey.

A key measure is the number of pedestrians moving past the proposed site. In any shopping centre development having the right anchor stores adjacent to the entrances will be crucial to manage customer circulation. Typically there is an imbalance in traffic flows between the upper and ground floors of a shopping centre. One way centre design managers can try to overcome this is to play around with the siting of some major entrances at the upper level. At the Meadowhall Centre in Sheffield the entrance from the Passenger Transport Interchange, where trains, buses and supertrams operate, is at the upper level (McGoldrick 2002). If your service derives a lot of its customer traffic from public transport then an analysis of the types currently and potentially available needs to be factored in, in any site evaluation.

Environmental concerns are having an impact on the acceptability of car usage and a range of measures to deter it have been introduced by a number of UK local authorities. These include priority bus lanes, high parking costs and the congestion charge in London. City authorities in the UK and other parts of Europe are following with interest all the issues concerning the implementation of congestion charging in London. As number plate recognition technology continues to improve, some form of road use charging may well be introduced.

Successful stores need to be visible. Sites that are not visible from outside the shopping centre or which are only accessible via escalators or subways will struggle to succeed despite their location.

Access is also an issue from the point of view of access for delivery vehicles. Local authorities may impose restrictions on loading times as a condition of planning permission.

Attributes also considered under the accessibility heading include security/lighting and the appearance/image of the location. The latter should complement the brand values being offered through this service location.

Competition

Competition may be both direct and indirect in the retail sector, but both need to be considered. The anchor stores in shopping centres, whether Sheffield's Meadowhall or The Mall, Ilford, may present competition to the proposed store but they are vital ingredients in the strategy of maintaining customer flow within and to the centre. Comparison shopping is quite common when it comes to clothing shops and department stores. Shoppers want to visit several stores on the single shopping trip so grouping similar stores together can be successful. Car showrooms are also often co-located.

The Meadowhall Centre has broken down its huge area into six distinctive areas such as The Arcade, anchored by a Marks & Spencer flagship store and comprising 44 stores over two levels. The theme here is on fashion and accessories. Park Lane is Meadowhall's exclusive area, with a select retail mix, anchored by House of Fraser, Next and Debenhams. Traditional names including Crabtree & Evelyn, Laura Ashley and Jaeger share Park Lane with designer boutiques such as Karen Miller. Major high street names including Bhs, H&M, Argos, Sports World and a large Mothercare, all situated in the Market Street area (http://www.meadowhall.co.uk/website/).

Part of the evaluation of alternative sites should include an analysis of trading strengths and weaknesses. You need to assume that competitors will respond to any new store opening and may well have their own development plans. A plan B and a plan C are necessary as well as plan A.

Costs

McGoldrick's fourth heading was costs. Likely turnover can be projected when the evaluation of population, accessibility and competition factors are combined. To be able to calculate profit potential requires you to calculate the likely development and running costs. These figures are produced after negotiations with developers or lease owners and from detailed estimations of construction or refurbishment costs. Site preparation may cost far more than the actual land costs: for example, decontamination of the Greenwich peninsula site for the Millenium Dome or the removal of waterlogged ashpits at the Gateshead MetroCentre site.

Multi-level stores need lifts and escalators, which will incur substantial maintenance costs. Locations with high crime rates push up the security costs for stores and the shrinkage rate through theft. These areas are most easily identified by their high insurance ratings.

The cost analysis should also consider the possible impact of the new outlet on existing branches.

Other factors that impact on costs are rent, management calibre, operations policies (such as hours/shift patterns and wage rates).

A poorly chosen site can lead to higher distribution and production costs and a lower than anticipated revenue stream. Location decisions are all about identifying the revenue potential of operations and minimizing the spatially variable costs of the operation. Convenience for the customer is a major determinant of customer contact and thereby revenue.

The assumptions made are that location is a major determinant of cost, that most major costs can be identified explicitly for each site. It is also assumed that low customer contact allows a focus on identifiable costs and that intangible costs can be evaluated.

Having collected all this information, the operations manager must analyse it and use it to make decisions; data for data's sake is just a waste of money.

TABLE 11.2 EXAMPLE OF FACTOR RATING METHOD

Factor	Factor weight	Factor score Location 1	Location 2	Weighted score Location 1	Location 2
Cost of living	10	5	2	50	20
Climate	30	2	5	60	150
Proximity to family	10	4	2	40	20
Good transport links	20	5	3	100	60
Quality of life	30	3	5	90	150
Total	100			340	400

Factor rating method

The most widely used location technique is the factor rating method. It works whether considering either service or industrial locations. Under this method factors are rated and then the scores for the locations under consideration are compared (see Table 11.2). Both tangible (quantitative) factors such as short-term and long-term costs and intangible (qualitative) factors such as education quality and labour skills can be compared using this technique. The steps to follow are:

- List all relevant factors.
- Assign importance weight to each factor (such as 0–1).
- Develop a scale for each factor (such as 1–100).
- Score each location using the factor scale.

- Multiply the scores by the weights for each factor and arrive at the total.
- Select the location with the maximum total score.

> *Over the past four years the author has observed various attempts to run a successful restaurant business in the London Borough where she lives. The selected site is on a main trunk road, close to the junction with the local High Street. A bus station and London Underground station are within 5 minutes' walk. Any footfall analysis of the area would have shown that there is a lot of pedestrian traffic past the shopfront.*
>
> *The restaurant has been aimed at a customer segment of those interested in eating out, wanting quality food, with both time and money to spare. It has gone through a number of relaunches, with changes in décor and name. My favourite was Appetito. Currently it is empty again.*
>
> *So why has it not worked out? One consideration in making location decisions is often referred to as suitability of the site. Here we had a site that found itself in the same road as a multitude of fast food restaurants. It always looked out of place, given that its position alongside a multitude of fastfried chicken outlets did not support the brand values of a sit-down restaurant with tablecloths on each table.*
>
> *Private car parking was very difficult, no off-road parking facilities were provided and there were severe restrictions on street parking.*
>
> *The menu offered was what passed for sophistication in the 1980's. It is an object lesson in that the menu offered and the price charged have to complement each other and be appropriate for the chosen target market. The selected site has to reinforce these values not undermine them.*
>
> *Successful restaurants are often located adjacent to each other. Potential customers can compare menus and prices. While a restaurant is building up its reputation, it is dependent on passing traffic. Being located in a known restaurant quarter rather than in a line of fast food outlets is more likely to attract the right type of clientele.*

Locational breakeven analysis

A breakeven analysis will show the amount of sales revenue necessary for a given situation to cover the costs of the operation. Costs are divided into fixed costs, i.e. those costs that will not change no matter how many sales are made, and variable costs, which are those costs that increase or decrease in line with the sales activity. The breakeven analysis technique is commonly used for industrial locations.

The steps to follow are:

- Determine the fixed and variable costs for each location.
- Plot the total cost for each location (Cost on vertical axis, Annual Volume on horizontal axis).
- Identify ranges of output for which each location has the lowest total cost.
- Solve algebraically for the breakeven points over the identified ranges.
- Select the location with lowest total cost for expected production volume.

Remember the breakeven equations used for calculation of total cost of each location and for calculating the breakeven quantity Q.

- Total cost = F + cQ
- Total revenue = pQ
- Breakeven is where Total Revenue = Total Cost

The suitable choice of location is the one above the breakeven point.

Centre-of-gravity method

This method sets out to identify the location of a *single* distribution centre which will serve several destinations. It is used primarily for services and considers the location of existing destinations, e.g. retailers, the volume to be shipped, the shipping distance (or cost). It involves placing existing locations on a coordinate grid. The grid has an arbitrary origin and scale. It maintains relative distances. The X and Y coordinates have to be calculated for 'centre of gravity'. Thus it generates the location of the distribution centre in such a way as to minimize transportation cost.

Place existing locations on a coordinate grid. Calculate X and Y coordinates for 'centre of gravity'.

X coordinate =

$$C_x = \frac{\sum_i d_{ix} V_i}{\sum_i V_i}$$

dix = x coordinate of location i

Vi = volume of goods moved to or from location i

diy = y coordinate of location i

Y coordinate =

$$C_y = \frac{\sum_i d_{iy} V_i}{\sum_i V_i}$$

Plot X and Y coordinates on the grid. This should give the minimum cost location.

Transportation model

This model sets out to find the optimal amount to be shipped from *several* sources to several destinations which will minimize those shipping costs. It is used primarily for industrial locations. It is a form of linear programming model. Linear programming finds the best solutions to problems that can be formulated mathematically. The objective is to minimize total production and transport costs. The constraints are production capacity at source (factory) and the demand requirement at destination. The transportation costs are recalculated for each location-capacity combination under consideration. The transportation method is often used to evaluate the cost impact of adding potential location sites to the existing network of facilities. It can also be used in an evaluation of the option of adding more than one new site to a network or of a complete redesign of the network.

The transportation method finds the best shipping pattern between plants and warehouses for a particular set of plant locations. However, distribution costs are only one element to be taken into account in evaluating potential location options.

Geographic Information Systems (GIS)

Geographic Information Systems enable the combination of many parameters. More and more retailers are making use of Geographical Information Systems to help find the most suitable locations. Object-oriented GIS products allow planners to link dynamically the spatial information stores in their maps to data stored in other IT systems such as customer databases or enterprise planning systems. These systems can create intelligent maps which can analyse the factors that affect location such as journey times, catchment areas and distance from competitors.

Tesco takes Ordnance Survey maps and then adds data about routes and speed limits, direction and location or one-way streets and how junctions are controlled. Ten different demographic models based on information from census, commercial databases and their loyalty card database can be run simultaneously and results plotted on the GIS.

Traffic management systems and optimization programmes for good delivery all use GIS applications. CACI, which was one of the pioneers in developing a computerized database from the census, have gone on to develop a number of products aimed at retail location analysis. Their Shopping Centre Planner is a tool to identify competition in an area and can provide an insight into suitable areas. Experian has developed a system for classifying residential neighbourhoods using a fusion of a number of different data sources.

A study of location techniques used by 100 retailers by Hernandez and Bennison (2000) found that most preferred to use experience or 'gut feel' and checklists: techniques that have the merit of being low cost as well as low tech. The same study also identified a growth in the use of GIS.

Having chosen the best location for your business in terms of costs and customer convenience the next decision to be taken is the design of the layout of the premises.

Layout

Consideration of possible layout designs for an operation are tied up with considerations about what sort of process is being organized. In terms of manufacturing processes there are project processes, jobbing processes, batch processes, mass process, continuous or line process. The differing ways of organizing production processes are dictated to by the volume of their output and how varied that output is. In the services sector we tend to talk of professional services, such as legal, tax advice or mass services. It could be argued that service shops mimic the batch production of manufacturing. In jobbing or project processes the finished goods output is small. Bespoke tailoring, made to measure, is one example. It is common where there is a high degree of customization. Batch production, as the name suggests, is organized around batch or lot sizes which are of moderate volume. Line, continuous or mass production exists where there is a high volume of standardized finished goods. Examples of this would include beer production, most chemical production, volume car manufacturing assembly plants and oil production.

Effective layout designs can avoid bottlenecks and accidents occurring from safety hazards. Basic designs are:

- Process layout
  Machines or workstations are grouped by the process they perform
- Product layout
  Workstations are organized in a linear sequence to produce a specific end product
- Fixed position layout
  Used in projects where the product cannot be moved
- Cellular or hybrid layout
  A mixed form of layout

There are three principles which govern layout decisions for the operation. The first is to optimize the physical flow of people or materials. The second is to minimize congestion wherever possible and the third is to maximize the use of space.

Reducing movements can minimize the need for materials handling equipment. Reducing movements of customers can result in fewer accidents as people do not have the chance to maintain their confidentiality. In some settings such as supermarkets, of course, it makes sound business sense to revamp which product lines belong where in the latest reorganization. Supermarket layout designers seek to come up with a design that forces customers to travel up each aisle of the proposed location. This exposes them to more merchandise as they are forced to vary their normal route round the store. Of consideration is how best to facilitate the entry, exit and placement of materials and people within the operation. Can efficient materials handling reduce manufacturing cycle time or customer service time? Good layout designers will examine the impact their design will have on materials handling so as to eliminate wasted or redundant movements.

Congestion can lead to queuing, which is a non-value-adding activity. Time spent waiting in a queue does not add to sales and may result in customers balking at the queue and leaving.

Good operations layout can facilitate communication and interaction between workers, between workers and their supervisors, or between workers and customers. This aids the delivery of high quality products and services. Safety and security considerations are also incorporated into layout design. The positioning of alcohol products in a supermarket setting requires a balancing between materials handling issues and security.

In business, time and space means money, so it is important to make the best use of the space available. Design the layout so more space is given to customer, front office, activities and less to back office functions.

Fixed position layout

This design is suited for a stationary project, where the project is too delicate to move. Under this design workers and equipment come to the site. Physical limitations as to the worth of the contract vary in their impact. There are two key complicating factors: limited space at site and changing material needs. In fact all sites have some physical constraints in terms of space, and different items become crucial as the construction process goes through various phases. Open heart surgery would come under the 'too delicate to move' category. Another example of a fixed position layout would be shipbuilding or aircraft manufacture; the product may not be delicate but it is certainly too large to move and requires that materials and staff are brought to it rather than the other way round.

Equipment may well be left on-site because it is too expensive to move frequently. Workers on such job sites are highly skilled at performing the special tasks that they are requested to do. In fixed position layouts the fixed costs would be low and variable costs would be high.

Process layout

This layout design is used where there are departments or production phases with large flows of material or people together. Operations of a similar nature are grouped together. For example, department areas having similar processes are located in close proximity, for example, all X-ray machines in the same area. Examples of process layout can be found in hotels, supermarkets and warehouses. Workers are skilled at operating their department's equipment. Where companies are producing customized, low volume products these may require different processing requirements and sequences of operations which are going to be best dealt with through a process layout.

The chosen layout has to cope with the varied processing requirements. Its flexibility is a big advantage. It is not particularly susceptible to equipment failures. Usually the equipment employed is less costly. Workers get to perform a variety of tasks on several machines, which is a positive contrast to the boredom of performing a repetitive task on an assembly line. It is possible to use individual incentive plans under this design.

The disadvantage of this design is that the in-process inventory costs can be high. Using this design makes challenging demands on routing and scheduling of both materials and labour. Utilization rates are low. Back-tracking is common. Materials handling sometimes requires specialist equipment such as conveyor belts to transport heavy and bulky items. Some materials are so delicate that frequent handling could result in a deterioration in their condition. Material handling under this layout tends to be more inefficient and slower.

Product layout

In the product-oriented layout the operation is self-evidently organized around the product. The design aims to reduce any line imbalances or delays between workstations. In a product layout standardized processing operations are used to achieve high volume flows of finished goods. This is the layout design chosen when the operations are continuous or repetitive processing. Examples are: fabrication line and assembly line. This design minimizes floor space. The classic example of the self-service fast food outlet such as one might find at a motorway service station sees the person being served moving from one phase to the next.

Line balancing occurs where tasks are assigned to workstations in such a way that the workstations have approximately equal time requirements.

A high rate of output is possible using this design. The high degree of utilization of labour and equipment and the high volume of output leads to the low unit cost. Under this design it is also possible to have a degree of specialization among the workforce; the reduced training time that results leads to lower costs. The routing and scheduling of materials and labour is easier under a product layout.

The disadvantages are clear and reflect what we said in Chapter 3 about the design of certain jobs. All too often under a product layout the division of labour results in dull, repetitive jobs. There can be a danger that a poorly motivated workforce with perhaps inadequate skills will not maintain their equipment or the quality of output. Not surprisingly, since this is a layout designed for mass production operations, it lacks the flexibility to respond to changes in volume. This sort of production is also highly susceptible to shutdowns. Preventative maintenance, which is needed under many quality management programmes and under Just-in-Time, is difficult to organize under a product layout. It is more difficult under this system to implement individual incentive plans.

Hybrid or cellular layout

It is difficult to follow a single layout design in all circumstances. A mixed form of layout may be more appropriate for a restaurant, for example. Pizza Hut, the franchise pizza restaurant chain, follows this sort of mixed format. There is a buffet self-service salad area, also used for lunchtime selections, which is a product layout and an at-table service is also offered which would be classified as process layout. Within a number of stores it is quite common to see a cellular layout displayed, for example all lunchtime products being grouped together, from sandwiches to salads, to drinks to snacks.

A cell layout tends to be a product layout being treated carefully as part of a larger process design. The design consists of *different* machines brought together to make a product. Some argue that this is a temporary arrangement only. Examples of low cost differentiation are a specialist process manufacturing cell or internal audit group in a bank. The shop within a shop cell layout is quite common. In manufacturing, machines are grouped into a cell that can process items that have similar processing requirements.

In planning service layouts the aesthetic appeal for customers and the need to incorporate spatial clues for customers have to be factored in to the design. Physical surroundings affect the behaviour of both customers and staff.

In office layouts the aim is to optimize the physical transfer of information (paperwork). Communication also can be enhanced through the use of low-rise partitions and glass walls. When designing the layout of warehouse facilities, for example, the same principle of minimizing materials handling holds true. Using Pareto principles it is straightforward to identify which items are ordered most frequently. These should then be placed close together near the entrance of the facility, while those ordered less frequently remain in the rear of the facility. Since 20% of the items typically represent 80% of the items ordered, it is not difficult to determine which 20% to place in the most convenient location. In this way, layout enables order picking to be more efficient.

SUMMARY OF KEY POINTS

- Facility location factors influence both the costs of the operation and customer service. Factors influencing costs are supply side factors: labour costs, land costs, energy costs, transportation costs and quality of life factors. Factors influencing customer service are demand side factors: suitability of the actual site, the image of the location, the available labour skills and convenience for customers.
- An existing operation should relocate only when the costs and disruption of moving are less than the benefits it will gain from its new location.
- The weighted factor scoring method takes a range of considerations into account when choosing a location. The method works whether considering either service or industrial locations. It is the most widely used method and can take account of both tangible and intangible factors.
- To identify a location that minimizes distribution costs the centre of gravity method is used. This method sets out to identify the best location for a *single* distribution centre which will serve several destinations and minimize transportation costs.
- A breakeven analysis will show the amount of sales revenue necessary for a given situation to cover the costs of the operation. This is usually done in conjunction with one of the other location analysis techniques.
- The transportation model is based on linear programming and is used to determine an allocation pattern that will minimize the cost of transporting products from two or more plants, or sources of supply, to two or more warehouses, or destinations. Its focus on transportation costs is a useful input to a location analysis but only gives a partial insight into location factors.
- There are four basic types of layout design: process layout – machines or workstations are grouped by the process they perform; product layout – workstations are organized in a linear sequence to produce a specific end product; fixed position layout – used in projects where the product cannot be moved; cellular or hybrid layout – a mixed form of layout.

STUDENT ACTIVITY 11.1

1   Imagine that you are planning a location for a new pizza restaurant.
   What sort of information do you need to inform your decision?
   Where will you get this information?
   What decision-making techniques will you use to decide between alternative locations?
2   Investigate the location decisions taken by the Hard Rock Café chain.
   What factors do they take into account in making their decisions?
   Is their strategy successful and why?

FURTHER READING

Clarke I. and Rowley J. (1995) 'A case for spatial decision support systems in retail location planning', *International Journal of Retail and Distribution Management*, 23 (3): 4–10.

Hernandez T. and Bennison D. (2000) 'The art and science of retail location decisions', *International Journal of Retail and Distribution Management*, 28 (8): 357–67.

Heizer J. and Render B. (2004) *Principles of Operations Management*, 7th edn. Upper Saddle River, NJ: Prentice Hall.

McGoldrick P. (2002) *Retail Marketing*, 2nd edn. New York: McGraw Hill.

Salvaneschi L. and Akin C. (eds) (1996) *Location, Location, Location: How to Select the Best Site for Your Business*. Gilmour Drummord Publishing.

Waters C.D.J. (1999) *Global Logistics and Distribution Planning*. London: Kogan Page.

www.meadowhall.co.uk/website/images/RetrieveAsset.aspx?AssetDocument ID=2015 (accessed 15 February 2006).

12 MANAGING CAPACITY AND VARIATIONS IN DEMAND

We need to understand what is the operational capacity of an organization so we can plan it properly. Capacity issues form an integral part of operations strategy. In this chapter we will be considering short to medium-term capacity issues. These are about ensuring that we have sufficient capacity of the right type available to meet demand for the planning period. Variations in demand will affect the use we make of that capacity.

LEARNING OUTCOMES

When you have completed this chapter you should be able to:

- Define capacity.
- Evaluate strategies for reconciling capacity and demand.
- Understand approaches to demand management in services.

Capacity

Capacity planning can mean different things to different people. Clearly, agreeing on a common, formal definition of the process is key to the design and implementation of an effective capacity planning programme. Here's an example of such a definition:

A process to predict the types, quantities, and timing of critical resource capacities that are needed within an infrastructure to meet accurately forecasted workloads.

Planning capacity requires the operations manager:

- To measure capacity
- To measure demand
- To evaluate alternative methods of reconciling capacity and demand and select the appropriate one.

TABLE 12.1 EXAMPLES OF MEASURING CAPACITY

Type of business	Input measures of capacity	Output measures of capacity
Hospital	Beds available	Number of patients treated per week
Beer producer	Volume of fermentation tanks	Litres produced per week
University	Number of students	Students graduated per year
Retailer	Floor space in square metres	Sales per square metre
Car manufacturer	Labour hours	Cars per shift

We usually use the word capacity in the sense of the space in a building, the volume of a container for example. An operations manager will talk of a multiplex cinema with 20 screens and a total seating capacity of 3,000, or of the maximum tonnes of output from a factory. These measures draw attention to the scale of operations but do not reflect processing capacities as long as they do not take account of time. Hence, capacity can be described as the 'throughput', or number of units a facility can hold, receive, store, or produce in a period of time. For example, a car park may only be fully occupied during the working day when it is used by office workers. Slack et al. (2004) define capacity as the maximum level of value added activity achievable over a period of time under normal operating conditions. Capacity can be expressed in terms of inputs or outputs, as in a retail store that has an input measure of sales floor area and an output of number of items sold per day; a brewery counts the volume of its tanks as an input measure, the output is then the number of litres brewed per week (see Table 12.1).

The output and capacity have to be in the same terms, e.g. units or customers etc. Product-focused firms talk about outputs, e.g. barrels of beer per year, car plants about 1,500 cars per day capacity. A service like a restaurant might consider how many sit-down and how many take-away customers it can cater for, then it can plan for the best combination.

How do we measure demand?

The first stage of capacity planning will be measuring demand. For operations managers this means having to deal with forecasts of demand which may well be inaccurate. In many organizations it is the sales or marketing department which is responsible for demand forecasting. However, since such forecasts form an essential ingredient in capacity planning the operations manager needs to understand the basis of such demand forecasts.

Forecasts need to be expressed in terms that can be used for capacity planning and control rather than only expressed in monetary terms. The aim is a forecast that gives some idea of the demands to be placed on the operation's capacity. Given that there will be a time delay for any operation between deciding to change capacity and that change taking effect no matter how flexible the operation is, it is important that the forecast is as accurate as possible. In some cases operations managers are called on to decide output in advance in an attempt to meet a demand forecast that might change before the demand occurs or, worse, prove not to reflect actual demand at all. Forecast levels of demand can lead the operations manager to recruit extra staff or put on extra shifts, yet if the forecast differs considerably from the actual demand unnecessary costs can be incurred or unsatisfactory customer service. So the operations manager will want to know what the limits to the forecast certainty are, i.e. being able to work out that there is a 5% chance of demand being higher than this and only a 5% chance of demand being lower than this.

> *In 1982 a new English soft blue cheese, called Lymeswold, was launched on to the UK food market. Clever marketing made the launch a success. Unfortunately, the brand owners, the Milk Marketing Board, interpreted those initial high sales as indicative of long-term demand for the cheese and expanded its capacity to produce Lymeswold. When those initial sales petered out, the unsustainable surplus capacity affected the cost base for the product adversely.*

Forecasting

So how will these projections of future demand be generated? There are qualitative forecasting, the quantitative approach and the causal approach. In most forecasts we are using the past to help us predict the future. It is therefore a matter of judgement to decide which past events are relevant to the future.

It has to be acknowledged that there is no way to state what the future will be with complete certainty, and regardless of the methods used there will always be an element of uncertainty until the forecast horizon has come to pass. Completely new technologies for which there are no existing paradigms tend to be off the radar screen and therefore are not be forecastable, creating a blind spot in the forecast.

Qualitative forecasting Using qualitative techniques requires judgement, past experience and existing past and current data. The most commonly used methods of qualitative forecast are:

- Expert opinion
- Market surveys
- Life cycle analysis
- Time series forecasting.

One of the most successful forms of expert opinion is the Delphi method. It is best used by large organizations due to its cost and time-consuming nature. The Delphi method was developed by the Rand Corporation and named after the ancient Greek oracle. Under this method a set of questions are put to a group of managers, or experts, who then give their individual opinion as they work without collusion. A coordinator then collates the answers and if there is a significant difference the results are fed back to the panel with a further set of questions. No names are revealed to prevent panel members being overly influenced by the reputation of certain contributors. The process is repeated until consensus is reached. Generally questions continue for four rounds with the questions becoming more specific with each round. The advantage of this method is that a group opinion is obtained without the need to actually bring the panel together physically. It has the advantage of being able to maximize the use of a geographically dispersed panel and avoid group dynamics and team-think, persuading group members in particular directions. The downside is that there can be a tendency for the feedback questions to force a convergence towards the group centre.

Other examples of expert methods are to obtain the views of the sales force and to establish a jury of executives. Sales force opinions tend to be influenced by recent events and be over-optimistic. Using the jury of executives approach, the estimates from a panel of company experts are averaged out. The positive side of expert opinion approaches is the making use of the experience and judgement of several experts. The negative side is the danger of the panel being swayed by a single dominant person.

Market surveys are a source of qualitative data which are best used to determine aspects of a new service or to find out why an existing service is not performing as it should. They are generally not used for forecasting demand for capacity management.

Many products and services have a time-based life cycle. Few sales are experienced at the launch stage, there is a rapid increase in customers at the growth stage and demand is relatively stable at the maturity stage. Life cycle analysis involves an assessment of a product's position on the life cycle. Experienced managers in the fast-moving consumer goods or fashion sector can predict how long a fashion item will stay at each stage of the life cycle, thereby enabling plans to be made to stockpile items in anticipation of a spurt in demand at the growth stage.

Quantitative forecasting Time series forecasting takes demand data from a few past time periods and projects those patterns into the future. It is based on the assumption that future behaviour is a function of the past. The simplest way is to take last period's actual demand and use that as the forecast for the next period's demand. Fine if the trend is upward; the forecast will be going in the same direction, just lagging behind a bit. On the other hand, if there happens to be distinct seasonal variations in the demand pattern it will be an inaccurate forecast.

It is also possible to average past results. The accuracy of the method can then be tested by measuring its deviation from the actual. The moving average forecast provides a reasonable response to trends and dampens fluctuations. It is a matter of judgement as to the number of periods that should be used for averaging. Examining the pattern of demand will identify whether there are definite cycles and if so the number of periods in the cycle can be used to determine the number of periods for averaging. The drawback to the moving average method is that equal weight is given to each of the historical figures used and it is necessary to have a history of data to test against and to forecast from. New factors in the future may throw the forecast out.

Other quantitative methods are: exponential smoothing (single exponential smoothing, double exponential smoothing); a type of weighted moving average that allows inclusion of trends, etc.; mathematical models (trend lines, log–linear models, Fourier series, etc.); linear or non–linear models fitted to time-series data, usually by regression methods and Box–Jenkins methods; autocorrelation methods used to identify underlying time series and to fit the 'best' model.

Causal method   The purpose of a forecast is to predict what might happen in the future. So consideration is given to what is happening or is likely to happen in the economy, which will impact on demand. Indicators such as interest rates, inflation rates, saving rates, employment rates, the entrance of new competitors and planned marketing campaigns will have causal effects on future results. It is important to know the causes for changes in demand levels. The causal model explores the relationship between variables affecting demand, e.g. lawn mower sales and new housing starts, advertising budget and competitors' prices. Multiple regression analysis is used to model complex systems involving relationships between two or more variables.

Understanding the demand pattern

There is some seasonality of demand for most products and services. As suggested earlier, capacity planning is about adjusting to those seasonal demand fluctuations. There used to be seasonality of supply for seasonal agriculture products but now in a global market place supermarkets source their salads, soft fruits, other vegetables etc. so they are available all year round, no matter what the season in the UK.

Possible causes of seasonality are climatic, festive, behavioural, political, financial and social factors (Slack et al. 2004). It is well to understand the causes because it may be possible to influence some of them.

While seasonality of demand is apparent over the year there is also the question of whether the demand for the service is consistent throughout the day, or week. Banks, supermarkets, even electricity utilities have weekly, daily, even hourly demand fluctuations that require capacity adjustments. How long an organization's customers are prepared to wait for their products or services affects the extent to which an operation has to cope with short-term demand fluctuations. (see Figure 12.1)

Take as an example the tube trains in London. The London Underground can do very little to alter its demand pattern. It can alter prices at times when demand is lower (travel cards), it can promote flexitime working in order to try to spread the load or it can promote trips to the theatre or to London sights to attract tourists, who tend to travel out of rush hour. It can also attempt to park some of the trains at times of lower demand, as long as large numbers of trains do not end up at either end of the line. Another approach is to undertake maintenance and judge the success of that by the number of trains that are back in service by 4.30 in the afternoon, before rush hour gets

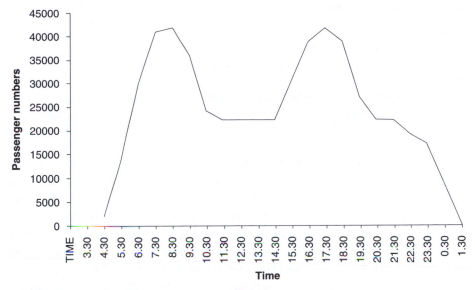

FIGURE 12.1   VARIATION IN HOURLY DEMAND FOR A LINE ON LONDON UNDERGROUND

under way. The supply of trains could be increased at rush hour, if the trains could operate closer together. This would require a heavy investment in computerized signalling.

Design capacity and effective capacity

Design capacity is the theoretical output of an operation which its designers had in mind when they commissioned the operation. This is rarely achieved due to a combination of planned and unplanned factors. Planned factors include maintenance, training and machine setup time whose timing can be determined in advance but, of course, while these are happening the output from the operation is lost. Losing output like this can be minimized by operations managers adopting the technique of undertaking as much of the setup process as possible while the operation is still in use. Similarly, training of personnel can be scheduled when seasonal demand is low. Effective capacity is that remaining after planned factors such as maintenance and training have caused a loss of output. Unplanned factors that impact on capacity are machine breakdowns, quality problems and absenteeism. This means that the actual capacity achieved is lower still than the design or effective capacity once the planned and unplanned factors are taken into account. Preventative maintenance will have a role in preventing or minimizing machine breakdowns. Looking at job design and how to improve motivation could impact on worker absenteeism.

Two measures often used in relation to these capacity measures are utilization and efficiency. Utilization is the proportion of time a process is in actual use compared with its design capacity. Efficiency measures the proportion of time a process is in use compared with its effective capacity (see Table 12.2).

TABLE 12.2 CAPACITY PLANNING

Design capacity
    The maximum output rate under ideal conditions
    A bakery can make 30 customized cakes a day when pushed at holiday time
Effective capacity
    Maximum output rate under normal (realistic) conditions
    On average this bakery can make 20 customized cakes per day

---

Utilization is a key measure of the performance of the operation. Different sectors may refer to utilization by different names such as room occupancy level in hotels, load factor for aircraft seats or uptime in some factories. In many businesses high utilization levels are necessary before investment in additional capacity is authorized. Yet low utilization levels can be a result of plant breakdowns, running out of materials, or low demand. There is also the case that an emphasis on high utilization in batch type operations is likely to lead to a build-up in process inventory. Also if the emphasis on utilization reduces the speed and volume flexibility of the operation this can have a detrimental impact on customers.

Benchmarking the organization's utilization and efficiency ratios against others in the sector will give a good insight into its performance.

Capacity management strategies

Having examined the influences on demand and understood the effectiveness and utilization of capacity, the operations manager needs to consider alternative methods of responding to demand fluctuations. There are three options available for dealing with such variations:

- **Level capacity plan** – ignore the fluctuations and keep activity levels constant.
- **Chase demand plan** – adjust capacity to reflect the variations in demand.
- **Demand management** – attempt to change demand to fit capacity availability.

Business realities mean that most organizations use a mixture of all these pure plans, although quite often one plan might dominate.

One of the most difficult aspects in planning is caused by variation in demand for products and services. Much of the literature on operations management tells the reader to optimize production but this is rarely possible due to the varying demand throughout the year, week or even day that customers want to buy a product or use a service. This becomes obvious as soon as one looks at particular types of product.

Level capacity plan

Let us consider the theoretical possibility of **level capacity plans**. Adopting a level capacity plan sets the processing capacity at a uniform level throughout the planning period despite fluctuations in forecast demand. Under this plan the same number of staff using the same equipment, operating the same processes, should be able to produce the same aggregate output in each planning period. This then requires output to be transferred to finished goods inventory until such time as demand improves and sales occur. In this way output is set at a fixed rate on the understanding that inventory is used to absorb variations in demand. The obvious drawback to such plans is the increase in the cost of holding inventory and the cost of discarding any perishable items. Firms using this plan prioritize creating inventory where future sales are relatively certain and not susceptible to sudden changes in fashion. Level capacity plans can result in stable employment, high process utilization, high productivity and low unit costs.

Since service organizations cannot store their output as inventory, a level capacity plan requires running at a uniformly high level of capacity. This has the drawback of high costs as staff resources are wasted as the staffing necessary to service all the rooms, run a full restaurant etc. are employed despite demand being forecast to be well below capacity.

Many service organizations can find level capacity plans too expensive because of the high under-utilization levels, yet feel they have to adopt them because of even higher opportunity costs of lost sales, e.g. estate agents or the high-margin end of jewellery retailing. Attempts to staff at levels just below the forecast peak demand may improve the utilization rate but can result in poorer customer service and queues when that peak demand is experienced.

Chase demand

Chase demand is the name given to the plan that attempts to match capacity closely with the varying levels of forecast demand. Such a plan is very demanding for the operations manager since it requires different working hours, different staffing levels, different amounts of equipment in each period. Given this, such plans do not suit operations that manufacture standard, non-perishable products in large volumes. Pure chase demand plans are adopted by organizations that cannot store their output such as customer processing operations. The wasteful provision of excess staff that occurs in a level capacity plan is avoided.

The chase demand approach requires that capacity is adjusted. Not all methods of doing so are suitable for all types of operations. This has sometimes been written of as 'flexing' the capacity.

Hire and layoff, or to put it more delicately, varying the size of the workforce, is achieved by hiring extra staff during periods of peak demand and then laying them off as demand falls. In the agriculture sector seasonal employment like this is common. There are considerable costs associated with this tactic. The obvious one is the cost of recruitment, then there are the costs of low productivity while new staff are recruited and trained. Laying staff off may result in the need for severance payments as well as having an adverse impact on staff morale. Then there is the ethical consideration, in treating fellow human beings as a commodity in this way.

Overtime or idletime: usually the quickest way to extend capacity is to vary the number of productive hours worked by staff. When demand is higher than the capacity the workforce may be asked to work an extended day and when the demand is lower the amount of time spent by staff on productive work can be reduced as staff are switched into cleaning or maintenance. Costs come from overtime payments that are necessary to secure staff's agreement to work extra hours or the costs of paying staff who are not engaged in productive work.

Recruiting staff to work on a part-time or temporary basis ensures that extra staffing resources are available at the times when there is an increase in demand. Such staff work less than a normal working day. Service operations such as fast food restaurants, supermarkets and other retailers use this method extensively. In some circumstances manufacturers use this method to staff an evening shift after the normal working day. Organizations have to weigh up whether the fixed costs of employment for each employee are so high that this method may not be worthwhile. Use of such staff gives the opportunity to develop greater flexibility in the schedule and to smooth the work demand.

Subcontractors can provide additional capacity to meet the forecast demand. One example of how additional capacity is obtained from external sources is the use made of doctors' deputizing services to provide on-call cover over the weekend.

Multiskilled staff increases flexibility in capacity decisions. In a hospital setting it might be desirable to have some floating capacity which can be shifted from one department to another if the number of patients or the amount of nursing attention required varies. In a supermarket setting multiskilled staff may be shelf filling as well as able to operate checkouts and moved from one task to another in response to peak demands.

Likewise, if you can *predict* that there are times when you are not so busy, spare labour is available and so you can schedule other work for these people, such as drawing up your demand curve for the year. This happens in Post Offices where, during busy times, back room staff help out on the front desk.

Demand management

For those who work mainly in the service sector and with services the problem is even more difficult, as services cannot be stored. The demand here changes by the hour. Because you cannot store services you must try to make the supply match the demand. The same rules apply, try to meet demand or alter demand – but by the hour.

A key tool in demand management is **varying the price**, offering discounts in times of low demand to stimulate demand and increasing prices for those times when demand is higher than the capacity limit.

Advertising and other promotional activities can be employed to boost sales during low demand periods.

Introducing an **appointment system** would achieve a uniform utilization of the service capacity despite the pattern of demand variations over the long term. The point of an appointment system is to be able to move demand into available time slots. Any delay between requesting an appointment and the actual time of the appointment depends on the backlog or queue of waiting work.

Existing processes can be used to make or sell **alternative products** during low demand periods. Garden centres sell Christmas trees and decorations at a time when traditional gardening activity is low. Universities fill their accommodation and lecture halls with conferences and company events during vacation periods. Ski resorts develop mountain activity holidays to be taken during the summer period. Snow mobiles and tractors are complementary products.

A city wine bar has far more options. They can open for early breakfasts for workers and later breakfasts for tourists. In the afternoon they can offer teas for tourists and in the evening meals and snacks for theatre-goers, before and after the performance. 'Happy hours' are quite common, where drinks are reduced in price, at times of the day when customers are few. Customers can be encouraged to stay later if entertainment is held, such as music or quizzes. Having some 'slack' in the system can also be a good thing, as quiet times are useful to allow the place to be tidied up, cleaned and the shelves restocked.

The demand variation at a hairdresser's shop tends to be over the week, with Friday and Saturdays being the busy days. Demand may be so low on Mondays that many hairdressers stay closed.

The key is to plan. With any example start by considering the following:

- How does work come in?
- How much is expected (planned) and how much is unexpected breakdowns?
- What happens to the demand in winter, summer?
- By what time must work be completed?
- Do certain parts break down more than others?
- Can you divide typical jobs into three broad types and how long do these three types take?

If you can identify all the likely factors that affect demand you can then enter them on a 'calendar' or chart. This will show you when you are most busy and also times when you are less busy. If you then see that there are times when you cannot cope, you can call for help *early enough* for something to be done about it.

Yield management

Yield management is an approach to revenue maximization. It is the use of demand techniques aimed at maximizing customer revenue in service organizations. It is a system designed to maximize revenue for capacity-constrained services by using reservation systems, overbooking, price manipulation and partitioning demand.

Yield management works best where there is relatively fixed capacity, an ability to segment the markets, perishable inventory, a product that can be sold in advance, fluctuating demand, low marginal sales costs and high marginal capacity change costs.

Given the perishable nature of airline seats – once the flight has departed the potential revenue from selling seats on it is gone forever – offering a discount to fill the aircraft becomes attractive. Of course if all seats are offered at a discount then you do yourself out of the opportunity to sell some at full price. Yield management attempts to allocate fixed capacity of seats on a flight to match potential demand in various market segments in the most profitable manner.

Overbooking happens because the organization knows that not every passenger who has booked a seat on a flight will actually show up, not every patient will attend for their appointment with their doctor. Airlines regularly book more passengers on flights than the number of seats. If they overbook by the exact number of passengers who fail to turn up then they have succeeded in maximizing their revenue. If more passengers turn up than expected some will be extremely irate at not being able to fly out as planned. Airlines have strategies in place to deal with these contingencies, such as offering financial inducements to take another flight.

Organizations using yield management such as Holiday Inn, airlines, restaurants etc. use specialized software that helps do the calculations, for example the **critical fractile model**. This is the cumulative probability of demand formed by the ratio of the cost of underestimating demand divided by the sum of the costs of underestimating demand and overestimating demand.

The yield management optimization equation used by Holiday Inn looks at seasonal occupancy patterns, local events, weekly cycles and current trends to develop a hurdle price – the lowest point at which rooms should be booked at that hotel. The software system predicts full occupancy and filters out discounted requests. It helps management balance the ability to charge full price for a room and still maintain satisfaction from a loyal customer base.

Generally yield management is used to anticipate when temporary demand and capacity imbalances will occur. Yield management as practised by American Airlines is a mixed strategy because the company integrates supply and demand management using the information contained in its computer reservation system. So it has a real time ability to sell a class of service to the right customer at the appropriate time and the most competitive price.

Managing queues

Time spent queuing is time wasted forever.

Hall (1991)

With a tangible product, such as cars, if you do not sell them today they will be available for sale tomorrow, but with services this usually is not the case – if a hotel room is not booked, that day's 'profit' is lost. What is more, 'stock', in the service sector, is often people queuing, and people do not like to queue: the customers start to moan and then they seek an alternative supplier.

Queues may form in the operations process of materials, work in progress, or customers … Queues form bottlenecks – where the next process is working at a slower rate and cannot keep pace with the arrival of materials, components or customers. (Bedward et al. 1997)

The operations manager has a major responsibility in providing the most efficient and effective service to the customer and in satisfying their demand through the point of sale. However, Johnston and Clark (2001: 4) expands this responsibility to encompass operations management being concerned not only with the actual process itself, but also with the people and resources necessary in order for the process to be regarded as successful. As such, for operations to be regarded as successful, an over-demand of customers may create an uncontrollable situation and be non-preferred. This view is in contrast to the position sought by the marketing manager whose major responsibility is creating the maximum demand for their product or service, which will mean 'getting the customers in and retaining them'.

Why do we have queues. Well queues form as a consequence of poor scheduling, badly designed systems, the system reaching saturation, irregular patterns of customer arrival and unknown service times. Analytic queuing models do not closely match the real situation of interest although they do have the advantage of being simpler and less costly than simulation methods. Analytic queuing models may be used to obtain the first approximation to a queuing problem or to make low cost analysis.

Characteristics of queuing consist of the source population, whether it is finite or infinite. With an infinite population, the customer pool is so large that subtractions or additions to the pool do not significantly affect the system probabilities. The second consideration is the way customers arrive at the service facility. Is the pattern controllable or uncontrollable? The queue or physical line itself, should it be organized in a single line or multiple lines? Then there is the question of how customers are selected from the line, is it first come first served or emergencies first or customer behaviour in the queue? Selection from the line should be on the basis of a policy which is seen as fair by users. Then consideration is given to the characteristics of the service facility itself, in terms of how many channels and servers are required to meet the forecast customer demands. Service systems are usually classified in terms of their number of channels (i.e. the number of servers) and the number of phases (i.e. the number of service stops that have to be made). Do all customers await their turn patiently? Human nature being what it is, it is likely that some customers arrive, see the queue and depart without ever joining it because they cannot abide queuing. Some customers will join the queue but lose patience before they get to the end of it and depart without completing their transaction. We call this balking or reneging. Do customers exiting the system return to the waiting population or not?

When arrivals occur at random the information of interest is the probability of n arrivals in a given time period, where $n = 1, 1, 2 \ldots$ If arrivals are assumed to occur at constant average rate and are independent of each other then they occur according to Poisson probability distribution.

The nature of the queue affects the type of queuing model formulated. The number of servers selected is affected by the rate of arrival of customers and the normal service time required. Queuing models help operations managers make decisions that balance capacity costs with queuing costs. (see Figure 12.2).

Examples of different queues are:

- **Single phase:** one cashier for cash transactions. In the single phase system a customer receives service from only one station before exiting the system. A restaurant where the same person takes the order, brings the food and takes the money is a single phase system.
- **Multiple phase:** health centre, one nurse, one doctor. If a restaurant required customers to place their order at one station, pay at a second, and pick up the food at a third stop it would be operating a multi-phase system.
- **Multiple channel, single phase:** passport office. Several assistants to serve the queue. The single queue system is in operation in most financial services outlets, airline check-in counters and post offices. Each customer waits in a single line for the first available server. This model seems to work faster than the same number of servers, each with its own queue (Van Looy et al. 2003). Customers perceive this form of queue as fairer.
- **Multiple channel, multiple phase:** queue at airport terminal – immigration control → customs, at each stage several operators. Under this model a company could differentiate services and allocate more experienced, trained servers to those queues with more difficult transactions.

A number of theoretical models have been developed to cover many queuing situations. In practice, managers will be less interested in the details of theoretical differences and more in what can be done to improve their operations. An understanding of queue behaviour and a way of testing alternative approaches helps with this. Simulation models avoid some of the pitfalls of mathematical modelling.

Bedward (1997) identifies two approaches to managing queues as (i) reducing the queue length and/or waiting time, and (ii) managing queue behaviour to make the wait more acceptable to customers. In (i), different strategies may be deployed such as optimizing service outlets; matching processing speed to queue length; structuring the service priorities and controlling distribution of services through ordering systems. Further improvements are made through the physical design of the distribution layout, which will aid the characteristics of control and speed. These measures may be considered to be operational approaches, and indeed, Johnston and Clark (2001: 194–195) offers advice dealing with queues applying his framework to manage the capacity (or overcapacity as it might well be) – giving consideration to resources, service demand, service output, and capacity leakage.

Lovelock discusses the analysis of the demand over a time period and discusses how operations may be adjusted to suit consumers' lifestyle patterns (Lovelock et al. 1999). Importance is placed on the well-being of the customer, ensuring

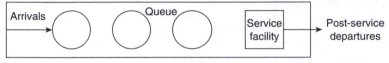

Single channel, single phase system

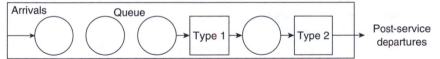

Single channel, multiple phase system

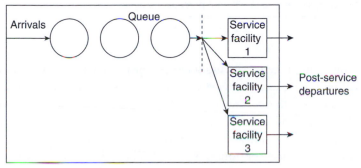

Multiple channel, single phase system

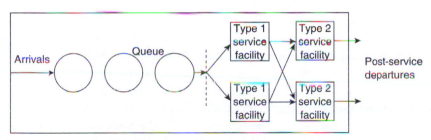

Multiple channel, multiple phase system

FIGURE 12.2   MODELS OF QUEUE STRUCTURES

their satisfaction with the provided service. Keeping the customers informed and entertained throughout the queuing process are popular methods used.

Introducing pricing strategies could be seen as a control measure in the example of a small football club hosting a cup game with higher division opposition. There is finite capacity within the ground and a surge of demand for tickets because of the opposition. Long queues are likely to form for tickets putting pressure on the local area. Staggering prices throughout the day or even off-peak periods may have assisted; different prices for different customers such as season and non–season ticket holders may also have been considered. However, FA regulations on ticket pricing for cup games does not allow this degree of flexibility. Clubs in this position usually operate a reservation system for season ticket holders. Other considerations may have

TABLE 12.3   PERCEPTIONS OF QUEUING

Queuing before the process feels longer than waiting during it
Uncertainty makes queuing seem longer
Unexplained queuing seems longer than explained queuing
Unfair queuing seems longer than when lines seem to be fair
Uncomfortable waits seem longer than comfortable ones
Idle time seems longer than occupied time
Anxiety makes the wait seem longer
The more valuable the service, the longer the customer is prepared to wait
Queuing alone seems longer than queuing in a group
Customers' current attitudes lead to particular perceptions of the wait
Customers' different value systems lead to different perceptions of the wait

been ticket outlet distribution centres being staggered or moved away from the residential area, or setting up a telesales service would have provided other options.

Focusing examination on the characteristics of queuing systems such as service rate, customers' arrival rate and number of servers in the system and their performance, e.g. average queue length and average waiting time per customer, has resulted in improvements in the service consumers received. There are other factors that affect customers' perceptions of the queue and their wait. Carmon (1991) considered factors that affect consumers' attitudes towards the time they spend waiting for service. Within the context of his studies, he showed that providing information about the expected duration of the wait, or about the causes of the delay, can reduce dissatisfaction with waiting, whether or not this information can lead to an alternative utilization of the time. Customers' prior expectations of the likelihood of a queue and the duration of a wait influence their level of dis/satisfaction.

While the operations manager cannot easily change customers' attitudes and values systems, they can take account of the research around the perceptions of waiting (for example Maister, 1985; Davies and Heineke, 1994). Table 12.3 sets out some of the theories about perceptions of queues. The operational response to these would be to reduce the anxiety that comes from uncertainty by providing timely, accurate information; to influence the perception of queuing time by providing distractions; to identify the stress elements in the environment such as temperature and noise and relieve them; to make the queuing time part of the service such as taking orders; use ticket numbers to enable people to leave the queue confident that the principle of first come first served will be observed, as at the delicatessen counter in a supermarket.

SUMMARY OF KEY POINTS

- Capacity is measured by output produced (number of cars per week) or availability of input resources (number of hotel rooms available). Utilization and efficiency are important measures of capacity.

- Most organizations face fluctuations in demand for their services. They can choose to cope with this by: keeping output level, which will result in under-utilization of capacity and increased costs as inventory has to be stored; varying the output level through varying the size of the workforce, overtime or subcontracting; trying to influence demand through advertising and promotion, developing complementary products. A mixture of these approaches is commonly used.
- In service operations the queuing approach is adopted to deal with a mismatch between variable demand levels and capacity levels.

STUDENT ACTIVITY 12.1

Think about the demand for your local police service. Are there any seasonal fluctuations in demand? What do you think they are caused by?

STUDENT ACTIVITY 12.2

You are setting up a firm to retail and service domestic appliances. It is intended that the servicing and repair should be done either at the customer's premises or, where necessary, in a workshop attached to the retail store.

What sources of variability of demand would you expect to see, and what strategies could you adopt to cope with this variability?

STUDENT ACTIVITY 12.3

Find an opportunity to observe a queue. This could be in a bank, post office, ticket booking office, fast food outlet or shop. Try to return to look at this activity at different times.

   Is there always a queue?
   How long does the average customer have to wait? From your observations, what do you think might cause the queue?
   What were the customer's reactions to the waiting time?
   How do you think the waiting time might be reduced or eliminated?
   Are there any ways that the queue could be managed to improve the quality of the waiting time for customers?

STUDENT ACTIVITY 12.4

Think of an occasion when you had to queue for a service.
How long did you have to queue?
How acceptable was this to you?
What were your feelings while you queued?
How could the organization have:

a)   Avoided this queue or made it move quicker?
b)   Made your queuing time less uncomfortable or frustrating?

STUDENT ACTIVITY 12.5

Think about an organization where you regularly encounter queues. Is there any way that the layout and provision of the service could be improved to reduce the queuing time or make it more efficient?

FURTHER READING

Carmon Z. (1991) 'Situational determinants of consumers' dissatisfaction with waiting', *Advances in Consumer Research*, 18: 703–5 .

Davies M.M. and Heineke J. (1994) 'Understanding the roles of the customer and the operation for better queue management', *International Journal of Operations and Production Management*, 14 (5): 24–31.

Hall R.W. (1991) *Queuing Methods for Services and Manufacturing*. Englewood Cliffs, NJ: Prentice Hall.

Maister D.H. (1985) 'The psychology of waiting lines', in J.H. Czeipel, M.R. Solomon and C.F. Surprenant (eds), *The Service Encounter*. Lexington, MA: D.C. Heath.

Van Looy B., Gemmel P. and Van Dierdonck R. (2003) *Services Management*, 2nd edn. London: FT/Prentice Hall.

13 EVALUATION AND PERFORMANCE MEASUREMENT

If you think good design is expensive, look how much bad design costs.

Martyn Denny, Sales and Marketing Director, Aqualisa

'Benchmarking is the continuous process of measuring products, services and practices against the toughest competitiors or those companies recognised as industry leaders (best in class).'

The Xerox Corporation

In this chapter aspects of performance measurement will be covered. The McKinsey consultancy firm are renowned for their belief that what cannot be measured cannot be managed. So the question arises, how can a manager decide what to measure to shed light on how the organization is performing.

LEARNING OUTCOMES

When you have completed this chapter you should be able to:

- Identify key performance measures.
- Explain the Balanced Scorecard.
- Assess the role of benchmarking.

So, managing successful products and services is simply about finding out what people want, all the attributes necessary to make the product better than the competition, at a price people are prepared to pay but will also provide a sufficient profit – and then supplying it. It sounds easy when put like that. Well, perhaps not, but at least knowing what you have to do is half the battle. And do it sooner rather than later – because your competitors may be doing it now!

Performance assessment

The main measure of the *success* of most services is profitability but with services there are more exceptions than with a manufactured product (e.g. public transport, education, NHS) and others that are created for the good of society where the importance of the service performance often outweighs (but does not exclude) financial considerations.

It is still necessary to ensure the service is operating to its full potential. To do this it needs to be analysed, evaluated and, if necessary, improved. The service may be expanded or enlarged. Eventually, plans must be implemented for its withdrawal from the market.

To do this, managers in the organization must arrange for the collection of an analysis of feedback from external sources and from within the organization. This should lead to an improvement/refreshment/revolution (new concepts and innovation) of the service if acted upon. If it is quickly found that significant or radical improvements can be achieved, this is probably an indication that the new product development process used in the first place was inadequate. There used to be great improvements claimed for value analysis, but here the same reasoning applies. If great improvements are possible shortly after the product or service is introduced, one ought to ask why it was not done like that in the first place. That does not mean of course that one ignores the suggested improvements.

In any case, there should be an evaluation of the development process to learn from what has gone before and thus implement improvements. Much of this evaluation will centre on the service success (or otherwise). Evaluation should encompass the outcomes of the design activities, especially the extent to which design and corporate objectives have been fulfilled. This will include financial measures and also the contribution and support to the corporate mission, strategies and objectives.

Questions that may be asked will include:

- Were the original targets met? (This will involve evaluation against the original specification.)
- Was it properly resourced?
- Was there good integration with all disciplines involved?
- Was the service effectively introduced to the market?
- What should be changed for the next service design programme?

All this might lead to process improvements. Such evaluations can also lead to triggers for new services as well as management decisions on potential service improvement, potential for service extensions or potential for service enlargement.

Such evaluations may also include performance of executives with responsibility for design. This might lead to revisions of their job description or revision of corporate or design investments. As the sales continue there should be improvements made to customer relationship management and this will involve datamining, which is the collection of quantitative information on customer behaviour.

Assessing service portfolio performance

Although already considered as part of the process, it is only after a period on sale that it will be possible to make management decisions on termination, and disposal where necessary. It may be possible to sell on the ownership of the service, license out, franchise or even sell the entire business. These considerations are a natural part of managing products and services.

Considering whether a product/service should be deleted from the product portfolio requires an assessment of the actual performance, of how well the product/service still fits in with the organization's strategic objectives, and of external triggers. Targets in terms of sales-related criteria, market-related criteria, profit-related criteria and operating criteria are set and performance evaluated against.

Performance management is a fundamental part of building effective organizations. Standards and objectives need to be identified and then performance measured against those goals so as to record whether progress has been made or not. The operations manager is used to measuring and controlling performance in terms of product/service quality.

There are four areas commonly measured in operations management. First, profitability and other financial metrics. (in the not for profit sector this includes consideration of keeping within allocated budgets and funds). Second, market performance, underlying yet again the close links the operations function has with the marketing function. Third is usually a consideration of the utilization of resources within the organization. The final area is people performance.

Financial metrics

All organizations aim to improve their levels of efficiency and can be held accountable for the funds and assets deployed within the business. Profit-making bodies seek profits so as to make a return to the owners of the business, the shareholders, to service any debts and to provide the funds for investment in new resources for future growth.

Most financial metrics are measured by the specialists in the finance department. A lot of this information is collected at the behest of outside bodies such as the Inland Revenue, Companies House, the Stock Exchange and other regulatory bodies. Yet the operations managers should also know how the information was collected and be able to read standard accounting reports.

Market performance

Sales growth and market share are important indicators of how well an organization has performed in the market place. Effective analysis of sales data can identify key customers and examine their spending over time. This is one of the building blocks of customer relationship management. The marketing department are responsible through the latter for identifying what is important to customers, e.g. speed of delivery. Other frequently stated suggestions were delivery times, cycle times and length of

TABLE 13.1   ELEMENTS OF THE EFQM EXCELLENCE MODEL

Leadership: How leaders develop vision and values for the organization

Policy and strategy: How mission is implemented: policies, plans, objectives and targets

People: How staff are managed and developed; how HRM strategies are planned

Partnerships and resources: How external partnerships and internal resources are planned and managed so as to support strategy and operations

Processes: How processes are designed, managed and improved so as to support strategy and create value for stakeholders

Customer results: Customer loyalty and perceptions of quality, image, after sales service

People results: Employee motivation, satisfaction and performance

Society results: Involvement in the community in which the organization operates, corporate responsibility, any external recognition received

Financial results: Profit, cash flow, meeting budgets, success rates, value of intellectual property

queues. These types of measurement are identified as being key to effective implementation of the operations strategy.

A key determinant of market performance will, of course, be robust quality management. As we have discussed earlier, in Chapters 4, 8 and 9, quality is a vital differentiator in a crowded market place. Often quality of product and service will be what ensures repeat purchases. The Excellence Model developed by the European Foundation for Quality Management has proved to be a very popular performance measure. The model seeks to aid organizations to identify how results are being achieved as well as defining results in terms of people, customers, financial performance and impact on society. Table 13.1 sets out the elements of the model.

Resource utilization

No organization has unlimited resources. Even Chelsea Football Club talk of their plan to break even by 2009–2010, despite Roman Abramovich's billions.

> Since Abramovich took over as owner of Chelsea Football Club in 2003 and paid off the club's 80 million pound (US$140.8 million) debts, Chelsea has spent 300 million pounds (US$528 million) on 20 new players. Chief executive Peter Kenyon is vowing to make Chelsea, which saw a loss of £88m in 2004, break even by the 2009–2010 financial year. (Alex Kleiderman, BBC News business reporter, February 2005)

Resources should be allocated to the areas where they are most needed or will be most effectively used. In theory, it is in organizations in decline where the budget is set on the basis of what was spent last year plus an appropriate percentage figure. In practice many organizations use last year's spending profile as the basis for the subsequent year's budget-making process. This is particularly the case where the discretionary spend is relatively small and most of the organization's budget is allocated to staffing, which does not vary a great deal from year to year.

Generating a budget to ensure departments have the necessary resources to achieve the overall objectives of the organization is the common example of resource planning. This naturally leads into using the budget as a control mechanism. Operations managers will be concerned about the impact of cost-cutting on the key areas of quality, innovation and customer service.

An approach more likely to lead to sustainable success for an organization is to focus on cost-effectiveness rather than cost-cutting. Fundamental to such a focus would be to understand the strategic drivers of cost: volume/capacity, variety and variation and their impact on the competition. Any proposed saving measures should be assessed in terms of their impact on quality, innovation and customer service. Before work on cost-effectiveness can begin there has to be an examination of the organization's cost structure. This may well include organizational-wide value analysis, restructuring or site rationalization.

People performance

The fourth element in performance management is, of course, looking at people performance. This demands soft performance measures in contrast to the harder-nosed quantifiable criteria which are, of course, easier to measure. This does not mean the operations manager can afford to ignore what the figures tell him or her about the number of mistakes, scrap and wastage levels, number of customer complaints, warranty claims, days taken to collect money from debtors, the cycle time of customers in the service system, cycle time of materials flowing through production, inventory value, number of days of inventory held or delivery days, for example.

As discussed in the chapter on quality (Chapter 9), the key differentiator in the delivery of services is usually the person implementing the service. Numerous market research studies have identified soft criteria such as aesthetics or empathy as being key determinants as to whether there is a repeat purchase of the service or a positive referral to other potential purchasers. In a quality culture, staff genuinely believe in the value of their product offering. They are able to reassure potential purchasers of the genuineness of their staff–customer interface. The smile is real, the member of staff *really does* want the customer to have a nice day.

Examples of soft criteria include colour, taste, smell, ambiance and feel as well as levels of finish and political sensitivity. Some organizations prioritize training in new skills, such as basic manners, acceptable language and grooming, in order to drive up delivery according to these soft criteria.

Keeping the score

Performance management should be about measuring what is important, and only if it has a direct impact on the product/service quality. The leading quality gurus, such as Deming, Juran, Crosby, Feigenbaum and Oakland, have all recognized the importance of measurement in achieving quality. Without keeping score, how is it possible to track what improvement might be occurring? Score cards also enable the performance of different units within the organization to be compared. Most departments/units improve at differing rates. Scorecards record this and can provide the public recognition needed to keep teams well motivated.

The balanced scorecard

Kaplan and Norton's Balanced Scorecard (1992) has proved to be a successful mechanism for many organizations to draw together disparate key performance indicators and subsequently review and revamp the organization's strategy. It aims to identify the measures to drive performance, acknowledging that financial measures are not the only way to assess the performance of successful firms.

The Balanced Scorecard looks at financial measures, customer measures, learning and growth, and internal business processes. Under each of these four headings the performance reviewer will look at objectives, measures, targets and initiatives.

- **Finance:** The question to consider is, to succeed financially, how should we appear to our shareholders?
- **Customer:** To achieve our vision, how should we appear to our customers?
- **Learning and growth:** To achieve our vision, how will we sustain our ability to change and improve?
- **Internal business process:** To satisfy our shareholders and customers, what business processes must we excel at?

Addressing these questions help organizations develop their business strategy.

There is an acknowledgement that as we move from an industrial economy to a knowledge-based economy, what becomes more important is human and intellectual capital, innovation power and the R&D pipeline, brands and relationships.

To be successful and maintain competitive advantage an organization has to make the most of its resources. Organizational resources comprise: physical resources, monetary resources, human resources, relational resources (suppliers and customers) and structural resources (processes, organizational culture and value).

Good operations management affect all of these.

Kaplan and Norton in their 2004 book *Strategy Maps* have a template which links the learning and growth perspective with the internal processes perspective, then the customer perspective and then the financial perspective.

Typical metrics in the financial services sector include:

- Number of customer contacts per employee
- Duration of each contact
- Number of contacts per member of staff
- Number of transactions processed each day
- Control of budget expenses
- Cycle time for approval of loan application/mortgage application/overdraft application.

The latter metric is the one that will be valued by customers. Some organizations find it easier to define metrics that enhance policing and control rather than design some with the customer in mind. These organizations probably also pay more attention to Taylor (1911) in their approach to job design rather than empowerment and other notions from the behavioural school (Mullins 1999).

Performance measures may be imposed top down, sometimes from an external source, or developed bottom up through discussion of what is important to customers in quality terms.

In the public sector in the UK since the late 1990s, there has been a culture of the government imposing targets on individual services as a way of attempting to drive service improvements. Often this has been in response to poor publicity about performance. This strategy has not been as successful as the politicians envisaged.

The danger is that employees work to achieve the specific targets set. In the health service, in response to poor PR about the length of time people are waiting on trolleys in hospital accident and emergency departments, a target was introduced which said that patients should be seen within 4 hours. In 2002, before any target was set, 23% of patients spent over 4 hours in accident and emergency, but by 2004 only 5.3% stayed that long. The downside of this was that medical staff were instructed to comply with the target at the expense of exercising their independent clinical judgements. Patients who were about to reach the deadline of 4 hours were admitted, despite the clinical need of others. Extra staff were drafted in to work in A&E departments on the occasions when the measurement was taking place. Operations were cancelled and in some well-publicized cases patients stayed aboard ambulances in the car park before being brought into the hospital when staff were confident that they could meet the target. In a world of restricted resources this is wasteful.

Benchmarking

Benchmarking can be done in a number of different ways. The performance of different parts of the organizations can be compared with each other, e.g. sales per square metre at Tesco stores within regions and between regions. Comparing the performance of your organization with another might mean looking at companies not necessarily in your field. This can get round the fact that not all organizations are willing to share the secrets of their success with their competitors. Back in the 1980s a DTI-sponsored programme to encourage the take-up of benchmarking facilitated what was then the Jobcentres Agency benchmarking their performance with supermarkets. The aim was to improve the Jobcentres' performance in updating their displays of job vacancies by learning from those whose success depended on speedy replenishment of their shelves. (Figure 9.2 sets out the key stages in implementing benchmarking.)

One of the easiest ways to benchmark performance is to analyse the audited financial reports and accounts of your competitors. Looking at ratios such as stock turn, return on investment or cost of sales enables you to position your organization's performance vis-à-vis the competition. For example, British Airways compared how long it took other airlines to turn round a Boeing 747. It took the evidence that a Japanese airline could do it in 40 minutes to spur their own workforce to improve their performance of 3 hours (Wright and Race 2004).

Unilever, the fast-moving consumer goods giant, has entered into formal benchmarking agreements with other world class manufacturers whereby each agrees to share information about critical success factors. The names of those participating are not published and everyone signs confidentiality agreements. The information gained is used internally to identify areas for improvement.

There are organizations such as **IndustryWeek** which collect data that they then reorganize and repackage and sell as new information. Their Best Plants benchmarking database seeks to highlight how the top manufacturers set themselves apart. What are their tactics? How do they measure their performance? This Best Plants database derives its information on successful practices in areas such as operations, quality, maintenance and worker productivity from some 250 benchmarks.

The Cabinet Office and HM Revenue & Customs have developed the Public Sector Benchmarking Service to meet users' needs for information and advice. Public sector organizations are able to access the members' website and benefit from the full range of PSBS services and facilities. Registration is free. This service is designed to promote knowledge transfer and effective benchmarking, supply practical advice and information on improvement tools, broker learning through sharing knowledge and good practices, and support public service improvement projects.

Collaboration with and between users is a core principle necessary to encourage the use of benchmarking. Benchmarking is a tool to facilitate the sharing of information and good practice. A partnership approach in which there is openness, trust and commitment to share, underpins successful benchmarking:

- **Openness:** Each partner needs to be prepared to reveal data and information.
- **Trust:** Each partner needs to be confident that information revealed will be properly safeguarded.
- **Commitment:** Each partner has to be committed to providing information in a timely manner as mutually agreed.

One method of engendering this within the PSBS is to encourage those undertaking benchmarking to abide by the European Benchmarking Code of Conduct. The PSBS helpfully gives definitions of the various benchmarking methods:

1 **Strategic benchmarking** is used where organizations seek to improve their overall performance by examining the long-term strategies and general approaches that have enabled high performers to succeed. It involves considering high level aspects such as core competences; developing new products and services; changing the balance of activities; and improving capabilities for dealing with changes in the background environment. The changes resulting from this type of benchmarking may be difficult to implement and the benefits are likely to take a long time to materialize.

2 **Performance benchmarking** or **competitive benchmarking** is used where organizations consider their positions in relation to performance characteristics of key products and services. Here partners are drawn from the same sector. However, in the commercial world, it is common for companies to undertake this type of benchmarking through trade associations or third parties to protect confidentiality.

3 **Process benchmarking** is used when the focus is on improving specific critical processes and operations. Benchmarking partners are sought from best practice organizations that perform similar work or deliver similar services. Process benchmarking invariably involves producing **process maps** to facilitate comparison and analysis. This type of benchmarking can result in benefits in the short term.

4 **Functional benchmarking** or **generic benchmarking** is used when organizations look to benchmark with partners drawn from different business sectors or areas of activity to find ways of improving similar functions or work processes. This sort of benchmarking can lead to innovation and dramatic improvements

5 **Internal benchmarking** involves seeking partners from within the same organization, for example, from business units located in different areas. The main advantages of internal benchmarking are that access to sensitive data and information are easier; standardized data is often readily available; and, usually, less time and resources are needed. There may be fewer barriers to implementation as practices may be relatively easy to transfer across the same organization. However, real innovation may be lacking and best in class performance is more likely to be found through external benchmarking.

6 **External benchmarking** involves seeking outside organizations that are known to be best in class. External benchmarking provides opportunities for learning from those who are at the leading edge, although it must be remembered that not every best practice solution can be transferred to others. In addition, this type of benchmarking may take up more time and resource to ensure the comparability of data and information, the credibility of the findings and the development of sound recommendations. External learning is also often slower because of the 'not invented here' syndrome.

7 **International benchmarking** is used where partners are sought from other countries because best practitioners are located elsewhere in the world and/or there are too few benchmarking partners within the same country to produce valid results. Globalization and advances in information technology are increasing opportunities for international projects. However, these can take more time and resources to set up and implement and the results may need careful analysis due to national differences.

(©Crown Copyright 2006, www.benchmarking.gov.uk/about_bench/types.asp)

Performance measurement is effective when it is linked to the objectives for the organization. In Chapter 2 we identified quality, cost, speed, dependability and flexibility as being the key strategic objectives for an organization. Table 13.2 shows some examples of possible performance measures.

TABLE 13.2 EXAMPLES OF PERFORMANCE MEASURES

Performance objective	Examples of measures
Quality	Number of customer complaints
	Scrap level
	Number of defects per item
	Warranty claims
	Customer satisfaction scores
Cost	Variance against budget
	Cost per operation hour
	Labour productivity
	Utilization of resources
	Added value
Speed	Customer query time
	Order lead time
	Cycle time
	Frequency of delivery
	Actual *vs.* theoretical throughput time
Dependability	Average lateness of orders
	Percentage of orders delivered late
	Proportion of products in stock
	Schedule adherence
	Average deviation from scheduled arrival
Flexibility	Range of products/services
	Time needed to develop new products/services
	Average capacity/maximum capacity
	Machine change over time
	Time to change schedules

SUMMARY OF KEY POINTS

- It is not enough to determine whether your performance matches your competitors. It is important to understand *how* your competitor is performing better and *what* is their method of improvement.
- Performance measurement involves taking a photo shot of the current position of the organization and then comparing that achievement with past performance, with target performance standards and with competitor performance standards.

STUDENT ACTIVITY 13.1

Taking a retailer of your choice, identify their main competitor and analyse their performance in terms of finance, market and resource utilization.

FURTHER READING

Brown S., Lamming R., Bessant J. and Jones P. (2005) *Strategic Operations Management,* 2nd edn. Oxford: Elsevier.

Kaplan R. and Norton D. (1992) 'The Balanced Scorecard: measures that drive performance', *Harvard Business Review*, Boston, MA: Harvard Business School Press.

Kaplan R. and Norton D. (1996) 'The Balanced Scorecard: translating strategy into action' *Harvard Business Review*, Boston, MA: Harvard Business School Press.

Kaplan R. and Norton D. (2000) *The Strategy-Focused Organization.* Boston, MA: Harvard Business School Press.

Kaplan R. and Norton D. (2004) *Strategy Maps: Converting Intangible Assets into Tangible Outcomes.* Boston, MA: Harvard Business School Press.

Liebfried, K.H.J. and McNair C.J. (1992) *Benchmarking: A Tool for Continuous Improvement.* New York: HarperCollins.

Longbottom D. (2000) 'Benchmarking in the UK: an empirical study of practitioners and academics', *Benchmarking: An International Journal*, 7 (2): 98–117.

Slack N. (1994) 'The importance–performance matrix as a determinant of improvement priority', *International Journal of Operations and Production Management*, 14, (5): 59–75.

Wright J.N. and Race P. (2004) *Management of Service Operations,* 2nd edn. London: Thomson Learning.

14 THINKING ABOUT AND MANAGING FOR 'THE FUTURE'

When you think about today, how much is visible to us? Almost nothing. In the world of nanotech, biotech, pharmaceuticals – all those areas where we can't see the technology – no wonder we are scared.

Chris Luebkeman, Director of Global Foresight
and Innovation, Ove Arup Foresight,
Innovation and Incubation (2004)

And the future is going to be even more scary!

LEARNING OUTCOMES

When you have completed this chapter you should be able to:

- Understand the importance of planning products beyond those currently being developed or sold.
- Know some techniques that enable an organization to plan into the future.

In this chapter we look at service design management for the future. Most managers do not know what they will be selling when the sales of the thing they are currently working on go into decline. Research has found that only one-third of companies in the UK and Germany actively plan the products beyond those they are currently developing (IBM London Business School 1996). If companies do not look beyond their next product then several things may happen. First, they will be caught out by possible changes that do occur or, secondly, they are doomed to become followers of others, making 'me-too' products. This policy has been known to be an area of poor profits and low growth for some time (e.g. Bellon and Whittington 1996; Thackaray 1997). As G. Peters (1996) has written:

> We are invariably caught unaware of the trends affecting our business because we don't spend enough time looking to the future. Our day-to-day lives are spent managing one crisis or another.

Innovation management for the long term

We are being advised in government White Papers and elsewhere to take a ten-year horizon on our new product development (UK Government 1994). It is important that organizations have plans. These strategic plans should include the changes in the parameters aligning with the anticipated growth (or decline) of the various parts or profit/product centres of the organization. Innovations in one area tend to 'snowball' into further innovations in allied (service) areas – each of which may be a new source of revenue. This was called 'serial innovation' by Alan Topalian (and mentioned in BS 7000-1: 1999).

Innovation is fundamental to corporate survival over a longer time span. To quote Cooper (1993):

> The annals of business history are replete with examples of companies that simply disappeared because they failed to innovate, failed to keep their product portfolios current and competitive, and were surpassed by more innovative competitors.

It is possible to survive a long time. Certainly it is necessary for organizations to be able to move, seamlessly, into the future through a constant supply of well-designed competitive products, and more likely in the future, services. To make sure organizations are moving forward in a logical manner there needs to be an estimation of what an organization's products and services are to be like more than ten years into the future. (Actually, ten years isn't *that* far ahead.)

> It is not the strongest of the species who survive, nor the most intelligent, but the ones most responsive to change.
>
> Charles Darwin

Such far-out planning sounds like an impossible task. We are blitzed with articles telling us that tomorrow will be very different from today. Change is occurring, yes, but not as fast in most areas as you are led to believe. Change happens fast in a few areas at different times. Look at the change that occurred in cars between 1895 and 1905. Compare that to the changes in cars in the past ten years. Far more conceptual changes were made at that earlier time, and more recently the main changes have been aesthetic.

> *Mike Jackson (2005) has noted 'a look at the last 250 years shows that cycles of change occur every 40 years or so, and that these changes have fundamentally altered human life cycles:*
>
> - *c. 1770 – industrial revolution*
> - *c. 1830 – steam and railways*
> - *c. 1875 – steel, electricity, heavy engineering*
> - *c. 1910 – oil, automobiles, mass production*
> - *c. 1950 – computing, telephone, television*
> - *c. 1970 – Information and communication technologies.*
>
> *A bit of a 'blunt-edged' analysis, but it does help to show that only certain areas change 'fast' at any particular time.*

People tend to assume that things will change faster than they do. Just look at films like *2001 A Space Odyssey* to see what was believed would happen, but just didn't. It was thought we were all going to dress the same, in shiny aluminium one-piece outfits. In fact, men are still wearing a pointless piece of cloth round their necks when they want to look 'smart' as they have been doing for a few hundred years. In reality, most people don't like too much change. The next DVD you buy you want to be able to play on your existing player; the next player you buy you want to be able to play your old DVDs. It's not that we're Luddites. It is not being said that things will not change, quite the reverse; but most people do not want *radical* change all the time.

There are currently five fast growing areas (Hollins and Hollins 1999):

- Electronics
- Communications
- Pharmaceuticals
- Biotechnology
- Some materials

Everything else is growing slowly and is therefore **Predictable**.

Much of the future is predictable. Try looking around your room. Excluding the five things listed above, surprisingly few things did not or could not, have existed 20 years ago. You have just taken your first step in understanding the future – which is only two stages away from being able to plan for it. Change is fast, but only in a few quite precise areas. In most other areas change is rather plodding, and this is how most people like it.

> *Radical change occurs in new ideas as they come to market, then the design settles down and general improvement occurs. Then, mainly through new technology, there is another surge in radical change and then things settle down again and change is*

> *(Continued)*
>
> *back to general improvement again. During the period of gradual improvement certain areas of design tend to change faster, such as aesthetics, ergonomics and process design. This means that if a company's products are on this 'plateau' they can focus efforts more in these areas of product development and design and thus spend less time seeking new concepts.*

Every company is in the process of becoming an anachronism irrelevant to the future.

Hamel and Prahalad (1994)

The future for service design?

People tend to concentrate on innovations within products but ignore the greater potential for innovation within services. Innovations within services are often more readily accepted by consumers as there is often less of an infrastructure (user standards) to shift. Domino Pizza in the United States first identified the potential for a doorstep delivery service. Through this innovation the company grew quickly and the idea was copied by many (as services cannot be patented), but their speed in implementation gave them the edge over their competitors in the market.

From designing just the product, companies should be moving towards designing the product, process and service interface. They should be moving towards Whole Life Design as a method for adding value and maximizing profit throughout the value chain right through to disposal. This places a greater emphasis on the post-production stage of products, distribution, marketing, customer and market support – the service end of the process – as well as corporate development. As a result, more emphasis will be applied to service design. Companies should be seeking opportunities for design at every stage of a product's life.

> *People buy 'benefits' and not 'technology' (Hollins and Hollins 1999). Too much emphasis on technology can result in the development of a working product that does not fulfil customer requirements – a major cause of product failure.*

More new technology will be used in services. This will make transactions faster, more efficient and more repeatable. The repeatability will make it easier to control and increase the quality of the service. The standardization brought about by the application of technology may reduce the personal interaction and thus the 'individual' nature of services. The 'service' dimension could be lost from the service transaction and that may not be to the satisfaction of all customers. The difference in the 'bespoke' nature of some services compared with some others (the difference between a restaurant and a 'fast food' outlet) will result in both types of service being available. The segmentation choices will be part of the service design.

On the other hand, further 'discrete' application of advanced technology (especially in communication) and IT in services can allow the benefits of apparent 'individual' service combined with the benefits that can be achieved with repeatability and 'selective' standardization. It can also allow the service providers to spend more time with customers.

FORECASTING FLOPS

We are not very good in predicting what the future will bring. We invariably guess too far ahead. For example, in 1935 it was predicted that by 1955 we would be able to fly 50 miles home from work in 5 minutes (600 mph) in our helicopters. Not only can't helicopters do that sort of speed but we are still using 'mph' instead of the long preferred 'miles/hr' when, anyway, we should be talking in kilometres/hr. And never mind a helicopter – we can't yet get a commuter train to arrive on time!

Pan Am were predicting in the 1960s that by the year 2000 they would be flying 'hyperjets' that would have a speed of 4,000 miles/hr. They didn't achieve that – they didn't even survive the end of the century, going out of business in 1997.

As recently as 1990 we were being told by the Department of Trade and Industry on the former popular BBC television programme Tomorrow's World that by the end of the century we would have domestic robots that would 'do the cleaning, clear away dirty dishes and put them in the dishwasher, and then vacuum the house'. If only.

It's very easy to predict the future, people do it all the time. The thing you can't do is get it right.

Norman 1998

If we are no good at predicting the future we are giving our designers little chance of designing the services for that future.

We will now look at some specific research that was undertaken into the way British companies plan their future products and services. (Thanks are due to Alan Topalian for many aspects in this section.)

Case Study: Planning long-term products and services

Here we describe some results of research into how companies plan their long-term products and services. This was the first time that such research had been attempted, and it explored what innovative organizations do, how they do it, who is involved and what they measure. This research was funded by the Department of Trade and Industry and the research was undertaken by Alan Topalian of Alto Design Management and Bill Hollins of Direction Consultants. It was discovered that it does appear to be possible to set up procedures to plan long-term products and services for three generations ahead but only the very best organizations are doing it.

The research cohort

In the first, and unsuccessful, stage of the research, 'captains of industry' were invited to give their views on how they could plan in the long term. It was found that few had any idea on how to approach this problem. Top managers who were consulted proposed that this should include activities such as market research, benchmarking and even Business Process Re-engineering. Whilst important, these are things for products being developed now, not for the products of ten years into the future. Market research can only tell you what people are already thinking and doing. Benchmarking compares an organization's operations with the 'best in class', which is fine for now but the best will have moved on a long way in the future. As for Business Process Re-engineering, this is now, fortunately, dead. It focused on the core products and this had the effect of stifling innovation and destroying new products that had potential. It was mainly used as a glorified redundancy scheme by companies that were unlikely to reach the future.

Perhaps the most difficult part was finding appropriate companies worth interviewing. The research was focused on companies that had a reputation for innovation and senior managers within these organizations were contacted. What was being sought were people who had serious plans on how to look at the longer-term future. The researchers were not interested in what these companies were planning for their future, but how they did it. What processes they adopted in looking at the long term.

A list of innovative companies was drawn up from winners of SMART Awards and the Queen's Award to Industry (Technology); the UK R&D Scoreboard; design award winners; enterprise companies known to the parties involved and those that responded to an article in *Ambassador* (the journal of the Association of MBAs).

Over 80 organizations that had won awards for design, innovation or technology were contacted. These organizations, at least, had a past record for successful innovation. Several chose not to become involved as they considered their innovation management processes to be confidential. Others stated that they were not interested in such planning.

Many more were found not to plan sufficiently far into the future and so were eliminated from the survey. The original cohort included well-known companies that you have heard of and that have a reputation for being at the forefront of their markets and at the cutting edge of technology. Most of these hadn't a clue when it came to long-term planning.

Data collection

After an initial telephone discussion with senior executives in each of the short-listed companies several companies were eliminated and those companies that appeared to be most active in planning the long term were contacted and 'invited' to become involved in the research.

> He that will not apply new remedies must expect new evils, for time is the greatest innovator.
>
> Francis Bacon

A final sample of 34 companies was investigated. The companies were geographically spread throughout Great Britain. Sizes ranged from three to over 58,000 employees. There was also a wide range in the annual turnover: £12,000 to £8.4 billion. The sample included organizations that were fairly new (2 years) and long-established (over 100 years); private, public limited companies as well as employee-owned enterprises. Their interests spanned a broad spectrum of industries and markets – pharmaceuticals, travel and tourism, hard and soft drinks, communications, IT, leisure activities and power generation. The research took the form of semi-structured interviews based around an extensive questionnaire and these interviews lasted 1–3 hours. Evidence of innovation was also sought not only with products but throughout the value chain.

Those interviewed were senior executives who were responsible for planning long-term products. In order to benefit from their knowledge and experience, executives were encouraged to talk and often the discussion extended beyond the set questions into areas of long-term product and service management that had not previously been anticipated. This aspect of **Grounded Theory** (Glaser and Strauss 1975) allowed the interviewers to explore new areas which resulted in interesting new findings. Virtually all who took part reported that it had been a worthwhile learning experience. These interviews were transcribed and more than 100,000 words were then analysed to find out what could or could not be useful in planning for the long term.

Findings from eliminated companies

Innovative thinking was short-term in nature in many organizations contacted. Most had no plans stretching far into the future; indeed, the thinking of many managers seems to be severely locked into the present. Often they are paid on short-term results, such as on profitability or share price. Also, those at the very top of organizations tend to spend fewer years working for their organization before moving on to 'pastures new'. As a result, they have little incentive to plan the long-term health and stability of the organization. This was found to be less true for smaller privately owned or family run enterprises. People at the top of these organizations were more concerned as to their organization's long-term health but even here planning tends to be in the hands of one, or a few, individuals.

WE JUST KEEP GETTING IT WRONG

On computers:

'I think there is a world market for about five computers' – Thomas Watson Snr, IBM Chairman

'There is no reason for any individual to have a computer in their home' – Ken Olson, President, Digital Equipment Corp., 1977

The total market for computers is 52 units – IBM, 1952
The total market for computers is 200,000 units – IBM, 1982
(Current IBM production of PCs is 200,000 units per week)

'640 K should be enough for anybody' – Bill Gates, 1981

It was also found that several apparently innovative organizations – some of which had won awards for their innovations – were referred to as 'one hit wonders' because they had often stumbled on a good idea but this was more by serendipity than by design. It was good that they had exploited these ideas and were making money from them but how often does lightning strike in the same place twice? Although they had developed a successful product and marketed it well, they seemed unable to take a long-term view beyond their one innovation and had no plans or processes for future innovations. These companies were also eliminated from the research.

Not all respondents agreed that a formal process was necessary to generate successful long-term products. One stated, *'product life cycles are so short there is no time to plan. Our competitors who do plan spend so much time on it that they are going out of business like light bulbs.'* This view was the exception, though it could be argued that companies should choose between detailed planning and agility to respond fast to change – perhaps they do not need to do both. If enterprises are sufficiently agile they may not wish to have constraining plans.

On the other hand, a company could build agility into its process so that it could change direction, or adapt, fast, to changing situations. A suitable process could increase an organization's agility allowing people to be 'fast on their feet' when technological breakthroughs occur. In any case, the process needs to be organic and flexible. Without any formal plan an organization may be limited to being a follower of others' innovations.

Some of the better organizations specified a direction in which they wished to go and this laid down the foundations for the type of products that would eventually be developed. Some organizations are compiling databases of possible products that might be developed, though the technologies required are not yet available. These propositions would be reconsidered at specific times in the future (for example, every three years) to see if the time was then right.

Overview of the research

There was broad acceptance among the enterprises surveyed that very little *cannot* be planned for ten years ahead. It is only the detailed specifications that were stated not to be possible There is also acceptance that it is worthwhile to attempt such planning so as to be better placed to deal with whatever future presents itself. Respondents had no sympathy with the view that it is not worth the effort to plan as the future will be very different from today and the chances of making the right predictions are minimal.

Plans should be sufficiently flexible but a clear vision of overall aims will increase the chances of 'staying on course' with a relevant development programme. The trick was to sharpen their analyses of what will be significant in the future and then apply the resources to work on those factors.

Future regulation and 'discontinuous change' that could destroy a company's markets were cited most frequently as factors that *cannot* be planned ten years ahead. However, executives also stated that these rarely occurred suddenly without any warning: there ought to be sufficient signs and time to do something about them. 'Curiosity-driven research which yields unique sparks' (Alan Topalian) might also have a major impact on carefully laid plans.

There may be prizes for those that make special efforts to effect change legislation in their favour by lobbying governmental and standards agencies in relation to, say, environmental, and health and safety issues. Changes in legislation (especially with regard to the environment) are a big opportunity that could be exploited for long-term product development.

Successful companies that planned their new products well into the future did not tend to look specifically at new technology. They were more likely to adopt one of two strategies. Either they would identify likely new markets and then seek the technology that would satisfy that market or they would find real potential markets that would use the technology that they had discovered and then 'aim' the development of that technology towards those markets.

Only one company had a complete system in place for planning in the long term, although most had parts of the 'jigsaw'. Also, few had company-wide planning for the long term in place. In many companies there were worthwhile practices going on but details were not even written down. To these companies it was suggested that without committing these systems and activities to paper (or electronic means) they were making their organizations vulnerable. Top managers must create an atmosphere within the organization so that there is company-wide acceptance that change will occur and that it will be supported from the very top. This means adequate time and finance to facilitate this planning.

The conclusions

This research has shown how some companies are actively planning their long-term products. As a result, these companies are better placed to survive and thrive in the future. As Gibson (1997) observed: 'Today a simple choice faces every individual, every corporation, every government and every society on earth. That choice is rethink the future or be forced to rethink the future.' Furthermore, the ideas for new products and services that emanate from such a system must also be effectively archived, so that they can be retrieved when the time is right. It must be remembered that the type of innovations being considered, in most cases, cannot be developed now. If they could, they would not be long-term products and services.

The high calibre results and information identified through the adopted methodology have given an insight into what might be considered 'good practice'. From the results obtained it was possible to piece together a 'system' for organizing long-term products and services for a period of ten years. These are given in the following section.

Some techniques on how to manage services for the future

1   The creation and sustenance of an **innovation–nurturing culture** is generated from the top and needs the support of most senior executives. The search for new products generally starts at director level: it is here that a specific initial budget should be allocated, which is then communicated to other relevant people around the organization.

2   Within these cultures there should be an enlightened **tolerance of failure**. Experimentation in new activities should be encouraged and no blame ascribed. Certain mistakes should be viewed positively as an inherent and valuable learning aspect of healthy long-term product planning. If punished for mistakes, individuals are likely to confine themselves to 'safe', low-risk options: this will prove to be more harmful to the enterprise in the long run.

3   Forward-thinking companies encourage innovation in all their change activities and seek opportunities to **innovate throughout the value chain**. As such, innovation is not restricted to technology but extends to business processes and marketing.

4   Senior executives should typically **spend 5% of their time** considering and planning the long-term future. This figure can vary widely from those who are involved full time in this activity to those who delegate it almost entirely to others. These people are generally linked to the product development or marketing departments.

5   The **costs involved** in planning for the long-term future are not great. Typically the budget for long-term product planning is between an additional 5% and 20% of budgets allocated to new product development. Depending on the type of products, this typically amounts to 0.5–2% of annual turnover.

This is adequate because the costs of planning over the long term are relatively low compared with other aspects of new product development. It involves mainly people's time and does not generally involve significant capital expenditure. Costs rise significantly when the decision is taken to develop a specific product and the project becomes part of the normal new product development process. The costs of *thinking* long term are not great and should not significantly affect the level of dividends paid to shareholders. Indeed, the costs of *not* planning are even greater if the company sets out in the wrong direction and/or invests in inappropriate initiatives.

6   There are **few threats** in planning the long term. Some threats could include the short-term economic climate and sudden changes in technology; however, changes in technology or legislation usually have lead times that allow plenty of time to act as long as there are people assigned to looking for potential threats.

7   It is important that the **process should be written down**. The future of a company may be very precarious if people leave, die, retire or simply forget. Perhaps a piece-meal approach to developing a long-term process is less disruptive, a case of 'continuous improvement' of the process over time.

8   The process also needs to **include personnel and communication** aspects, as well as a method for archiving ideas for future retrieval. This could include a short overview which then leads the user to greater details of each basic set of activities.

AND WE CONTINUE TO GET IT WRONG

On cars:
'The actual building of roads devoted to motor cars is not for the near future, in spite of many rumours to that effect' – Harpers Weekly, 1902

'The horse is here to stay; the automobile is just a novelty' – The President of the Michigan Savings Bank to Henry Ford's lawyer on the risks of investing, 1903

'With over fifty foreign cars already on sale here, the Japanese auto industry isn't likely to carve out a big slice of the US market for itself' – Business Week, 1968

On telephones:
Alexander Graham Bell, said that there would be a telephone in every American city.

On music:
'The Phonograph … is not of any commercial value' – Thomas Edison, 1880

'Radio is just a craze', Thomas Edison, 1922

'Groups of guitars are on the way out' – Decca Recording Co. executive on turning down The Beatles

On flying:
'Heavier-than-air flying machines are impossible' – Lord Kelvin, President of the Royal Society, 1895

By 2001 houses would be made of ultra lightweight material and be capable of flying – Arthur C. Clarke in Vogue, 1966.

---

9   **Central archiving** and effective sharing is essential. Websites and intranets open up considerable opportunities to exploit knowledge more effectively.

10   **Alliances** are a fact of life and will feature more prominently in the years ahead. A reason gaining prominence is that, increasingly, customers are seeking comprehensive solutions to larger requirements from their suppliers. Few companies can service such systems on their own therefore networks of suppliers are forming to offer such total support.

11 The system for managing the long-term products is not one that can be described through a design process model. A series of **inter-related 'layers'** is a more appropriate model, each contributing to the organization's management of the long-term future.

12 **Sufficient time** is needed for long-term product planning to flourish: time-scales that are too tight tend to kill off such activities.

13 Companies should have portfolios with mixes of **high risk/high return** and **low risk/low return** projects to safeguard their future. A marking system can be used to grade projects (e.g. 1–5) on several parameters, including possible returns, the likelihood of success, whether the required technology already exists, and whether the organization had the required skills to achieve the set goals. This risk assessment can be used for filtering ideas.

14 Ideas can be **evaluated** first by looking at the potential benefits to customers compared to existing products on the market and, second, by assessing whether customers are likely to find those ideas attractive. There are generally more ideas than resources to develop them, so an early mechanism for filtering ideas is important.

15 Evaluation of both successful and failed projects results in **feedback** that helps to adjust the design process and improve its future effectiveness.

IT TAKES A LONG TIME TO DESIGN FOR THE FUTURE

A long-term project may need a significant lead time before there is productive output. Consider a large project that takes ten years before it comes on stream. An example could be the 5th terminal at Heathrow Airport. In practice such projects are made up of many smaller projects, some may be planned now but others may not yet be possible. All such projects can be mapped out on the innovation highway and these may show serial innovations.

It may be that the longer-term ones are treated with less importance just because there appears to be a significant time before they need to be realized. Having been positioned on the length of the innovation highway it is then possible to identify the start and completion stages of the aspects of the project forward in time towards the present. As part of this plan will be shown the technology that will need to exist to be able to complete the project.

This may show the need for serial innovation. Several options are open to the project manager when planning for the technology that will be used:

(Continued)

(Continued)

> (a)   A stage may be designed in a 'sub-optimum' form using current technology but configured so that it can accommodate newer technology as it becomes available. This will involve actively seeking suppliers of that technology.
>
> (b)   Where a particular technology is needed perhaps it can be developed by the organization, if the skills and finance are available.
>
> (c)   It may be possible to enter alliances with other organizations or universities to develop the technology.
>
> 'You must have a clean desk to plan the future – otherwise you never get round to doing it properly.' (Research interviewee)

The only one who likes change is a wet baby.

Ray Blitzer, Educator

Setting the highway

There needs to be a long-term strategic plan or business plan stretching over the period under consideration which prescribes an overall direction for the organization at which new products and services can be targeted. This has become known as **'the length of the innovation highway'** (see Figure 14.1). Quite often this is then translated into five-year or three-year rolling plans. These can then be translated into a long-term product or service plan.

The start of the highway is determined by the organization's existing new product development programme and the life cycle of specific products. This highway dovetails into existing products and services that are currently being marketed and also the next product that is being developed. Generating ideas for new products over the long term does not seem to be a problem. The real challenges are to be found in identification of the right ideas and adequate resources to develop them.

The process for planning these long-term products generally includes a set of parameters inside which new products must be positioned. These necessary restrictions are generally financial or time restrictions but may also include the number of staff or type of skills that could be used. Smaller companies will have the most restrictions around areas that could be explored when looking at long-term products. This is known as **'the width of the innovation highway'** (Figure 14.2). This, in effect, is the specification for this type of product. The 'width' can be as open or restricted as necessary. The more that are specified the more restricted will be the subsequent allowable ideas that emanate from the system.

As implied, the length and width of the innovation highway has to be determined by senior managers – it is a responsibility of those at corporate level.

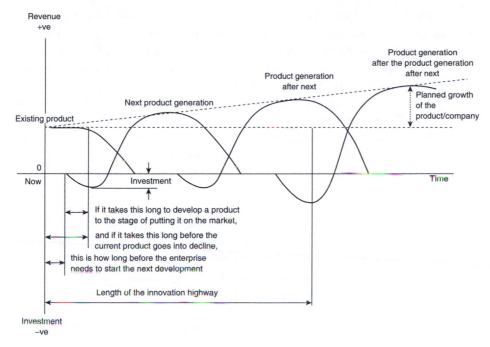

FIGURE 14.1 THE LENGTH OF THE INNOVATION HIGHWAY (REPRODUCED FROM BS 7000-1: 1999 WITH PERMISSION FROM BSI CSERVICES@BSI-GLOBAL.COM)

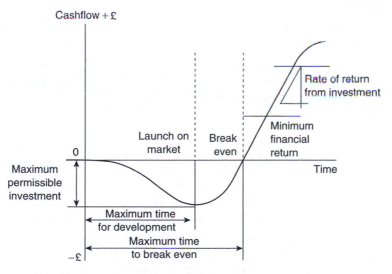

FIGURE 14.2 THE WIDTH OF THE INNOVATION HIGHWAY (REPRODUCED FROM BS 7000-1: 1999 WITH PERMISSION FROM BSI CSERVICES@BSI-GLOBAL.COM)

The 'width' is not cast in stone. Circumstances will alter and these may require 'fine tuning' to the parameters laid down: *'Competitors that have a rigid plan for their future tend to go out of business'*, said one research interviewee. On the other hand, wholesale and regular large changes probably, indicate that the initial parameters specified were poorly considered.

Parameters can be expanded as time passes to allow for growth within the organization. For example, it is possible to specify a particular maximum investment for the development of types of product. It may be planned for the maximum specified to increase over the length of the innovation highway. This may, or may not, include an additional figure to account for inflation. It is also possible to build in factors to allow for business cycles.

The more open the parameters or the fewer the specified restrictions the greater will be the freedom to innovate. Also, though, with less 'direction' the greater will be the risk of the organization taking a wrong turn. Brainstorming is the most commonly used way to determine both the width of the innovation highway and the subsequent products that could be fitted along the length of the innovation highway. The 'width of the innovation highway' is used to filter the ideas coming from the unrestricted brainstorming session, just as would be the case in the use of product specifications when planning the short term.

Mankind has run out of things to invent.

Sextus Julius Frontinus, AD 10

Conclusions

Bruce (1998) stated that the right culture for change included 'a clear vision of what success will look like, commitment in the form of necessary resources and budget, a clear and communicated plan of activities and a mechanism for validating the value at the end'. These have all been found to be true in the research reported here.

Without any plan, an organization will have to take a 'shot gun' approach to the future and can only react to situations as they occur – they will be 'fire fighting' for much of the time and following other competitors for almost all the time. No direction means that any direction is right. With a plan for the future and a system to bring the potential new products into reality, a company will be able to focus resources and skills towards making the future possibilities into realities. People within companies will have a shared direction and higher morale, and products and services can be planned along an innovation highway. Old products can be withdrawn and new replacements mapped out at future milestones. The resources (often financial) can be planned to be made available when they are needed.

Even if the direction given is not altogether correct, if properly considered in the first place it will probably be almost right and will only require 'fine tuning' as circumstances and situations change. Either the company has a plan that relates to future products and services for the future or the prospects of employment in that company are in a very vulnerable position. To be confident of corporate survival they need to know where they are going.

This information has contributed towards the formulation of an integrated process in the British Standard, BS 7000 1, *Guide to Managing Innovation* (British Standards Institution 1999).

If we don't change our direction, we'll end up exactly where we are heading.

Ancient proverb

SUMMARY OF KEY POINTS

- It is important that organizations plan beyond the services that they are currently selling or developing.
- Products and services change more slowly than most people realize.
- Currently, there are only five fast-moving 'areas': Electronics, Communications, Pharmaceuticals, Biotechnology and some materials.
- As most areas are changing slowly, it is possible to predict and plan new services for ten years into the future.

Act now, the future is almost upon us.

STUDENT ACTIVITY 14.1: EXERCISE ON THE EXTERNAL ENVIRONMENT

1   Taking a service or an industry of your choice, analyse the external factors which are affecting the industry now.
2   How might the factors change in the foreseeable future and what do you consider to be the likely impact on the future viability of the companies within the industry?
3   How can a company within this industry use such an analysis to guide their strategy?

STUDENT ACTIVITY 14.2: SHORT TERMISM

Dyson is quoted as saying:

There is a short-termism, perhaps brought about by failure, that demands a fast return, an immediate whopping turnover, a quick buck. Design and research and engineering are not about that. They offer a long-term way of regenerating a company – or building one.

Relating this to the service sector, discuss the validity of this statement. In your answer refer to how your organization (or an organization with which you are familiar) operates. From the literature, state how this situation could be improved within any chosen organization.

FURTHER READING.

British Standard (1999) BS 7000-1, *Guide to Managing Innovation*. London: British Standards Institution.

Gibson R. (ed). (1997) *Rethinking the Future*. London: Nicholas Brearley.

Hollins W. and Hollins G. (1999) *Over the Horizon*: *Planning Products Today for Success Tomorrow*. Chichester: Wiley.

Jackson M. (2005) 'Anticipating the future', *Strategy Magazine*, Issue 6 (December).

Mintzberg H. (1998) *Strategy Safari*. Englewood Cliffs, NJ: Prentice Hall.

Peters G. (1996) *Beyond the Next Wave: Imagining the Next Generation of Customers*. London: Pitman.

Schwartz P. (1998) *The Art of the Long View*. Chichester: Wiley.

Sheth J.N. and Sisodia R.S. (2006) *Tectonic Shift*. London: Sage.

PART 4

Case Study

15 'Trenbrover Football Club'
Here all the techniques are brought together in trying to manage a struggling foot-ball club.

Glossary
This section offers a list of definitions for some of the key terms used in this book.

> Our ability to invent, design and manufacture the goods and services that
> people want is more vital to our future prosperity than ever.
>
> Tony Blair, DTI Innovation Review, 27 November 2002

15 TRENBROVER FOOTBALL CLUB

This case study incorporates many of the ideas put forward in this book. If you find aspects difficult to understand then look back to the relevant chapter. As you read it try to think what would be the best way to save this club as a thriving going concern.

The case study is about a struggling football club. Outside of the Premier League, most football clubs are in financial difficulties and there are not many that can support their ambitions from the income derived just from the playing side. As a result, many have developed ingenious methods for increasing their income from other sources. Many of the smaller football clubs could be considered masters at Customer Relationship Marketing, with efforts that put the larger clubs in the shade. In this chapter, we describe one such club that is just coming to terms with the realities of football in the lower divisions.

www.farnhambee.co.uk

Scene 1:   April

It was not a happy time at the Trenbrover Football Club. They had lost their last two games and an away defeat at Wycombe Wanderers had sealed their fate.

'Look, we are relegated and, like most other clubs in the bottom two divisions of the league, we are broke', said Marvin Lunge, the Chairman and Chief Executive of Trenbrover. 'I've got everybody together because we have a crisis on our hands. We are spending too much, gates are falling and the bank is threatening to call in their money. We have to find a way out of this crisis or we will fold.

'Now, football clubs are not a lot different from any small company, except most small companies can control their futures. In football we need a bit of luck and we haven't been getting much recently. But good luck or bad, the only way out of this mess is to manage our way out of it.

This is what we are going to do, and it is not much different from any small business that finds itself in trouble. We are going to:

1   Analyse where we are now.
2   Realistically identify where we want to be.
3   Plan for it.
4   Then implement the plan.

'But, also, we need to survive the serious situation we find ourselves in. We need a short-term survival plan and a longer-term strategy, say, for five years. This is what I propose. You are each going to be assigned tasks. You can call on the help of everybody you can, but each named person will be responsible for seeing these tasks through.'

At this point Sid Bobbins, the team manager, came in late to the meeting. 'What I need is new players, good players, something with a bit of class if we are going to bounce straight back up next season. How much can you let me have, Marvin?'

'Sorry, the answer is very little. We are a club in trouble and unless we sort out this crisis now you will not have a club called Trenbrover starting the next season in August.'

'But, Marvin, you are always saying that. The money is not my problem, I just deal with the playing side. Just dip your hand in your wallet and I'll get you the players.'

'Sorry, Sid, not this time. I've put enough into this club and the losses have now gone beyond my means, especially as my property development business is also going through a bad patch at the moment. And what is more, it is everybody's problem and if we don't solve it we will all be out of a job – probably starting with you.'

Molly Kettle, the Commercial Manager, interrupted, 'Let's keep this friendly. We are all in the same boat and we need to plan our way out of it, just like you said at the start, Marvin. So where do we start, boss?'

'Well first, Molly, I would like you to get everybody to give you a list of things they can do, jobs they have held in the past and, even, details of their hobbies. We already have a lot of this information on people's CVs, but I want the information from everybody.'

SKILLS AUDIT

A skills audit is often a useful starting point when tackling any problem. This can be compiled at any time and, preferably, at quiet times. It need not be product-related, though, if you are considering particular products or service, giving this particular direction or focus is often quite useful. It is, also, helpful to include hobbies and it is surprising what skills people involve themselves with, just out of interest, that can also be used by the organization. Furthermore, if somebody is doing something unpaid as a hobby, they are often quite keen to utilize these skills within their main occupation and get paid for it.

Scene 2:   Two days Later

Molly entered Marvin's office. 'Well, I've got all the CVs and have been through them and we have quite a diversity of skills within this place. Did you know that the Communications Manager, Peter Dillon, recently obtained an MBA?'

'What's he doing in a job like this then?' queried Marvin.

'I asked him that. He said he actually likes the job and he says that his MBA helps him in his daily tasks.'

Marvin continued, 'Anyway, the point of collecting all this information is twofold. First to find out what we can do, but also to show, perhaps, what we shouldn't be involved in. If we don't have the skills available, it's going to take us time and money to get them. We have neither time nor money. In effect, what this does is set a parameter or boundary around what we can do. What I intend to do is to build up a series of these boundaries and, as a club, we must operate within these.

'Of course, the main boundary is going to be financial. What can we afford? How much can we borrow, over what period of time and how quickly can we get the money back? The next thing to do is to have a chat with Peter. With his knowledge he must be the best person to coordinate all this.'

BOUNDARIES

Organizations have to operate within a set of boundaries and most of these are not openly expressed, but are known in a vague, roundabout way. For example, a small organization, such as a small, privately owned machine shop, would be unable to design and manufacture aeroplanes. On the other hand, they may be able to make parts for aeroplanes. Likewise, an advertising agency is unlikely to become involved in manufacture at all.

(Continued)

(Continued)

If the senior managers in an organization agree a set of parameters, within which the organization will operate, these can be specific. Projects that are undertaken will fit into the area bounded by these series of specified boundaries. Any project that does not would, probably, not be started. With certain projects there may be areas that do appear to be right for the organization, but other areas which are not. For example, it may be that a particular organization can produce a product or service, but does not have the required means to market it. Knowing the area, which is outside the organizational boundaries, would require those within the organization to specify how they would overcome this deficiency before proceeding any further. It may be, for this one aspect alone, the project would be abandoned.

Marvin introduced the broad problem to Peter. Far from being full of bright ideas, Peter sat at his desk looking confused but then he said, 'I think the next stage should be to look at what we are going to do, just like developing a new service. We are going to go through a design process and we are going to manage this process just like it would be managed within any company. I'm going to state the various stages that we should go through and, using this design model, we can develop the various products and services to get us out of this mess. Of course, at the early stages, these will look a little "raw". When we have got the details together, we will then work on how to implement them'.

'A good starting point would be to look at what the customers want and then see what we can do to give it to them. Remembering, of course, that we have got to make a profit and a substantial one at that. And what is more, we have to survive as a club until we can turn things around.'

'But we know what the customers want,' said Marvin. 'They want a winning team.'

'Managers and designers do go seriously astray – when they begin to believe they can be effective arbiters of consumer needs without researching such needs sensibly – when, in ignorance or sheer arrogance, managers and designers begin to rationalize their private wants into fictitious or superficial consumer needs'. (Topalian 1980)

'Yes', Peter replied. 'We know what the customers want in simple terms, but beyond the obvious we only think we know what the customers want. When we get down to the fine detail to find out what they do want, we need to ask them. We need to do some market research and even this will not go far enough. This is all part of customer relationship marketing. We also need to tap into the needs of those people who aren't yet supporters. Even if we could keep our existing supporters, having just been relegated, we won't have a sufficient income. We need to find out what others want and supply that as well.'

'But how can we do market research when we don't know what we are doing market research on?' Marvin queried.

'This is the problem with many of the books I used in my studying. They put things down in such a way as to make it appear obvious. Real life isn't like that, even in a small club like this with a turnover of only 5 million pounds. The books also seem to ignore the fact that there are so many things going on at the same time. So many calls on the money available and all the books plead that their area is the most important, often completely ignoring all the other areas. Things don't happen in a simple sequence and in isolation. Everything is a muddle and intertwined. The more I think about it the worse it gets. I think an Operations Management approach would be best as this topic tends to look at the bigger picture.

'Just take market research. They all assume you start by looking at the market, but you can't until you have an idea of what you may want to offer them. Then you have to go back and see if you want to do that anyway and then you have to go back and ask the customers before you can start to think about what you are going to do. It all looks so simple in books, going neatly from one stage to the next. In practice it just seems a complete muddle and I am not even sure where to start.'

CHANGE IS ALWAYS FULL OF ITERATION

Which comes first, the concept session or the market research? Does design always start at the same stage of the process?

Marvin looked crest fallen. 'Do you mean you can't do it?'

'What? This is the opportunity I've been waiting for. I've got all the theory, I know this club inside out and, what is more, I'm the person to do it. Leave it to me, Marvin. You give me the support, the time and just a bit of pump-priming cash and watch me work. Everybody will need to get involved and if they do we will get this club going again.'

'Good man, Peter. You have my support and the cash, say £50,000, but there will not be any more when you have blown this.'

Scene 3:   A little later

Sid Bobbins burst into Marvin's office. 'What's all this about Peter getting 50 grand to play with yet there's nothing for me. That money would buy me an all-right midfielder. I want that money. No, I need it.'

'Sorry it is worse than that. To give him that money we will have to let some players go. We have been living beyond our means and no successful business can do that indefinitely. We have to pay our way from now on and if Peter gets some money to sort things out then it means there is less for Paul, or in this case, Sid.'

Sid fumed. 'But I won't take it – the fans won't take it.'

'We have just got to accept that we can't afford the new players for this coming season that will get us promotion. We need to keep as many of the existing supporters as happy as possible whilst we put in the systems to make us some money. By the following season we should be a more viable business with funds to "invest" in the team. It is a rough tough fact of life. At the moment the money is just not there to be able to go into the market.'

'Look, Marvin, I'm telling you straight. If I don't get some cash and pretty fast then I'm off.'

Marvin thought for a few seconds then invited Sid to sit down and talk things through. 'I don't want to see you go. OK, so we have just been relegated but I still think you are a good manager. I want you to stay but you have to face up to realities. There is no money unless we earn it. When we do then you can have your players. That is top priority, I promise. But until then we all have to turn our efforts to saving and planning, what we save can finance our plans. If we fail then we fold, if we succeed then you can be part of that success. Don't just walk out on us. Go away and think about it for a bit. If you do choose to leave you will need to find another job and there aren't too many for managers who have just had their team drop down a division.'

Sid was still not pleased. He rose slowly from his chair, was about to say something then changed his mind and left the office. Marvin could see from his window as Sid climbed in his car and drove away from the ground. 'I wonder if he'll be back,' he thought.

Scene 4:   Next day

Peter was discussing his ideas with all the office staff and barely looked round when Marvin walked in. 'To keep our existing supporters happy is going to take a very large dose of customer relationship marketing. In my studies I have noticed that CRM is a bit like Total Quality Management and "delighting the customer" [Deming 1986] and it also ties in with the main reason for services failing – market failure, "not understanding the customer requirements" [Cooper 1983]. So whatever we do we have to focus on our customers – and our potential customers.'

CUSTOMER *RELATIONSHIP MARKETING*

'There has been a shift from transaction to relationship focus in marketing. Customers become partners and the firm must make long-term commitments to maintaining those relationships with quality, service and innovation'. (Zeithaml and Bitner, 1996: 171)

> *(Continued)*
>
> *During this decade this has become one of the important parts of marketing and actually by following the introduction of relationship marketing various other new processes will be found to be necessary that can improve your existing services. The aim of relationship marketing goes beyond the traditional transaction or a focus on a single sale. As it has been shown that it is easier to retain customers than it is to find new ones, relationship marketing addresses how to keep customers through additional services linked to the original sale and re-purchase.*
>
> *One of the effects of relationship marketing is that it tends to 'stretch' the organization's involvement with mainly the service side of their offerings. This will be shown up in the blueprint.*

Suddenly Molly burst in to the office. 'Bad news Marvin. Have you seen the papers? Sid says he has been kicked out and you are holding the club back by not investing in new players.'

'I guessed something like this might happen after our talk yesterday. He is right about the second part but I was rather hoping that this information would come from me in a carefully worded press release.'

Molly looked glum. 'With all he has been saying it isn't going to do our customer relationship marketing initiative any good. I will knock up something and show it to you before giving it to the press. You had better talk to the players before they start to panic. We have to remember, as part of TQM, we must also think of our internal customers. That is, everybody who works here.'

'Good idea,' Marvin answered. 'Just make sure that the press release says he hasn't been sacked but don't include the usual bit about a vote of confidence as nobody believes that any more. Tell the lads we will have a meeting first thing tomorrow morning.' Then Marvin added, 'Well at least that saves us a wage bill and that gives us a bit more to play with. But we still need a Team Manager.'

Scene 5:   Next day

Albert Melnikoff, the accountant, was working on the finances to run the club. The outgoings were fairly clear if rather worrying. The income of any football club is far less predictable than it is from most businesses. A bad patch, like the club has recently experienced, can really hit the income. The gates were well down and this means all the associated income was also down. Fewer programme sales, the weekly club lottery sales and even sales from the tea and hamburger stands were well down. It was sales from the club shop which seemed to have been hit hardest. Who wants to be seen and ridiculed in the replica shirt of a team that has just been relegated?'

What was needed was an income from the club that was not so dependent on the success of the team. Something that could be set up without a lot of expense but could use some of the under-utilized facilities that the club owned. Albert broached his problem to Peter. Peter was quick to reply.

'This is a creativity problem. We can write a specification which will include all the things that the club has or can use. We can then 'dream' up some concepts in a brainstorming session, the concepts are possible ideas that can raise us some money.'

Albert was unfamiliar with this use of creativity but could see the logic in what Peter had suggested. 'A brainstorming session. I've heard of these. A few people getting together to thrash out some ideas. All the top management team should be involved.'

'Not necessarily,' interrupted Peter, 'the best ideas don't necessarily come from the most senior people. I think a group of players would make an ideal team to start this off. They aren't doing much at this time of the year. You sort out a list of the clubs assets and also some financial parameters such as how much we need and when do we need it. Realistic figures now. If you ask for millions then the whole thing will be a failure. It would also be a good idea to specify some boundaries around the scheme. This will give the sessions a clearer focus.'

BRAINSTORMING

Brainstorming is a group, problem-solving activity. The rules were devised by Alex Osborne in the late 1930s and published in the 1950s (Osborne 1953, republished 1993), although in its basic form brainstorming is probably hundreds of years old. He defined brainstorming as where a group of people 'attempt to find a solution for a specific problem by amassing all the ideas spontaneously contributed by its members'.

The rules are quite 'antique', but still valid. The group should consist of people from a diversity of backgrounds, working on a particular problem and following strict rules and guidelines. These are shown in Chapter 7.

STUDENT ACTIVITY 15.1

Working in groups, try brainstorming this problem yourselves.

Using the information shown and a maximum budget of £50,000, make suggestions how this can be made to grow to £200,000 in 6 months. Also, taking a long-term view, what other money-raising schemes can you propose to generate income for the club? The income needs to be generated away from the playing side so it is not dependent just on the club's success (or otherwise).

The property of Trenbrover Football Club PLC

Freehold football stadium, capacity 13,000, comprising 9,000 seated undercover and 4,000 standing, with 2,000 of these undercover.

Football pitch 110 x 85 yards, four food and drink stands – one at each side of the ground, club shop, bar and club house – capacity 400, 15 turnstiles, car park 80 x 60 yards.

Training pitch 50 x 90 yards, 6 old lock-up garages – positioned together under Railway arches – each 10 x 6 yards.

2 cars and 1 x 12-seat minibus. Fully equipped and manned secretarial function with printing facilities. Loudspeaker system that can be heard in all parts of the ground.

Following the brainstorming session Peter reported back to Albert Melnikoff. 'Actually it went very well. It started off as a bit of a joke and there were a lot of daft ideas but then they began to take it more seriously. One of the early ideas was to open a stud farm for lonely ladies and another was an escort agency. But at least they were thinking widely.'

'As the ideas began to dwindle we packed up for an hour and they had a training session. Then we started again and some good ideas came. Then after lunch we continued the session down the pub, the club paid for the drinks.'

'What? Is that wise. They are professional footballers.'

'They are adults as well and it has been shown that alcohol does improve creativity. You know this is true yourself. You go to a party, have a few drinks and suddenly the bright ideas flood into your head.'

'And the first, and worst, is that I think I can dance,' interrupted Albert.

'It has also been shown that marijuana and most other drugs do the opposite by reducing creativity. People begin to focus too much. It is always a problem to get people away from what they have seen before; to try to stop them relying too much on experience.'

'Well, was the investment in drink worthwhile?'

'It came to £47 for the eight of them so it wasn't too bad and I think we got some ideas that will work in both the long and short term. The first big idea is a bingo game. We have the seats, the loudspeaker system and can even print the cards here. A really big prize could be a car that we could drive onto the pitch at the start of the evening.'

'Good idea, Peter. I'll work out the costings. I know we fulfil the legal requirements because of our existing club lottery. I'll get Molly to work out the promotion aspects. It will need a good deal of work to make sure people know about it. Any other good ideas?'

'I'm still assessing them. Some look good in the long term. It seems wise to sell the lock-up garages and maybe sell the training pitch for housing. We could raise £15 million through that alone, but that would take a good bit of planning and a lot of time before the cash comes in. Marvin is in the property development business so he should be able to guide us in the right direction. Many small clubs practise in the local council-owned facilities and there is no reason why we shouldn't do the same.'

'That is a great idea, Peter, but we need money now. What can we do over the summer that will bring in some cash now?'

'A soccer school where the lads will give lessons. Not big money, but thirty kids paying £5 a day for ten short days during a couple of weeks of the school summer holidays could bring in a bit and it will get the local lads interested in the club. Some of the lads have volunteered so we can do it at ten sites throughout the borough. I reckon about £10,000 after expenses. We would need to promote it in schools. If the idea works we could repeat it every half term and holiday.

'The physio has said that he could run a sports injury clinic if we get him the insurance cover. Also the local council seem keen to support our activities through a "Football in the Community'" scheme.

'We can "sell" plots of the pitch for a fiver and issue fancy certificates of ownership. We can run a pop concert, we can hold car boot sales. There are loads of ideas.'

'With all these plans we can get the support of the local paper. Old Fred down at the *Gazette* is as Trenbrover mad as any and will do anything he can to help us in his rag.'

'There are quite a lot of good ideas amongst the bad. Too many have to be rejected because the set-up costs are too great, they damage the pitch or the club's reputation or they just have too long a pay-back period for the work involved. I will circulate a list of the best ideas and perhaps everybody will add a few more when they see what we are trying to do.

EVALUATION

Evaluating ideas from a brainstorming session involves first appraising the suggestions against the specification and then through a 'concept assessment matrix'.

'We also now need a specification for each. I know that normally the detailed specification usually comes first but in this really "blue sky" concept generation that we have been doing the brief we used was sufficient. We now have some firm ideas and to develop these properly we really need a thorough specification. This always looks like hard work at the start but it is easier to solve all the compromises when things are still on bits of paper than when we have gone further down the line and have started to invest money in them. If I can't write a sensible specification for any of the ideas at this stage then the idea can be abandoned and we won't have spent a lot of money on it. I will use a checklist to guide me, and this lists 35 elements that need to be considered for each idea.'

SPECIFICATIONS AND LISTS OF ELEMENTS

What do you think needs to be considered? Have a couple of goes at this as there is a lot more than one would at first think. Also, there needs to be more compromise between 'elements' than one would initially think.

How should these specifications be used and compiled?

Scene 6: Later that week

Less than a week has gone by since his crisis speech and things were really buzzing. Marvin was happy with the way things were going. He was also a bit busier himself, looking into the possibilities of building on the training pitch. Things had been going well except for the manager walking out. The trouble was that cuts had to be made and these had to start with the playing staff. Albert had supplied a list of the expenditure in each area and there were some parts of the club where savings could be made.

'The trouble with making cuts is the effect it has on everybody,' Marvin thought. 'It lowers morale throughout the organization and even those who are not directly affected become suspicious and this results in bitterness. People start doing only "their" bit and do not assist others unless they have to.' It was going to be a difficult patch ahead and Marvin had to face up to the fact that there would be some fierce squabbles before calm would eventually return.

He also had to streamline procedures to maximize the efficiency of the club. They were going to be a smaller club than they were before and people would need to take on more responsibility and have bigger roles. This situation was bound to remain for at least a couple of seasons. At least Marvin had made up his mind that he would do just one reorganization and not make it 'death by a thousand cuts'. Each reorganization can cause more problems of suspicion, lower morale and distrust. 'Do it once and do it properly,' he thought. 'This will be the strategy.'

Marvin had found the 'retained list' of players in Sid's office and thought that the pruning hadn't gone far enough. He agreed with those players identified as being allowed to go but should a few more be added? This was a difficult problem as he wasn't qualified himself to make the decision. 'Too many chairmen,' he thought, 'poke their noses into the playing side of football clubs and their actions are mostly purely based on their time spent in the stands watching the game on a Saturday.' He had to be more professional so he decided to stick with the list. It might make things easier when telling the players because he could say that it was not his choice but put the 'blame' on Sid. But that was too easy. Ultimately, it was his responsibility and he couldn't pass on the buck, or the blame, to another. ('The buck stops here,' had said US President Harry S. Truman.)

The salary structure was his responsibility, as was finding a new manager. When the players find out how their wages have been cut to match their new found 'status' no doubt there would be other departures and these would be amongst the better players whose agents could get onto the playing staff of clubs in a higher division.

One by one Marvin called in the players and announced whether they were staying or going. It was a horrible job and far worse than he could have imagined. 'Any company that announces redundancy must go through this exercise,' he thought. Some of the axed players, mainly the youngsters, looked heart-broken, some were defiant and argued their case forcefully and others turned quite offensive. Quite a lot of the retained players also made it clear that they wanted to go and these were asked to put their transfer request in writing. As expected, these tended to be the better players but not exclusively.

At the end of the exercise Marvin felt sick. He had prided himself on being a hard man but he was not so hard as he had thought. 'Sid had chosen his time to leave well,' he thought, but at least he had reduced the number of players to 24, and six of those were apprentices. That was just enough to keep the first team going and we would resign from the reserve team league. The juniors would make up the numbers if other players were injured or suspended. It was still a pretty big wage bill and further cuts might be necessary if the books still weren't balancing. The next stage would be to go through the permanent office staff and look for cuts there. This was going to be even harder. How could he raise the morale and get everybody working together with the threat of redundancy hanging over their heads?

As a rule, **never try to introduce change whilst making redundancies**. *When people fear losing their jobs they will view any change as a threat and will not cooperate.*

A little while later Peter looked in on Marvin and found him deep in thought. 'A penny for them, Marvin,' said Peter.

'I was just thinking about the manager problem. We need someone inspirational. We want someone who can carry us all forward and I don't see anyone who will fit the bill. In a small organization like this the personality of the person at the top is so important, the right man or woman can lead by example and can take everyone along. In a large organization the top person can act as a figurehead but the actual personality of the person perhaps isn't so important.'

'I remember back in the late sixties there was a football club in the old Third Division who were just as broke as we now are. They pruned right down to only 14 professional players and almost no other staff. They had an inspirational manager called Jimmy Sirrel who did everything. He even cut the grass and fixed holes in the roof of the stand! On match days he would whip up his players into a real team. They would run through brick walls for him. They were never going to win any trophies but it was great to see a bunch of underpaid lads running their hearts out for each other, the fans, the club, the manager and themselves. They showed real pride and the crowd loved it.'

'But things are different now,' said Peter. 'Players are only out for what they can get and you can't tell me that there is a common purpose or even a common direction running through this club.'

'Bit of a hero is he, this Jimmy Sirrel?' Peter teased. 'I thought your heroes would be successful building contractors.'

'Our heroes aren't always the most obvious people', Marvin was quick to reply.

'I do have an idea, actually, said Peter. Our captain is young but inspirational – I've seen him in action during training. Could we make George Towers the Player Manager? He may not be the obvious choice, but the other players like him and he does have their respect.'

'That's a good idea', said Marvin, and he was one of the better lads who wanted to stay. On the wider front we also need a clearly expressed common purpose.'

Peter answered, 'Do you mean a "Mission Statement" to give us a common purpose? I've seen quite a few Mission Statements and they tend to take up a lot of management time, which we haven't got, and are usually no more than a bland set of words put in a bright frame to adorn the foyer of the company, alongside their ISO 9000 certificate. Save us from that.'

'But they don't have to be,' Marvin rejoined. 'Heaven knows we have the perfect mission statement for right now, and that can focus our ideas. When we have achieved it we can scrap it and have another that suits that period and that set of circumstances. I agree with you about Mission Statements in most places. They try to write something that is the mission for all time and the top directors spend an age compiling it. It must cost a fortune in their wasted, expensive time. We will have something short and pertinent.

'I know as the chief executive I shouldn't make the Mission Statement on my own, but I suggest that it ought to be, at the moment, **'The survival of Trenbrover FC through profitable short-term ventures'**.

Peter frowned. 'It doesn't sound right to me, but at least it will get us focussed. Survival is the top priority and we can only do that by making money.'

'OK,' said Marvin, 'print it up and stick it on the notice board but no fancy frames. Also tell people to send their ideas to you or me for money-making schemes. Perhaps you could knock up a suggestion box and we could go through the ideas once a week.'

Scene 7: A week later

Marvin returned after a week of working abroad on his latest construction venture. It had not gone well. The market throughout Europe was flat and if any business was to be obtained then profits would be cut to the bone. On Marvin's first day back Peter arranged to see him. Peter came in to Marvin's room looking rather smug.

'It's all going rather well and we already have quite a lot organized. There is only one thing, Marvin. The set-up costs have come to £60,000 so we need another £10,000.'

Marvin was quick to retort, 'You can't have it because I haven't got it and even if I had you still couldn't have it. I said £50,000 tops and I meant it. There is no more so some of your plans will have to go. Use Pareto for a start – the 80:20 rule. Most of the money will come from just a few ideas so concentrate on those.'

Peter could see that Marvin was in an unshakeable mood but he tried to persuade his boss. 'A lot of the plans are quite a long way down the line and will cause problems if we try to call a halt on them now.' (See Figure 15.1).

'You should have thought of that. Go and work something out with old Melnikoff. I've got more on my plate at the moment than I need and this club is not even on the agenda today.'

Albert Melnikoff was in a better mood and listened to what Peter had to say. 'I'm on Marvin's side but I sympathize with you,' he said. 'You have worked hard on these plans but we have to be realistic. There really isn't any more than the £50,000 and you should have worked within that. That doesn't mean that your plans have to be

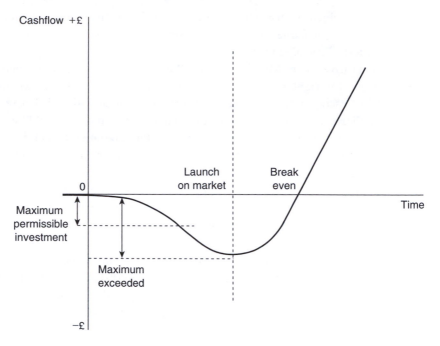

FIGURE 15.1   THE PROBLEM: THE INITIAL INVESTMENT REQUIRED EXCEEDS AVAILABLE FINANCE

scrapped, just rescheduled. I'll explain. Delay some ideas and the use of income from one venture to pay for another. Some of the ideas have to fit into certain times but others can be rearranged so that they can be fitted into a more suitable time. You can build all this into a Gantt chart and this can be developed to show when the expenses will occur and when the cash should come in.'

> *It is possible to schedule plans so that the income from one can pay for the next – and so on – but it doesn't always work. Back in 1985 Sir Clive Sinclair planned a series of three battery-driven cars and the profit for the first was supposed to pay for the second and then the third. Unfortunately, the first was a disaster and didn't pay for anything, not even itself!*

'Consider all the priorities of what we are trying to do. Some of the fund raising schemes must be done immediately and some can be delayed a bit. It may not be ideal but some of the ideas may even need to be cancelled, although probably only a couple at the most. By stretching out the plans you need never go over the magic £50,000 ceiling and what is more, the income from one project can go to finance subsequent projects. Two things to remember: the first is that people do not pay their bills as quickly as they should, and so you must avoid a cash flow crisis. This is an aspect of my job. (See Figure 15.2).

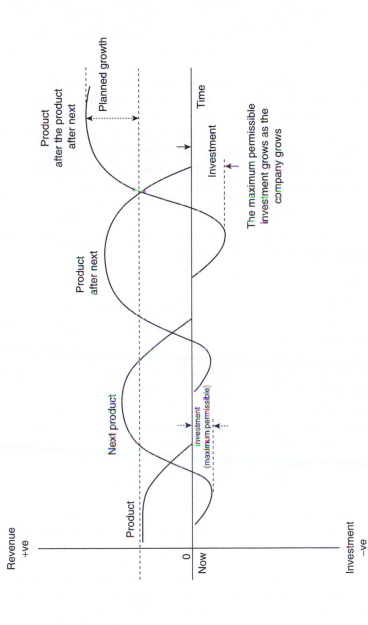

FIGURE 15.2 INITIAL INVESTMENT SPREAD OVER TIME, WORKING WITHIN AVAILABLE FINANCE. (NOTE: THE FIGURE DEMONSTRATES HOW THE INVESTMENT CAN GROW AS THE PROFITABILITY GROWS. ALSO NOTE THAT IF OPERATING WELL, THE EXPENDITURE WILL NEVER DROP AGAIN BELOW ZERO – BUT THE FIGURE AS DRAWN IS FOR CLARITY OF THE PRINCIPLE)

OVERTRADING

Overtrading occurs when (successful) companies take on too much and extend their finances. If there is a delay in the money coming in then the immediate bills do not get paid, there is a cash flow crisis, the company goes into debt and the bank can foreclose. More people used to go bankrupt from overtrading than anything else.

'The second thing to remember is that many of your schemes, sorry, *our* schemes, will be a failure. You must be realistic and anticipate that more than half of your plans will probably not be profitable. If you assume that they all will be profitable then you probably will not have generated sufficient funds from the early schemes to pay for the later ones. You will need to include on your Gantt chart a large factor for expediency to allow for the failures that are bound to occur. Always choose the worst case scenario if your company survival is in jeopardy, and this club is!'

Research has shown that companies need (on average) to put 2.6 products/services on the market for each success.

'We also need to develop a resource plan and also a Roles and Responsibility Matrix to take some of the load off your shoulders, otherwise you will work yourself into an early grave.'

Peter knew what Albert was saying. He had been working from seven in the morning until after ten at night every day for the past fortnight and it was clear that it was showing. He knew he couldn't go on like this indefinitely but there wasn't enough time to delegate. Of course, this was stupid; of course there was time to delegate. An afternoon to develop the Roles and Responsibility Matrix would enable him to share out the work fairly and leave him a lot more time to oversee the progress of the total strategy. This is what management is all about, planning, delegation and evaluating. The lessons of his MBA were beginning to come home to him.

'And,' Albert continued, 'as well as developing a type of Gantt chart to show the activities that need to be done, you probably need a blueprint as well.'

Peter interrupted, 'I've already developed a plan for each of the fund raising schemes and on each of these is shown the anticipated times of each of the stages.'

There is a link between a Gantt chart and a design model. The design model shows the activities that need to be undertaken to develop a new service. These activities can be shown on a Gantt and this will be to a base of time. This can show the 'concurrencies' (what can be done in parallel). It is then necessary to identify a cost for each of these (and can also show the maximum expenditure at any one time) and then the people who should be involved in a 'Roles and Responsibility Matrix'.

Scene 8:   Two days later

Peter had been working hard and his head started to spin. He was tired. To break the muddle he strolled over to the notice board to collect the suggestion box. He noticed that someone had scrawled over the Mission Statement and added their own rather personal comments. 'Perhaps this is why they always protect these Mission Statements under the cover of a frame', he thought. The suggestion box didn't encourage him either. Jobs were being lost and several of the staff were broadcasting their feelings anonymously through the suggestion scheme. Peter was feeling depressed as he read the various comments.

Then one caught has eye. It said, 'I know that Molly collected details of the skills in this place and we have all listed what we think we can do, but what about our supporters? There are at least 4,000 people who want to see Trenbrover a success. Why not ask through the local paper for help and ideas for fund raising? Also, what skills do local businesses have which they can share with the club? Special deals for supporters or donations to the club? There are 4,000 lists of skills just waiting out there to be collected.'

Peter was further pleased to see that the idea had come from one of the players. Perhaps they weren't all just interested in themselves as he had originally thought. This also showed one of the ways in which a football club was different from most other organizations. How often would customers be expected to rally around to help out a company that gets itself into trouble?

There was more good news when he got to his office. There was a message from a local businesswoman and fan who offered reduced price programme printing, and an offer from another for training facilities at a local health club, all through the good publicity of the local paper. All the businesswoman wanted was an advert for her company on the edge of the pitch. Peter thought, 'I wonder if anyone will pay to put an advert on the roof of the stand?'

Of course companies can form alliances with others to assist them in their aims and this is becoming more popular. Outsourcing is one area in which this occurs, but increasingly organizations are joining together to develop new products or, along the lines of a vertical integration tie-up, to develop improved forms of marketing. Could Trenbrover do something similar? A ground share with another club was the most obvious idea that came to mind.

By the end of the week Peter had rescheduled his plans and had plotted the anticipated expenditure against time and (conservatively) the anticipated income from each of the planned activities. This was drawn up for the next year by which time Marvin should be well on the way to putting up those houses on the training pitch. He had also plotted the cumulative expenditure and anticipated income and this showed that at no stage did the total cumulative outgoings exceed £50,000. Things were beginning to go right and he felt that he was getting things under control.

STUDENT ACTIVITY 15.1

Try to schedule the ideas selected from your brainstorming sessions into a chart complete with likely income and expenditure. Then rearrange it so expenses do not exceed £50,000 at any one time. Then identify the concurrencies and the Roles and Responsibilities Matrix.

Peter's design model and Roles and Responsibility Matrix were also working and this was taking some of the pressure off him. He was back to working sensible hours, getting a decent amount of sleep as well and was, therefore, being far more efficient during his working hours.

'It was stupid to try to do so much by myself at the start,' he thought, 'I was walking around like a zombie for some of the time and just making mistakes. It certainly pays to delegate to all the experts within the organization and then specialize on the bits that I can do best.'

Peter knew that it wasn't the beginning of the end of all the problems, but he realized that it was the end of the beginning. 'So much still to do but at least I now see the light at the end of the tunnel,' he thought.

STUDENT ACTIVITY 15.2

Is the club going in the right direction?
What would you do differently?
What more would you do?

Good reading for this is any match programme, in which one can see the lengths that some clubs go to ensure their survival with limited resources. It should be remembered that football clubs in the lower divisions are actually very small businesses, typically with turnovers of less than £10 million. Most of the players in these clubs will be earning less than £30,000 per annum.

Postscript

A Football club that prides itself on its customer relationship marketing is Brentford, winners of 'The Football Club Community Club of the Year 2005/6', and they are the inspiration behind this case study.

As an example of just one comparison between different approaches, consider this exchange of e-mails:

From: Bill Hollins

Sent: 18 November 2005 16:43

To: Peter Gilham
Subject: What a good service!

Hello Peter

I never realized what a really good service I (and presumably others) have been getting from you lot at Brentford – until I tried Arsenal.

My lad wants to see their game against Reading to see again the old Brentford players. It is a low cost game so I can afford it but not sure if work will allow me to get there and I won't know until the afternoon of the match.

Ten days ago I went to their website to find if tickets were available on the night, but it didn't tell me.

I then rang their 'help' line. After a long wait I gave up and sent an e-mail. Today I got a reply that just repeated lots I had already read from their website but still I didn't get the info.

I answered their reply with a question asking 'are tickets available at the door on the night – yes or no?' A couple of hours later I got a reply saying that they were very busy and my e-mail would be answered when they get round to it. Arsenal customer service joins my list of oxymorons like airline food, military intelligence and computer help desk.

What a joy to support Brentford! I needed an incident like that to make me realize just how good you and those around you are.

Thanks

Bill

Fifteen minutes later I got this reply:

Hi Bill

Thank you for your email … we will get round to looking at it when we get time …!!!

Best regards.

Peter

(Note to readers not familiar with English humour: this was irony!)

Glossary

ABC inventory control an approach to inventory control that classes inventory by its usage value and varies the approach to managing it accordingly

benchmarking comparing methods and performance with other processes in order to learn from them

blueprinting mapping out of a service customer journey and parallel processes that constitute the service, isolating possible fail points and establishing the time of the various stages for the journey; a 'process broken down chronologically into sequential constituent stages' [BS 7000-1 1999].

brand visual or verbal representation of an organization or product

bull-whip effect tendency of supply chains to amplify small changes at the demand side of the supply chain such that the disruption at the supply end of the chain is much higher

capacity maximum level of value added activity that an operation is capable of producing over a specified time period

cause–effect diagrams technique to identify root cause of problem requiring systematic questioning; also known as Ishikawa or fishbone analysis

cell layout resources with a common purpose put together in close proximity (e.g. in a cell)

centre-of-gravity method of location technique to determine location that balances weighted importance of the other operations with which the one being located has a direct relationship

chase demand a medium capacity management technique which tries to adjust output/capacity to reflect fluctuations in demand

concept options that might fulfil the trigger for the service

core service central or main body of the service

corporate identity articulation of what an organization is, what it stands for, what it does and the way it goes about its business (especially the way it relates to its stakeholders and the environment) [BS 7000-10 1995, definition **22008**]

customer relationship marketing (CRM) all marketing activities directed towards establishing, developing and maintaining successful relational exchanges, (Morgan and Hunt 1994)

customer service blueprint method for exploring the mainly qualitative components during different stakeholders' experiences with the service

design (noun) (a)   set of instructions (specifications, drawings, schedules etc.) necessary to construct an artefact or service

(b)   artefact or service itself [BS 7000-10 1995, definition **21006**]

design (verb) generation of information by which a required product or service can become a reality [BS 7000-10 1995, definition **21007**]

a multidisciplinary, iterative process that takes an idea and or market need forward into production/implementation and through to disposal [author's working definition]

design management totality of the design activity, its administration and contribution to an organization's performance

NOTE: Design management encompasses the organization and implementation of the process for developing new products and services.

design process stages that a service or product will pass through during its design

NOTE: The stages are generally shown in chronological order but the process is highly iterative in practice.

ethnography the qualitative measure of human social activity which is obtained mainly through observation of people performing activities in places where the activity normally occurs

failure mode and effect analysis (FMEA) technique to identify features of product/service/process which are crucial to determine effects of failure

fail safeing building in simple devices which make it difficult to make mistakes that could lead to failure; *poka yoke* in Japanese

innovation (a)   the transformation of an idea into a novel saleable product, operational process or new service in industry or commerce

NOTE 1: It consists of all scientific, technological, commercial and financial steps necessary for the successful development and marketing of novel manufactured products, the commercial use of new or improved processes and equipment, or the introduction of a new service.

(b)   the employment of design or construction techniques, or materials that do not have a proven history of performance or are not covered by the organization's current practice [BS 7000-10 1995, definition **23011**]

NOTE 2: Definition (b) applies mainly to the construction industry.

industrial design the professional service of creating and developing concepts and specifications that optimize the function, value and appearance of products and systems for the mutual benefit of both users and manufacturer [Peter B. Clarke, President and Founder, Product Ventures USA]

internal customer person influenced by, affected by, or who one works directly with inside an organization

iteration revisiting an earlier stage of the design process to update the information and approaches in the light of new knowledge, experiences and changing circumstances

ISO 9000 set of worldwide standards for quality management systems, last updated in 2000

job design the way the content and environment of a job is structured within a workplace and its interface with technology and facilities

Just-in-Time (JIT) method of planning and controlling that aims to meet demand instantaneously with no waste

kaizen Japanese term for continuous improvement

kanban Japanese term for signal or card; used to authorize the release of materials in a pull control system like JIT

level capacity plan medium-term capacity management technique that tries to keep output constant, irrespective of demand

logistics supply chain management term for the total process of moving goods from suppliers to customers in the most timely and cost-efficient manner possible

moment of truth defining experience with a service that makes a significant impression on the customer

multidisciplinary team group of people with an appropriate range of skills and experience drawn from within, and sometimes outside, an organization

multi-sourcing obtaining same type of product/component from more than one supplier in order to maintain bargaining power or continuity of supply

pilot test prototype trial or test marketing

product champion (a) a person dedicated to the promotion and introduction of a new product, although not necessarily responsible for any aspect of the programme [BS 7000-10 1995, definition **21018**]
(b) a design leader who is a constant member of the design team, responsible for ensuring that communication is effective, that the design process is well coordinated, the right decisions are taken, and who ultimately will make the decision to abandon failed projects [Hollins and Hollins, 1991]

reverse logistics the process of planning, implementing, and controlling the efficient, cost-effective flow of raw materials, in-process inventory, finished goods and related information from the point of consumption to the point of origin for the purpose of recapturing value or proper disposal.

scenario **(a)** description and configuration of what the user is anticipated to do with the service

(b) likely future circumstances in which the service might feature

service **(a)** any activity or benefit that one party can give to another that is essentially intangible and does not result in the ownership of anything; its production may or may not be tied to a physical product [Kotler 1986]

(b) a set of functions offered to a user by an organization

NOTE 1: This definition is identical with **191-01-04** of BS 4778-3.2 1991.

(b) results generated by activities at the interface between the supplier and the customer and by supplier internal activities to meet the customer needs

NOTE 2: The supplier or the customer may be represented at the interface by personnel or equipment.
NOTE 3: Customer activities at the interface with the supplier may be essential to the service delivery.
NOTE 4: Delivery or use of tangible products may form part of the service delivery.
NOTE 5: A service may be linked with the manufacture and supply of tangible product.
NOTE 6: This definition is identical with **1.5** of ISO 8402 1994. This definition is taken from BS 5750-8 1991, with the exception of Note 4.
[BS 7000-10 1995, definition **21023**]

service design brief documentation that describes the primary purpose of a service and gives guidance

NOTE 1: Guidance can relate to such matters as its style, grade, performance, appearance, conditions of use including health and safety considerations, characteristics, packaging, conformity, reliability, maintenance.
NOTE 2: The service design brief is often the result of a feasibility study and forms the basis of the design.
[BS 7000-10 1995]

service specification documentation that prescribes the requirements to which the service has to conform.

NOTE: A service specification should refer to or include drawings, patterns or other relevant documents and should also indicate the means and criteria whereby conformity can be checked. [BS 7000-10 1995]

specification element area that needs to be considered when compiling a design specification

stage gateway milestone and decision point relating to the continuation, or otherwise, of a service development project

stakeholder organization, or individual, from inside or outside an organization, involved with, having an interest in or affected by a service

supply chain management the management of activities that procure raw materials, transform them into intermediate goods and final products and deliver these products to customers through a distribution system [Lee and Billington 1992]

tangible evidence all the material aspects of a service that stakeholders use to evaluate its effectiveness

team a number of individuals who share explicit common objectives

Total Design a multidisciplinary iterative process that takes an idea and/or market need forward into a product or service and through all stages to disposal. [Hollins and Hollins 1991]

total quality management (TQM) defined as managing the entire organization so that it excels on all dimensions of products and services that are important to the customer

touch-point different points of contact and interactions that stakeholders might have that make up the experience of a service

trigger catalyst that prompts action that might lead to a new product or service

vertical integration extent to which an operation chooses to own the network of processes that produce the product/service

yield management techniques that can be used to ensure that an operation maximizes its profit-generating potential

BIBLIOGRAPHY

Akao Y. (ed.) (1990) *Quality Function Deployment: Integrating Customer Requirements into Product Design* (trans. Glenn Mazur). Portland, OR: Productivity Press.

Anderson N.G. (1975) *From Concept to Production: A Management Approach*. London: Taylor and Francis.

Andreason M. (1994) *Design Model*. WDK Workshop on Evaluation and Decision in Design. Technical University of Denmark, Lingby, 2–3 May.

Andreason M. (1994) Personal Correspondence with author.

Badke-Shaub P. and Stempfle J. (2004) 'Analysing leadership activities in design: how do leaders manage different types of requirements?' *Design 2004 Conference*, Cavtat, 17–20 May.

Baxter M.R. (1997) *Product Design: Practical Methods for the Systematic Development of New Products*. London: Chapman and Hall.

Bedward D., Rexworth C., Blackman C., Rothwell A. and Weaver M. (1997) *First Line Manager*. Oxford: Butterworth-Heinemann.

Belbin R.M. (2003) *Management Teams: Why They Succeed or Fail*. Oxford: Butterworth-Heinemann.

Bellon B. and Whittington G. (1996) *Competing Through Innovation*. Cork: Oak Tree Press.

Bennett R. (1996) *Corporate Strategy*. London: Pitman.

Best R.J. (2005) *Market-Based Management*, 4th edn. Englewood Cliffs, NJ: Prentice Hall.

Brown D. and West M. (2006) 'Pride and groom', *People Management*, 26 January.

Brown M.A. (1993) 'Why does TQ fail in two out of three tries?', *Journal for Quality and Participation*, 16 (2).

Brown S., Lamming R., Bessant J. and Jones P. (2005) *Strategic Operations Management*, 2nd edn. Oxford: Elsevier.

Bruce A. (1998) 'Aiming for change? Stay on target', *Professional Manager*, September.

Brysland A. and Curry A. (2001) 'Service improvements in public services using SERVQUAL', *Managing Service Quality*, 11 (6): 389–401.

BS 4335 (1999) *Vocabulary of Terms Used in Project Management* (proposed). London: British Standards Institution.

BS 5750 (1979) *Quality Systems*. London: British Standards Institution.

BS 6079 (1996) *Guide to Project Management*. London: British Standards Institution.

BS 6079 (2000) *Guide to Project Management*. London: British Standards Institution.

BS 7000-1 (1989) *Guide to Managing Product Design* (now withdrawn). London: British Standards Institution.

BS 7000-1 (1999) *Guide to Innovation Management*. London: British Standards Institution.

BS 7000-2 (1997) *Design Management Systems: Guide to Managing the Design of Manufactured Products.* London: British Standards Institution.

BS 7000-3 (1994) *Guide to Managing Service Design.* London: British Standards Institution.

BS 7000-3 (2006) *Guide to Managing the Design of Services.* London: British Standards Institution.

BS 7000-4 (1996) *Design Management Systems: Guide to Managing Design in Construction.* London: British Standards Institution.

BS 7000-6 (2004) *Guide to Managing Inclusive Design.* London: British Standards Institution.

BS 7000-10 (1995) *Design Management Terminology.* London: British Standards Institution.

BS 7373-3 (2005) *Guide to Identifying Criteria for Specifying a Service Offering.* London: British Standards Institution.

BS 7750 (1994) *Environmental Management Systems.* London: British Standards Institution.

British standard 7373 (2001) *Guide to the Preparation of Specification* Parts 1 and 2. London: British Standards Institution.

BS EN ISO 9000 (2000) *Quality Systems.* Geneva: International Organization for Standardization.

BS EN ISO 14000 (1997) *Environmental Management Systems.* London: British Standards Institution.

Bush S.A. and Sheldon D.F. (1993) *Whose Cost Is It Anyway?* Proceedings of an International Conference on Engineering Design, The Hague, August.

Carmon Z. (1991) 'Situational determinants of consumers' dissatisfaction with waiting', *Advances in Consumer Research*, 18: 703–705.

Chaffey D. (2002) *E-Business and E-Commerce Management.* Englewood Cliffs, NJ: Prentice Hall.

Christopher, W. (ed.) (1993) *The Service Quality Handbook.* New York: The Amacom Press.

Clarke I. and Rowley J. (1995) 'A case for spatial decision support systems in retail location planning', *International Journal of Retail & Distribution Management*, 23 (3): 4–10.

Clausing D. (1998) 'Reusability in Product Development', Design Reuse: Engineering Design Conference '98. Brunel University, 23–25 June.

Cooper R.G. (1983) 'A process model for industrial new process development', *IEEE Transactions on Engineering Management*, 30 (1): 2–11.

Cooper R.G. (1988) *Winning at New Products.* London: Kogan Page.

Cooper R.G. (1993) *Winning at New Products*: Accelerating the Process from Idea to Launch, 2nd edn. Reading, MA: Addison-Wesley.

Cooper R.G. (1999) 'The invisible success factors in product innovation', *Journal of Innovation Management*, 16.

Cowell D. (1985) *The Marketing of Services.* London: Pitman.

Crosby P.B. (1979) *Quality Is Free: The Art of Making Quality Certain.* New York: McGraw-Hill.

Davies M.M. and Heineke J. (1994) 'Understanding the roles of the customer and the operation for better queue management', *International Journal of Operations and Production Management*, 14 (5): 24–31.

de Bono E. (1993) *Handbook for Positive Revolution.* New York: Harper Business.

de Brentani U. (1991) 'Success factors in developing new business services', *European Journal of Marketing*, 25 (2): 33–59.

De Geus A. (1997) in Michael Johnston, 'Managing for profit or survival', *Strategy*, Issue 12 (Feb.).

Deming W.E. (1982) *Quality, Productivity and Competitive Position.* Boston, MA: MIT Center for Advanced Engineering Study.

Deming W.E. (1986) *Out of the Crisis*, 2nd edn. Cambridge: Cambridge University Press.

Design Council (1985) *Innovation: Study and the Problems and Benefits of Product Innovation*. London: Design Council.

Design Council (1998) *Designed to Compete: How Design Can Make Companies More Competitive*. Red Paper 1. London: Design Council.

Design Council (2002) *Knowledge Cell Asset: Service Design*, Hollins W. London: Design Council.

Design Council (2004) *Touching the State. What Does It Mean to Be a Citizen in the 21st Century?* London: Design Council.

Dibb S., Simkin L., Pride W.M. and Ferrell O.C. (2006) *Marketing Concepts and Strategies*, 5th edn. New York: McGraw-Hill.

Drucker P.F. (1955) *The Practice of Management*. London: Heinemann.

Dumas A. (1990) 'Why design is difficult to manage', in Gorb P. (ed.) Design Management. London: Architecture, Design and Technology Press.

Edvardsson B. and Olsson J. (1996) 'Key concepts for new service development', *Service Industries Journal*, 16 (2): 140–164.

Elliot C. (1993) 'Turning dreams into specifications: Part 2', *Engineering Management Journal,* April, p. 3.

EMAS (1995) *EC Eco-Management and Audit Scheme for Local Government*. London: Department of the Environment.

Ettlie J.E. (2006) *Managing Innovation: New Technology, New Products and New Services in a Global Economy*. Oxford: Elsevier.

Feigenbaum A.V. (1986) *Total Quality Control*. New York: McGraw-Hill.

Feilden G.B.R. (1963) Engineering Design.

Fisher E. (1994) 'Total quality: hit or myth?', *Accountancy,* April.

Gibson R. (ed.) (1997) *Rethinking the Future*. London: Nicholas Brearley.

Gisser P. (1965) 'Taking the "chances" out of product introduction', *Industrial Marketing*, 50: 327–341.

Glaser B.G. and Strauss A.L. (1975) *The Discovery of Grounded Theory*, 7th edn. New York: Aldine.

Grant R.M. (1995) *Contemporary Strategy Analysis*. Oxford: Blackwell Business.

Greasley A. (2006) *Operations Management*. New York: John Wiley.

Gregory S. (1966) *The Design Method*. London: Butterworth.

Hague P. (1993) *Questionnaire Design*. London: Kogan Page.

Hague P. (2004) *Do Your Own Marketing Research*. London: Kogan Page.

Hall R.W. (1991) *Queuing Methods for Services and Manufacturing*, Englewood Cliffs, NJ: Prentice Hall.

Hamel G. and Prahalad C.K. (1994) *Competing for the Future*. Baston, MA: Harvard Business School Press.

Hart S. (1996) *New Product Development – A Reader*. New York: Dryden.

Hauser J.R. and Clausing D. (1988) 'The house of quality', *Harvard Business Review,* 53 (Jul–Aug).

Hayes R. and Wheelwright S. (1984) *Restoring our Competitive Edge*. New York: John Wiley.

Heizer J. and Render B. (2004) *Principles of Operations Management*, 7th edn. Upper Saddle River, NJ: Prentice Hall.

Henley-Incubator (2003) *Going Beyond the Idea: Delivering Successful Corporate Innovation*. Henley Management College.

Hernandez T. and Bennison D. (2000) 'The art and science of retail location decisions', *International Journal of Retail and Distribution Management*, 28 (8): 357–367.

Herzberg F. (1966) *Work and the Nature of Man.* Cleveland, OH: World Publishing.

Herzberg F., Mausner B.S. and Snyderman G. (1957) *The Motivation to Work.* New York: Wiley.

Heskett J., Sasser W.E. and Schlesinger L. (1997) *The Service Profit Chain.* New York: Free Press.

Hill T. (1993) *Manufacturing Strategy,* 2nd edn. London: Macmillan.

Hollins G. and Hollins B. (1991) *Total Design: Managing the Design Process in the Service Sector.* London: Pitman.

Hollins B. and Hollins G. (1995) 'Reassessing the lone designer and creativity', European Academy of Design Conference Design Interfaces, University of Salford, 11–13 April.

Hollins B. and Hollins G. (1999) *Over the Horizon: Planning Products Today for Success Tomorrow.* Chichester: Wiley.

Hollins B. and Hurst K. (1995) 'Research into user-friendly specifications for effective design management refining and simplifying the process', *Journal of Engineering Design,* 6 (3).

Hollins W.J. (2000) 'The Bill Hollins Column: The Millennium Dome', *Engineering Designer,* 24 (6): 24.

Hollins W.J. (2000) 'The Bill Hollins Column: Failures – a bridge too far?', *Engineering Designer,* 26 (4): 21.

Hollins W. J. and Hollins G. (1992) 'An international perspective on keys to managing the people side of design', The Design Management Institute's West/92 Conference, Santa Cruz, California, USA, March 1992.

Hollins W.J. and Pugh S. (1990) *Successful Product Design: What to Do and When.* Oxford: Butterworth.

Hollins W.J., Blackman C. and Shinkins S. (2003) 'Design and its management in the service sector – updating the standard', 5th European Academy of Design Conference, 28–30 April, Barcelona.

Huda F. (1997) 'Total quality management in voluntary service organizations: residential and nursing care', PhD Thesis, University of Westminster, London.

Hurst K. and Hollins W.J. (1995) Improved Product Design Specification Compilation, Proceedings. International Conference on Engineering Design, Prague, August.

IBM London Business School (1996) *Made in Europe 2: An Anglo-German Design Study.*

Ishiwaka K. (1979) *Guide to Quality Control.* Tokyo: Asian Productivity Organization.

Jackson M. (2005) 'Anticipating the future', *Strategy Magazine,* Issue 6 (December).

Janis I. (1972) *Victims of Groupthink: A Psychological Study of Foreign-Policy Decisions and Fiascoes.* New York: Houghton Mifflin.

Japan Management Association (1987) *Canon Production System* (trans. Alan T. Campbell, ed. Constance E. Dyer). Cambridge, MA: Productivity Press.

Johnson G. and Scholes K. (1984) Exploring corporate strategy: text and cases. FT Prentice Hall.

Johnston R. (2004) 'Towards a better understanding of service excellence', *Managing Service Quality,* 14 (2/3): 129–133.

Johnston R. and Clark G. (2001) *Service Operations Management.* Englewood Cliffs, NJ: Prentice Hall.

Juran J.M. (1989) *Juran on Leadership for Quality, and Executive Handbook.* New York: The Free Press.

Juran J.M., Gryna F.M. and Bingham R.S. (eds) (1988) *Quality Control Handbook*, 4th edn. New York: McGraw-Hill.

Kandampully J. and Butler L. (2001) 'Service guarantees: a strategic mechanism to minimize customers' perceived risk in service organizations', *Managing Service Quality*, 11 (2): 112–120.

Kaplan R. and Norton D. (1992) 'The Balanced Scorecard: measures that drive performance' *Harvard Business Review*, Boston, MA: Harvard Business School Press.

Kaplan R. and Norton D. (1996) 'The Balanced Scorecard: translating strategy into action', Harvard Business Review, Boston, MA: Harvard Business School Press.

Kaplan R. and Norton D. (2000) *The Strategy-Focused Organization*. Boston, MA: Harvard Business School Press.

Kaplan R. and Norton D. (2004) *Strategy Maps: Converting Intangible Assets into Tangible Outcomes*. Boston, MA: Harvard Business School Press.

Kare-Silver M. (1997) *Strategy in Crisis*. London: Macmillan.

Katz A. (1993) Eight TQM pitfalls. *Journal for Quality and Participation,* 16 (4).

Kelley S.W., Donnelly Jr J.H. and Skinner S.J. (1990) 'Customer participation in service production and Delivery', *Journal of Retailing*, 66 (3): 315–325.

Kingman-Brundage J. (1993) 'Service mapping: gaining concrete perspective on service system design', in Scheuing E. and Christopher W. (eds), *The Service Quality Handbook*. New York: The Amacom Press, pp. 148–163.

Kotler P., Armstrong G., Saunders J. and Wong V. (1986) *Principles of Marketing*, 3rd edn, FT Prentice Hall.

Lee H.L. and Billington C. (1992) 'Managing supply chain inventory: pitfalls and opportunities', *Sloan Management Review*, 33 (3): 65–73.

Lee H.L., Padmanabhan V. and Whang Seungjin (1997) 'The bull-whip effect in supply chains', *Sloan Management Review*, Spring, pp. 93–102.

Levitt T.H. (1960) *Marketing Myopia. Harvard Business Review*, July–Aug: 45–56.

Liebfried K.H.J. and McNair C.J. (1992) *Benchmarking: A Tool for Continuous Improvement*. New York: HarperCollins.

Lockwood T. (2000) 'Designing automobiles for global markets: ten market trends', *Design Management Journal,* 12 (4).

London Business School (2004) *EU Spend Management Study*. London: LBS.

Longbottom D. (2000) 'Benchmarking in the UK: an empirical study of practitioners and academics', *Benchmarking: An International Journal*, 7 (2): 98–117.

Lopez-Mesa B., Eriksson S. and Thompson G. (2004) 'The Decomposition and Linkage of Design Methods and Problems', Design 2004 Conference Cavtat, 17–20 May.

Lovelock C., Vandermerwe S., Lewis B. (1999) *Services Marketing: A European Perspective*, 4th edn, Prentice Hall.

Luk Sh.T.K. and Layton R. (2002) 'Perception gaps in customer expectations: managers versus service providers and customers', *The Service Industries Journal*, 22 (2): 109–128.

Lynch R. (1997) *Corporate Strategy*. London: Pitman.

Lyons Review Team (2004) *Well Placed to Deliver? Shaping the Pattern of Government Service.* www.hm-treasury.gov.uk/Consultations_and_Legislation/Lyons/consult_lyons_index.cfm

MacDonald J. (1992) 'Reasons for failure', *TQM Magazine*, August.

Machiavelli N. *The Prince*. Oxford: Oxford University Press.

Madanayake R. (2002) *Strategic Marketing Plan: The 12 'P' Model*. Sri Lanka: Vishva Lekha.

Maister D.H. (1985) 'The psychology of waiting lines', in Czeipel J.H., Solomon M.R. and Surprenant C.F. (eds), *The Service Encounter*. Lexington, MA: D.C. Heath.

Maslow A. (1943) 'A theory of human motivation', *Psychological Review*, 60: 370–396.

Mattsson J. (1994) 'Improving service quality in person-to-person encounters: integrating findings from a multidisciplinary review', *Service Industries Journal*, 14 (1): 45–61.

McAloone T.C. and Andreasen M.M. (2004) 'Designing for Utility, Sustainability and Societal Virtues: Developing Product Service Systems', Design 2004 Conference, Cavtat, 17–20 May.

McGoldrick P. (2002) *Retail Marketing*, 2nd edn. New York: McGraw-Hill.

McQuasrie E.F. (2005) *The Market Research Toolbox*. London: Sage.

Meyer M.H. and De Tore A. (2001) 'Creating a platform-based approach for developing new services', *Journal of Product Innovation Management*, 18: 188–204.

Mills P.K. (1990) 'On the quality of services in encounters: an agency perspective', *Journal of Business Research*, 20, pp. 31–4.

Mintzberg H. (1994) *The Rise and Fall of Strategic Planning*. Prentice Hall.

Mintzberg H. (1998) *Strategy Safari*. Englewood Cliffs. NJ: Prentice Hall.

Morgan R.M. and Hunt S.D. (1994) 'The commitment-trust theory of relationship marketing', *Journal of Marketing*, 58: 20–39.

Mullins L. (1999) *Management and Organizational Behaviour,* 5th edn. London: Pitman.

Munoz T. (2004) 'Disgusted of Dallas', *Financial Times*, London, 14 December.

Nesbit P. (1992) 'Common barriers to succesful TQM implementation', *Quality Forum*, 18 (2):

Norman A. (1998) 'Open Saturday', BBC 2, 19 September.

Oakland J.S. (1993) *Total Quality Management*, 2nd edn. Oxford: Butterworth-Heinemann.

Oppenheim A.M. (1993) *Questionnaire Design, Interviewing and Attitude Measurement*. London: Heinemann.

Osborne A. (1953) *Applied Imagination*. New York: Scribner.

Osborne A. (1993) *Applied Imagination*, 2nd edn. New York: Scribner.

Pahl G. and Beitz W. (1996) *Engineering Design: A Systematic Approach*, 2nd edn. Berlin: Springer-Verlag.

Parasuraman A., Zeithaml V.A. and Berry L.L. (1985) 'A conceptual model of service quality and its implications for future research', *Journal of Marketing,* 70 (3): 201–230.

Parasuraman A., Zeithaml V.A. and Berry L.L. (1988) 'SERVQUAL: a multi item scale measuring customer perceptions of service quality', *Journal of Retailing*, 64: 12–37.

Parasuraman A., Zeithaml V.A. and Berry L. (1990) *Delivering Quality Service: Balancing Customer Perceptions and Expectations*. New York: Free Press.

Parasuraman A., Zeithaml V.A. and Berry L.L. (1994) 'Reassessment of expectations as a comparison standard on measuring service quality: implications for further research', *Journal of Marketing*, 58 (1): 111–124.

Peters G. (1994) *Benchmarking Customer Service*. London: Pitman.

Peters G. (1996) *Beyond the Next Wave: Imagining the Next Generation of Customers*. London: Pitman.

Peters T. and Austin N. (1985) *Passion for Excellence*. New York: Random House.

Platts K. and Gregory M. (1990) 'Manufacturing audit in the process of strategy formulation', *International Journal of Operations and Production Management*, 10 (9).

Porter M. (1980) *Competitive Strategy: Techniques for Analyzing Industries and Competitors*. New York: The Free Press.

Porter M. (1985) *Competitive Advantage: Creating and Sustaining Superior Performance*. New York: Free Press.

Pugh S. (1982) *Total Design Model*. Loughborough University, UK.

Pugh S. (1991) *Total Design*. Reading, MA: Addison–Wesley.

Quinn F.J. (1997) 'Team up for supply chain success', *Logistics Management and Distribution Report*, 1 October 1997.

Radosevich L. (1996) 'The once and future of EDI', *CIO Magazine,* 1 (6): 66–77.

Randall L. (1993) Customer Service Problems: Their Detection and Prevention. Service Superiority Conference, Warwick Business School, 25–26 May.

Reekers N. and Smithson S. (1994), 'EDI in Germany and the UK: strategic and operational use', *European Journal of Information Systems*, 3 (3): 169–178.

Rich H. (2004) 'Proving the practical power of design', *Design Management Review*, Fall.

Rogers D.S., Lambert D., Croxton K. and Garcia-Dastugue S. (2002) 'The returns management process.', *International Journal of Logistics Management,* 13 (22): 5.

Rohatynski R. (1990) 'Process of Technical Design Operational Approach', Proceedings International Conference on Engineering Design, Dubrovnik, August.

Sakao T. and Shimomura Y. (2004) 'A Method and a Computerized Tool for Service Design', Design 2004 Conference, Cavtat, 17–20 May.

Salvaneschi L. and Akin C, (eds) (1996) *Location, Location, Location: How to Select the Best Site for Your Business*. USA: Oasis.

Scheuing E.E. and Christopher W.F. (eds) (1993) *The Service Quality Handbook*. New York: The Amacom Press.

Schwartz P. (1998) *The Art of the Long View*. Chichester: Wiley.

Schein E.H. (1969) *Process Consultation: Its Role in Organization Development*. Reading, MA: Addison–Wesley.

Sheth J.N. and Sisodia R.S. (2006) *Tectonic Shift*. London: Sage.

Shewhart W. (1931) *Economic Control of Quality Manufactured Product*. New York: Van Nostrand.

Shingo Shingeo (1986) *Zero Quality Control*. Connecticut: Productivity Press.

Shostack G.L. (1984) 'Designing services that deliver', *Harvard Business News*, Jan–Feb, pp. 133–139.

Simchi-Levi D., Kaminsky P., Simchi Levi E., (2003) *Designing and Managing the Supply Chain*. New York: McGraw-Hill.

Slack N., Chambers S. and Johnston R. (2004) *Operations Management*, 4th edn. London: FT Prentice Hall.

Slack N. (1994) 'The importance–performance matrix as a determinant of improvement priority', *International Journal of Operations and Production Management*, 14 (5): 59–75.

Smith A. (1776) *An Inquiry into the Nature and Wealth of Nations*, Book One, 6th edn. London: Methuen.

Smith D.G. and Rhodes R.G. (1991) 'Specification Formulation – a structured approach', Poster Session., International Conference on Engineering Design, Zurich, August.

Sohal A. (2002) *Total Quality Management Text with Cases*. Oxford: Butterworth-Heinemann.

Starr M.K. (1963) *Product Design and Decision Theory.* Englewood Cliffs, NJ: Prentice Hall.

Taguchi G. and Clausing D. (1990) 'Robust quality', *Harvard Business Review*, 68 (1): 65–75.

Taylor F. (1911) 'The principles of scientific management', cited in Boone L.E. and Bowen D.D. (1987) *The Great Writings in Management and Organizational Behaviour*. New York: McGraw-Hill.

Tan Gek Woo and Shaw M. (1998) Applying component technology to improve global supply chain network management. *ICIS 1998*: 296–301.

Thackaray J. (1997) *Winners: How Today's Successful Companies Innovate by Design*. Aldershot: Gower.

Topalian A. (1980) *The Management of Design Projects*. London: Associated Business Press.

Topalian A. and Hollins W. (1998) 'An Innovative Approach to Developing the New British Standard on Innovation Management', Conference: Quantum Leap – Managing New Product Innovation. University of Central England, September.

Tosi H.L., Mero N.P. and Rizzo J.R. *Managing Organizational Behavior*, 4th edn. Oxford: Blackwell.

Trott P. (1998) *Innovation Management and NPD*. London: Pitman.

Turban E., King D., Lee J., Warkentin M. and Chung H.M. (2002) *Electronic Commerce: A Managerial Perspective*, 2nd edition. Upper Saddle River, NJ: Prentice Hall.

Turner R. (2002) 'Design as interface', *Design Management Journal*, 13 (1).

UK Government (1994) *Helping Business to Win*. Government 1st White Paper on Competitiveness, May.

Ulrich K. and Eppinger S. (1995) *Product Design and Development*. New York: McGraw-Hill.

Van Looy B., Gemmel P. and Van Dierdonck R. (2003) *Services Management*, 2nd edn. FT London: Prentice Hall.

Vroom V.H. and Yetton P.W. (1973) *The New Leadership: Managing Participation in Organizations*. Englewood Cliffs, NJ: Prentice Hall.

Walker D. (1989) 'Design or Decline'. Video, Design Management Series, Open University.

Warihay F. (1993) 'Total quality in service organizations', *Journal for Quality and Participation*, 16 (3).

Waters C.D.J. (1999) *Global Logistics and Distribution Planning*. London: Kogan Page.

Whittington R. (1993) *What is Strategy – and Does It Matter?* London: Thompson Business.

Wikstrom K. and Erichsen S. (1990) 'Design Models Used in the Development of North Sea Oil Installations Compared with Theoretical Design Models', Proceedings International Conference on Engineering Design, Dubrovnik, August.

Womack J. and Jones D. (2005) *Lean Solutions: How Companies and Customers Can Create Value and Wealth Together*. London: Simon and Schuster Ltd.

Wood J., Wallace J., Zeffane R., Chapman J., Fromholtz M. and Morrison V. (2003) *Organizational Behaviour: A Global Perspective*, 3rd edn. Chichester: Wiley.

Wright J.N. and Race P. (2004) *Management of Service Operations*, 2nd edn. London: Thomson Learning.

Zeithaml V.A. and Bitner J.M. (1996) *Service Marketing*. Singapore: McGraw-Hill International Limited.

INDEX